# THE ORNAMENTAL KITCHEN GARDEN

# THE ORNAMENTAL KITCHEN GARDEN

# GEOFF HAMILTON

BBC BOOKS

GEOFF HAMILTON trained in horticulture before going to work in many different branches of gardening, including vegetable growing, and landscape gardening. He now cultivates a five-acre garden at Barnsdale in Rutland where he has planned, built and planted his own ornamental kitchen garden, as well as growing a wide range of vegetables, fruit, flowers, trees and shrubs.

Geoff Hamilton's career as a gardening journalist began over twenty years ago on the weekly magazine *Garden News*. From 1974 to 1979 he was the editor of *Practical Gardening*. He writes regularly for several gardening magazines and is the author of many books on gardening, including *Successful Organic Gardening*, *First Time Garden* and *Gardeners' World Practical Gardening Course*. He is the regular presenter of the very successful BBC TV series *Gardeners' World*.

Front cover photo: Geoff Hamilton in his ornamental kitchen garden at Barnsdale, near Oakham, Rutland.
Back cover photo: Mixed flower and vegetable bed at Barnsdale.
Photography by Stephen Hamilton.

Published by BBC Books,
a division of BBC Enterprises Limited,
Woodlands, 80 Wood Lane, London W12 0TT

First published in hardback 1990
Reprinted 1990 (four times)
First published in paperback 1995
© Geoff Hamilton 1990
ISBN 0 563 36763 6

Set in 11/13 Bembo
Printed and bound in Great Britain by
Butler & Tanner Ltd, Frome and London
Colour separations by Technik Ltd, Berkhamsted
Cover printed by Clays Ltd, St Ives plc

# ACKNOWLEDGEMENTS

## PHOTOGRAPHS

MALCOLM BIRKITT pages 82–119 *all*; BRIDGEMAN ART LIBRARY page 19; PAT BRINDLEY page 218 *left*; BRITISH MUSEUM page 22; BRUCE COLEMAN pages 134 *bottom*, 163 *bottom* Gordon Langsbury), 169 (Dennis Green), 210 *right* (Eric Crichton) & 242 (Jane Burton); GARDEN PICTURE LIBRARY page 187 *bottom*; HULTON PICTURE COMPANY pages 17 & 24; S. & O. MATHEWS pages 175 *bottom* & 191 *bottom*; KEN MUIR pages 226 *bottom*, 231 *right* & 234; NATIONAL TRUST page 26; BRIAN NICHOLLS pages 37, 40, 50–1, 53 *top*, 54–5, 56 *left* & *centre*, 60–1, 75, 77 *all bottom*, 80–1, 150, 170, 201 *bottom left*, 218 *right*, 231 *left*, 235, 236 & 237; PHOTOS HORTICULTURAL pages 127, 131, 143, 158 *top*, 159 *right*, 166, 183, 186, 190, 198, 199, 203 *right*, 210 *left*, 214, 215, 219, 221, 227 & 230; HARRY SMITH HORTICULTURAL PHOTOGRAPHIC COLLECTION pages 130, 184 & 195.

All other photographs were specially taken for BBC Enterprises Ltd by STEPHEN HAMILTON.

## ILLUSTRATIONS

LORRAINE HARRISON pages 14, 25, 34, 44, 45, 47, 57, 60, 62, 63, 69, 73, 74, 78, 178, 205, 206, 207, 214, 216, 220, 227, 230, 232, 234 & 237.
LYNN CHADWICK pages 38, 42 & 43.
CHARLOTTE WESS page 89: *Narcissus* 'Thalia'; page 93: *Chionodoxa sardensis*; page 97: New potatoes 'Home Guard'; page 101: *Papaver nudicaule* 'Garden Gnome'; page 105: Bay laurel *Laurus nobilis*; page 109: Cucumber.
MIKE GILKES page 30.

# CONTENTS

## Chapter 5: Decorative Plants

## Chapter 6: Herbs

## Chapter 7: Vegetables

## Chapter 8: Tree Fruit

## Chapter 9: Soft Fruit – and Some Others

## Chapter 10: Control of Pests and Diseases

## Useful Addresses

## Index

# FOREWORD

This book has been hatching in my head for a long time.

As a committed conservationist and a lover of nature since childhood, I have long felt uneasy about the use of chemicals in the garden. Somehow the wholesale slaughter of hundreds of thousands of living things sours my enjoyment. Because, as a gardener, I have developed a kinship with nature, I know in my bones that it's wrong.

Nonetheless, as a gardening advisor, I could hardly suggest methods that were doomed to failure. Nature in the raw may look fine in the wide open spaces, but in the confines of a garden it's a mess. Reconciling the two opposing points of view was quite a problem.

The answer came to me slowly. It began with the realization that all the problems of pest and disease control in agriculture come about because of monoculture. If you grow a large area of a single crop, it's bound to attract insect pests from far and wide.

When I began to look into it, I found plenty of evidence that simply hiding plants away amidst a camouflage of other species would reduce that advertisement for 'The best greenfly snack-bar in town'. Yes, said my *alter ego*, but in the vegetable plot a row consisting of half a dozen different kinds of plant would drive a good gardener mad!

Then, reading a book on the history of gardening, I came across the fact that medieval gardeners didn't differentiate between plants at all. A plant was a plant whether you ate it, smelt it or simply looked at it, and they were all grown together.

And why not? Why on earth should it be a rigid rule that flowers must be grown in one part of the garden, fruit in another and vegetables always hidden away somewhere round the back? Why not grow them all in the same border?

Finally, a talk with a naturalist had me convinced. I discovered that it isn't necessary to fill your garden with stinging nettles and thistles in order to attract butterflies and you don't have to grow native oaks to get birds to nest. Native plants are by no means essential to build up a population of wildlife that will help control pests and diseases and fill your days with delight too. Just grow as wide a diversity of plants as you can, all mixed happily together, and let nature do the rest.

Well, it all sounds a bit too good to be true, doesn't it? That's exactly what I thought too. But, please, read the book and then give it a try. You don't need to convert your whole garden overnight. Start with one border and I guarantee you'll be delighted with the results and want to do more.

It's perhaps a somewhat unusual method of gardening but it guarantees a stunningly beautiful garden, a virtual self-sufficiency in fruit and vegetables, a plot that's buzzing with fascinating wildlife and the most interesting and creative gardening I've ever been involved in. I honestly don't think you could ask for much more than that.

I hope you enjoy the book.

GH

*Geoff Hamilton in his ornamental kitchen garden at Barnsdale.*

# *Chapter 1*

# INTRODUCTION

 BASIC PRINCIPLES

If you want to grow perfectly clean, fresh and wholesome fruit and vegetables, you'll have to start by throwing your brain into reverse. Step back about 50 or 60 years and more or less start again.

Mind you, I'm certainly not suggesting that we take gardening back to the Dark Ages and turn our backs on modern science and technology entirely. Much progress has been made in growing techniques that are of benefit to the gardener, but we've made one great mistake.

Our error has been to follow blindly the methods of the commercial grower and the farmer. When they found it expedient to grow in long, straight rows, we did the same. Where they used poisonous sprays to control pests, we followed. And when they developed new varieties, we grew them too. And we did it without really stopping to realize that our growing conditions are different, our problems are different and even our requirements are different. Once you accept that, growing your own becomes easier than you ever thought possible.

## Growing in rows

Ancient farmers started by growing all their crops in big blocks. They simply broadcast the seed by hand and up it came where it fell. And the system worked perfectly well when there was little need to worry about labour costs. Corn would be weeded by hand, and an army of low-paid peasants could make

short work of hand-hoeing a field of turnips. It wasn't a very satisfactory method but it sufficed.

The revolution came with the seed drill. Now, instead of scattering seed by hand, it could be sown by machine in straight rows, enabling future hoeing to be done with a horse. This was much quicker than hand-hoeing, and with reduced competition the crops were heavier too.

The seed drill has remained until today, with new precision drills becoming so sophisticated that they can drop a single seed to within an eighth of an inch (3 mm) of where it's needed. So the efficient long straight row has become part of our growing pattern. On a farm scale it has been proved over centuries to be the most effective method. But is it really the best way for gardeners? I think not.

In a small space, it's incredibly wasteful. The trouble is that, however little land the crop may require to grow well, we need to space the rows at least a foot apart in order to walk between them with our hoe – even if they will do perfectly well at only half that spacing. Just imagine a couple of rows of radish with a foot between them. It's a complete waste of space.

Over the years I have compared the row method of growing with the ancient gardeners' way of growing in beds with the plants placed much closer together (see p. 16). The result is *always* a doubling of the yield and sometimes it's possible to triple it.

Of course, there are disadvantages. First of all, it's more time consuming. That's the reason the farmer could never consider it.

But gardeners do have the time, and indeed it's in order to spend time growing plants that we garden in the first place. In any case, on a small scale the extra labour involved is minimal. By the time you've got your hoe out of the shed, I'll have half finished the job by hand!

The other 'problem' is that a higher input of fertilizer and organic matter is necessary. In order to increase the amount taken from a bit of land, you need to keep it in a high state of fertility and that means putting more into it. But remember that you're also taking a lot more out, so in the end you'll win hands down.

There are all kinds of other advantages to growing in blocks rather than rows. You don't, for example, tend to fall into the trap of sowing too much just to complete the row, and finishing up feeding all the neighbourhood. You'll find that the maintenance of a small patch at a time is much more encouraging, so the job tends to get done at the right time. But you'll find all this out for yourself as you go along.

## Using chemicals

I have a theory that in a hundred years' time, just as we are now incredulous at, for example, the physicians of yesterday using leeches to draw blood as a universal panacea, our great-grandchildren will laugh at our use of chemicals. I can hear it now: 'Just imagine, they would soak their vegetables in poisons and then eat them! They all knew very well they were poisonous, but they did it anyway. Must have been mad!'

Well, I'm not so sure I could condemn farmers out of hand for using chemicals. Perhaps they have to. But for gardeners it's crazy.

If a farmer has an enomous field of cabbages attacked by caterpillars, perhaps he has no alternative but to douse them with pesticides. Yet the gardener with a dozen plants can simply go round and pick them off. But the marvellous thing with the growing system I'm going to suggest is that your cabbages won't get attacked in the first place.

The main reason why pests and diseases are so devastating in agriculture is that the crops are grown in such large quantities. First of all, a 20 acre (8 ha) field of cabbages is going to attract all the cabbage white butterflies in the area. They'll home in on them from miles around. And then, with such an enormous food supply around them, they'll lay clutch after clutch of eggs.

The ornamental kitchen gardener, on the other hand, actually hides his cabbages away among the flowers which, since the butterflies are attracted by sight, is a very effective way to avoid their attentions. What's more, because there is such a diversity of planting in the garden, a natural balance of life will be built up. The trees will attract a multitude of birds, for example, and they'll be very happy to clear up the odd few caterpillars which do find their way to the cabbages. That's if the ground beetles don't get there first!

## Choice of varieties

Over the last couple of decades, the plant breeders have really done the farmer and the commercial grower proud. They've beavered away to produce varieties with exactly the required characteristics. If, for example, the supermarket demands all its cauliflowers exactly the same size, the growers can do it by choosing the right variety. If they want a tomato to be virtually seedless, the growers can oblige there too. And now that genetic engineering is being used in plant breeding, that capability will increase. But very often what is a 'super-variety' for the farmer is a dead loss for the gardener.

Take Brussels sprouts, for example. It's essential for the farmer to harvest his crop by machine, all in one go. So he chooses a variety that will crop uniformly. But, of course, that's the reverse of what the gardener wants. He would prefer to pick a small amount each day or two, over a long period. So many of the commercial varieties are just not for him. Commercial tomatoes are grown all exactly the same size and are bred to crop right through the winter in heated and artificially lit greenhouses. But they taste like water. What we want is a variety that will make our mouths water *thinking* about it and never mind the uniformity of size.

But don't think I'm condemning all new varieties – far from it. One of the main features the breeders are trying to develop in new varieties is pest and disease resistance, and I see that as a major weapon in organic control.

## The primrose path

So what I'm suggesting is an entirely 'new' approach to kitchen gardening, which is completely divorced from the farmer or commercial growers' methods. I have proved to my satisfaction that it works much better.

Mind you, if you're going to be successful with this method, there can be no half-measures. You have to go the whole hog or not bother at all. And this is where I differ from most organic experts.

You'll find that organic gardeners suggest quite a few chemicals that can be used 'safely' in the garden. Their justification is that they are derived from plants and only have a short period of persistence. Try as I might, I simply can't see the logic in that argument.

The fact that they're derived from plants makes them no less dangerous than those cooked up in a laboratory. (Atropine, a strong poison, is plant-derived, and so is heroin for that matter.) And with short persistence or not, if poisonous chemicals will kill caterpillars, they'll kill bees, hoverflies and ladybirds – allies you simply can't afford to lose.

No, the only way is to co-operate with nature and let natural methods keep pests and diseases in check. Apart from a few physical

barriers, I'm going to suggest that you chiefly rely on growing really strong, healthy plants that will be able to shrug off pest and disease attack. You should also provide the conditions that suit a variety of natural predators that will do your pest control for you.

So you start by getting rid of the whole idea of mono-culture and you grow your food crops in small patches. This can take a bit of getting used to with some crops, like potatoes, for example. The natural tendency here is to put them all together in one spot where they can easily be earthed up and dug when the time comes to harvest. But you'll find that if you grow just three or four plants together in one place you can harvest those in about a week, leaving the space free for something else. Grown in one big block, you have to wait until the whole crop's lifted before you can use the land. So, that's another way you increase production. Indeed, I know a country gardener who, throughout spring and early summer, puts a potato tuber in whenever and wherever a space in her close-planted borders appears. That way she gets a succession of delicious early potatoes right through until early winter.

With successional crops like lettuce, the patch method is perfect. You simply sow or plant a fortnight's supply in one place, then wait a couple of weeks and sow another patch somewhere else. That way the land is always being used and you never grow more than you need. Again, the quantities required will take some getting used to, so keep a diary in the first season, noting what you sowed and when and also whether or not you got the quantities right. In a couple of seasons you'll get it spot on.

Around the patches of vegetables will be flowers of all descriptions – shrubs, herbaceous plants, bulbs, roses, etc. These will serve to camouflage the food plants and also to attract insect predators to control the pests. Provided you don't weaken and resort to the sprayer, they really will do the job for you.

There is just a point to make on the debit side. It does take a while to build up a natural balance of life that will police your plot and make sure that no one species becomes a problem. You will almost certainly have both pest and disease attacks in the first season but they will gradually diminish thereafter. However, you shouldn't expect them to ever disappear completely. They won't.

If you're one of these fussy eaters who throws a cabbage away if there's a hole in one of the leaves, or discards an apple because of a bird-peck, your only way is to do what the commercial grower does and keep a constant coverage of chemicals over the lot. Me, I'll take my chances with the bird-peck.

But once you do weaken and decide you simply *must* use chemicals, well you simply start again. You'll kill off the goodies as well as the baddies, bang go your allies and it's you and the sprayer against the world.

## Fertility

The other reason for the use of so much pesticide on commercial crops is that they're grown soft. As we all know if we read the papers, farmers and growers use large quantities of nitrogen, usually in the form of nitrates or sulphate of ammonia. Nitrogen is the element that creates rapid growth of leaves and stems and there's no doubt that by using more and more they've managed to increase yields tremendously. (The fact that the excess nitrogen runs into the land drainage system and eventually into our rivers to pollute our drinking water is another story I won't go into here.) But that nitrogen 'force-feeds' the plant, making for soft growth which is more attractive to pests and diseases and gives the plant little power to overcome attacks.

The organic way is to rely on feeding the soil rather than the plant. Natural manures and fertilizers tend to release their plant foods over a much longer period, so they remain in the soil where they're available to the roots as and when the plants need them. They don't get 'force-fed', so they remain shorter, tougher and fitter.

But it is necessary to maintain a really high level of fertility if this intensive system is to work well. You'll need lots of manure or, if you can't get that, spent mushroom compost or some other source of bulky organic matter, perhaps with the addition of a concentrated organic fertilizer. And it goes without saying that a compost heap is obligatory.

## Aesthetics

Of course, the first and foremost requirement is that the garden should be a thing of beauty and a place of leisure. However keen you may be on growing your own fruit and vegetables, you don't want to turn your garden into a scruffy allotment. And the great joy of this method is that it looks *wonderful!*

The rule must be that everything has to earn its place in the garden by looking beautiful as well as being productive. It really isn't as impossible as it sounds. There are lots of vegetable varieties that are attractive as well as being good eating. Fruit can be grown in very beautiful shapes to enhance a dull wall or fence or even to edge a border. And the flowers that provide your pest control and your pollination service will fill the plot with colour and perfume the whole year through.

*Mixed flowers and vegetable beds in the ornamental kitchen garden.*

## ✿ PAST GARDENS ✿

The Domesday Book tells us that, even as far back as the eleventh century, cottage gardeners were growing in much the way I'm suggesting – albeit for different reasons.

At the time there seems to have been little attempt to design the garden as an area for relaxation. Although there was often no shortage of space, the garths, as the kitchen gardens of country cottages and town houses were called, were crammed full of all manner of plants with no attempt at segregation. Cabbages were grown among marigolds and fruit trees underplanted with herbs. There was likely to be a beehive or two, a few chickens scratching about and even a pig.

At that time gardeners saw little difference between types of plants and could see no reason to separate them. While modern fashion dictates that the fruit and vegetable plot should be strictly divorced from the ornamental part and hidden from view if possible, to eleventh-century gardeners a plant was a plant, whether shrub, herb or vegetable. Most found a use, either as food or medicine, or as aromatics to alleviate the strong human smells that must have been all too pervasive in those days. So all of them were grown together.

### Companion planting

In a strange way, another factor that's also relevant to our system is the old theory of *sympathetic magic*. The belief was that like would attract (or sometimes repel!) like and also that the physical characteristics of plants could be transferred simply by growing them near to each other. Grow onions among the soft fruit, for example, and the fruit would transfer its sweetness to the onions. Whether the fruit would pick up the onion taste wasn't mentioned but is far more likely!

Of course, I don't suggest that this is a good reason for mixing plants together, but what is most interesting is that the theory also

extended to pest and disease control and that really *does* work.

I think it highly doubtful that medieval gardeners knew *why* their 'companion planting' was so effective. Some of their remedies were so outlandish that they must put the others into question. The practices of burying an owl's heart in the plot to keep away mice and planting the notoriously 'windy' lentils to reduce the damaging effect of gales are unscientific to say the least!

Nevertheless, by indiscriminately mixing their planting in this somewhat haphazard way, they were, perhaps unknowingly, diminishing the likelihood of pest and disease attack simply by reducing the area covered by a single crop. There's no doubt that a vast acreage of one type of plant is much more likely to attract pests than the odd one or two plants hidden among others.

What's more, they were building and maintaining a natural balance of wildlife which included predators as well as pests, so ensuring that no one species built up to unacceptable proportions.

They may have put their success down to other reasons, but, by adopting that ancient method of planting in 'controlled chaos' the modern gardener can certainly benefit.

### The formal design

By the fifteenth century, fashions in Europe had changed dramatically. The transformation from the Middle Ages to the Renaissance began in Italy and then spread through France to Britain. Through wool, cloth and a vastly increased international trade, to say nothing of successful wars and piracy, Britain, by the sixteenth century, was enjoying a period of unparalleled prosperity and freedom.

Elizabethan adventurers were sending back plants from all over the world and the newly prosperous middle classes were anxious to exploit them. While it was still necessary to raise fruit, vegetables and herbs for culinary and medicinal use, elaborate pleasure gardens began to appear too. With the sharp social division between the wealthy merchants and the peasants, there was no shortage of cheap labour to build them. Now it seemed that the wealthier folk wanted to disassociate themselves from the disorganized clutter of the cottagers' gardens. The trend then was for formality. Influenced by the Italians, the French and the Dutch, fashionable gardens were laid out in strictly geometric designs, with intricate networks of paths and beds.

Here again the modern gardener can draw inspiration, because although the carefully sculptured raised beds were purely intended to please the eye, they may be regarded as the forerunner of our 'deep-beds'.

They were deeply dug (sometimes *four* spades deep!), and liberally manured, raising them above the level of the paths, so ensuring free drainage and high fertility. All cultivations were carried out from the paths so that the beds were never compacted by treading. And that's exactly the principle of the 'new' method of deep-bed gardening. Modern research has shown that the method is actually capable of doubling productivity.

Still there was not much segregation of the plants. The beds were often edged with neatly clipped miniature hedges of box, lavender or rosemary, but inside the planting varied

*Sixteenth-century engraving showing the gardening activities of spring, including levelling beds, planting, sowing and raking raised beds.*

throughout the garden. One bed may have contained culinary or medicinal herbs while its neighbour on one side grew leeks and on the other the purely decorative flowers that were now becoming popular.

### Elizabethan science

As you would expect, some of the horticultural science of the sixteenth century was flawed. It was widely believed, for example, that by grafting a sour but prolific variety of apple on to another, sweet but poorly cropping one, you'd get the best of both worlds. The new tree would benefit from both 'parents' and produce sweet apples in profusion. We now know that the theory is something of a schoolboy howler, but it was a beginning. The concept of grafting one variety on to another has enabled us to progress to the modern fruit tree. Many types can now be grafted on to a special rootstock which will control the eventual size of the tree and encourage it to fruit more freely too. It's even progressed to the 'family tree', which has two or three different varieties grafted on to the same stem, making an invaluable plant for today's tiny gardens.

Many tender plants were grown in tubs and containers, even wheelbarrows, so that they could be protected. On calm, sunny days the exotic oranges and lemons imported from Spain were wheeled or carried outside to take advantage of the warm weather. When frost threatened they could be carried back again.

Well, that may sound like a lot of trouble, but it's still a valuable method for the modern gardener with limited space. These days, when the paved patio is *de rigueur* and a conservatory quite common, it's an ideal way to grow exotic fruits and flowers while at the same time decorating your living area both inside and out. In the purely organic garden, it's even effective in controlling disease – but more of that later.

## THE VICTORIAN GARDEN

The Victorians were a bit of a mixed blessing. Queen Victoria's own opinions and, dare I say, prejudices, had such a profound effect upon society that they influenced every part of life, even gardening. Amazingly, much of that influence remains today.

Despite what we would now consider quite inhuman conditions in the lives of working people, she was a 'super-moralist' – so much so that, taking their lead from the Queen, 'fashionable people' went to extraordinary lengths to avoid having their delicate sensibilities sullied by 'common' things.

It was quite normal, for example, for gardeners to be made to walk half a mile further with a barrowload of manure on a circuitous route which would hide them from the windows of their master's house. Had the mistress had the misfortune to rest her delicate eyes on such an offensive scene, she would immediately suffer an attack of 'the vapours'!

The very thought of seeing a beetroot or a lettuce from the house was quite *infra dig.* for gently brought-up young girls. So the vegetable garden was banished behind high walls where it would be well out of sight. And that was the beginning of the segregation of flowers and vegetables that still persists today.

Well, I don't think there are many of us who would blanch at the sight of a potato or swoon if we caught a whiff of good honest muck. There's no need to segregate flowers from vegetables, and they'll all grow much better and, I think, look better if you don't.

On some counts, I can forgive the Victorians anything. First of all, they left us some inspirational gardens. Because of the astonishing gulf between the living standards of the rich and the poor, with some employers earning in a day what they paid their workers in a *year*, labour was extremely cheap. So, though it was a high price to pay in human terms, their legacy was some of the best gardens in the world. And among the

*The Victorian cottage garden; painting by E. W. Waite (1854–1924).*

styles they developed was the 'romanticized' cottage garden – nothing to do with the real cottagers' gardens of the day, of course, which were in the main purely practical and used to grow food to supplement a bread-line diet. No, the 'chocolate-box' Victorian gardens were rather the wealthier classes' idea of what a cottage garden *ought* to have looked like. But what a wonderful way to garden a small, modern, estate-house plot. It wasn't but it could have been tailor-made. You need to add in the fruit and the vegetables of course, but the principle is perfect.

The Victorians paid great attention to detail in their gardens as with their buildings. Indeed, many would say they were over-fussy. Certainly you have to be careful: the architecture of modern houses is essentially plain and simple so the over-decorated Victorian style could look completely out of place.

A lot depends on personal preference of course, but for me, acres of crazy paving, so beloved of the Victorians, is anathema in the garden of a modern house. So is that terrible, twee rustic trellis they loved so much. You have to interpret and adapt, but there's still a lot we can learn from that era.

*Octagonal brick paving with a central design of concentric circles under the rose arbour.*

Brick paving is very Victorian, for example, but rightly making a strong comeback these days. What's more, it's very adaptable and easy to lay (see p. 54). I find it suits a modern garden well and I've used it widely. And in the centre of the octagon of brick paving under my rose arbour, I've used an idea from the most famous of all Victorian architects, Edwin Lutyens. I noticed it at Hestercombe House in Somerset and have reproduced it at Barnsdale. It's a series of concentric circles right in the centre of the octagon, and it's made by fitting a number of different sized flower pots one inside the other – simple, but very effective and typical of the Victorian attention to detail.

We must also praise the Victorians' marvellous inventiveness. Just as our 'boffins' today amaze us all the time with more and more mind-boggling electronic marvels, they bent their minds to the 'new' craze for mechanical engineering. Whatever it was they wanted to do, they had to make a machine for it, and some of their inventions can be a source of inspiration still. Furthermore, when they made anything they always did it *beautifully*. Just take a look at a real Victorian conservatory and compare the iron-work with our purely functional aluminium structures, cast an eye over an old wheelbarrow with an intricately decorated wrought-iron wheel or compare their lantern cloches with what we have on offer today. They were all works of art and, in a garden, that's just what they should be.

When I first started my ornamental kitchen garden, cloches were a source of great pain to me. There simply wasn't *anything* available that looked half decent, and in a small garden you can do without eyesores. I finished up making my own from rigid plastic and they're a great improvement (see p. 74). Of course they're not a patch on the Victorian equivalent, but they're not going to give me the vapours at least!

Coal was cheap and abundant in the nineteenth century so heated frames and glasshouses were common. It was nothing for gardeners to grow bananas, pineapples and other exotics alongside their grapes, figs and melons. Well, I can't see many modern gardeners being able to afford to grow bananas, but we can certainly emulate the Victorian passion for heated frames. They're useful all the year round and, if you do it the Victorian way, they're very cheap to run.

Apart from coal, those wily old gardeners would create cheap heat from a renewable and very common source of energy in those days – horse muck. And strangely, that's something that is becoming much more readily available to us too. These days there must be hundreds of thousands of youngsters with a pony and an ever-increasing pile of horse manure in the back garden. It's common to see roadside signs offering it for sale quite cheaply and it's also almost certain that there's a riding stable near you which could supply you some. To check, I looked in the telephone directory for riding stables in south London and found no less than 40, so it's likely that there will be a supply wherever you live.

Of course, I'm not suggesting that it's as cheap as the Victorian horse muck would have been. But the lovely thing is that you can get twice the value from it.

You'll need to use some manure on the garden each year and you'll want it well rotted. It's generally quite difficult to find manure for sale that has been piled up for six months or so, because most riding establishments need to make space by moving it much sooner. So you'll have to stack it yourself, which gives you the chance to make a proper Victorian hotbed.

Of course, their hotbeds were wonderfully complicated, brick-built contraptions, complete with air ducts and ventilators, etc. But that's not at all necessary unless you insist on growing pineapples! For most purposes, all you need do is to make a pile of manure and put your frame on top. Then you can grow a couple of crops of very early vegetables, follow them with something wildly luxurious like melons and still have your pile of well-rotted manure for use as a soil improver at the end of the season.

*Victorian lantern cloches.*

## 🦎 FORMAL GARDENS 🦎

The best way to take advantage of nature's help with pest and disease control and to make the kitchen garden a thing of beauty at the same time is to grow on the 'cottage garden' principle. Modern gardens don't have the room for anything on the grand scale, so the technique of growing everything together in the same border suits very well. I'm not suggesting that design and especially colour combinations should be left entirely to chance, and indeed there's plenty of opportunity to create some subtle visual effects with a combination of flowers, vegetables and fruit. But, though you may plan very carefully, the net result will be essentially informal.

There are some circumstances, however,

*Walled herb garden from a medieval gardening treatise.*

where you may prefer to take the strictly formal approach. It may be that in a tiny, square town garden you feel that the informal effect would look messy, or it may be that the garden is large and you have room for a change of tempo. You may simply prefer the formal, 'tidy' approach to gardening. Still, with a little thought, you can use the same natural principles to grow your fruit and vegetables organically and attractively. And once again, it helps to look to the past for inspiration. There are plenty of fine examples of restored formal gardens around the country and it may come as something of a surprise to realize that the present-day approach to gardening, with informal designs and 'random' planting, is a relatively modern phenomenon.

Once you go back beyond the Victorians, you'll find plenty of examples of formal gardening. In Elizabethan times there seemed to be such an obsession with geometry that all the gardens of the 'gentry' seem to have been designed with set square and compasses. I have no doubt that the cottage gardens of the peasants were much as they looked centuries later, but these were rarely illustrated.

I've mentioned how medieval gardeners would grow vegetables in rectangular beds. Though this no doubt started as a purely practical way of growing, it was developed over the years into something quite elaborate, with the beds being laid out in formal and highly decorative patterns.

While the borders were mostly devoted to vegetables and herbs, some flowers were included for the purely visual effect and, I suppose, to provide cut flowers for the house and for the fashionable posies of the day. It may have been that even in those days experienced gardeners recognized the value of attracting the natural enemies of garden pests with flowers. They were certainly aware of the importance of bees. But aware or not, it's certain that the flowers helped in their pest control and provided a lift to the spirits at the same time. I can think of no better reason for

following suit. One thing is sure, that today we have a far, far greater choice of flowers and, if we choose to grow them, of vegetables too. So we have the chance not just to emulate Elizabethan designs but, in the second Elizabethan age, greatly to improve on them too.

There's no doubt that the edging of beds with wooden boards makes the modern deep-bed garden far cleaner and tidier. And the paths between can be gravelled, so that you can dash outside for the lunchtime lettuce in your Sunday best and return without so much as a speck of mud!

Quite by chance I discovered another small but significant advantage. While edging the beds in my own garden, I tried to put myself in the mind of an Elizabethan gardener. In those days, and indeed right up to the beginning of this century, craftsmen paid more attention to perfection than we do today. There were not the financial constraints we seem to suffer now and this bred a different attitude to beauty. The craftsman and the artist gained the respect of their fellows for their skills, so they took enormous trouble over what we would now consider the most unpromising utility items. You only have to compare the elaborately carved gargoyles that served as drainpipes on medieval buildings with our own grey plastic!

So I felt convinced that an Elizabethan gardener would have finished the corners of his vegetable beds with finials in much the same way they decorated the apex of a roof or the top of a post.

It took a couple of telephone calls to find a supplier but, once installed, they looked good. Very Elizabethan! What I didn't realize until I came to do the watering was that they serve also as the perfect way to run the hose round the garden without battering down the plants. The hose lodges underneath the ball and slides round a treat. Hoses were, of course, unknown to gardeners in the days of Elizabeth I, but, if they'd had them, you can bet your life they'd have relished my finials!

Perhaps the most formal of all the Elizabethan fashions was the knot garden. These were marvellously complicated arrangements of low hedges, planted and clipped to form intricate shapes. Originally, a knot was a feature on its own – a piece of plant sculpture, with the low hedges, often box, santolina or lavender, cut to give the impression that the strands of the hedge wove in and out, over and under, in a fascinating three-dimensional tangle.

In Thomas Hill's book *The Gardener's Labyrinth*, published in 1577 and the first general gardening book written in English, he produces a couple of designs for knot gardens which are nothing if not optimistic. The patterns rival a Persian carpet for intricacy, and indeed it's quite likely that is from where the inspiration came. But unless your knot garden is to cover an acre at least, a pattern of such complication is to be avoided! If you do set out on such a grand project, you'll need deep pockets, because the hedging should be planted only a few inches apart and dwarf hedging is not cheap, though there are ways to economize. But more of that later (see p. 70).

Later the hedges were used as edgings to beds planted with flowers, herbs or vegetables. The French called them *jardins potagers* and the fashion soon spread to Britain. The designs were still complicated and the extreme of formality. They were intended, of course, to be viewed from above, so they were sited either below a raised terrace or where they could be seen from balcony or bedroom window.

*Watering a knot garden; illustration from*
*Thomas Hill's* The Gardener's Labyrinth *(1577).*

Perhaps the most famous and certainly the most extravagant of these formal vegetable gardens has been faithfully reconstructed at the Chateau Villandry in France. Seeing it should be considered part of a gardener's education and I urge you to go, though it's on such a grand scale that it'll need a fairly wild stretch of the imagination if it's to provide inspiration for the modern backyard gardener. Nonetheless, don't let me put you off. It's perhaps the best illustration in the world of the *principle* of this type of gardening, and there are many smaller features, like the decorative trellis and the arbours, which certainly had my imagination racing. I couldn't wait to get home and get started! There are, of course, plenty of 'potager gardens' in England on a more modest scale which are easier to relate to and well worth a visit.

These days they are more often seen planted with herbs, and very effective they look too. If your garden is big enough, you may find room for a small knot garden to house the herbs while you grow the vegetables in cottage-garden style. If you do use herbs, make sure you pick varieties which will not swamp the hedges, or you'll naturally lose their effect. The sages, thymes and marjorams will look fine, but lovage or angelica are definitely out.

Vegetables go well in small knot gardens too, but again you should choose the smaller ones like onions, carrots and spinach, and make sure you find some room for flowers mixed in amongst them to help with the pest control. The very thought of dousing a sweet-smelling Elizabethan knot garden with some evil-smelling modern pesticide out of a sprayer would have Thomas Hill spinning in his grave.

##  GROWING FRUIT ATTRACTIVELY

With the aid of modern technology, it's now possible to provide a supply of home-grown fruit right through the year. While the amateur gardener can't afford to store his apples and pears in refrigerated gas stores like the commercial grower, he can borrow some of those very techniques to make his fruit last well into the spring at least. And with the help of that most useful of modern gardening tools, the deep-freeze, and a few lessons from the past, there's no excuse for ever going short on vitamin C!

Research into commercial fruit growing has revolutionized techniques for the professional and at the same time greatly benefited the amateur. There's much we can learn from the fruit farmers, but the wise gardener will be very selective about which methods he borrows. Many modern varieties, for instance, have been developed for purely commercial reasons which don't affect the gardener. In many cases, the older ones are still much better.

'James Grieve' is a perfect example of a superb garden variety, shunned by commercial growers and therefore not as popular as it should be. It was introduced by Messrs Dickson of Edinburgh in 1890 and named after one of their employees who bred it. It has a wonderful crisp, juicy flesh and a superb, slightly acid flavour. And because of its profuse flowering it makes a very fine pollinator for other varieties. But one drawback has denied it a starring role in commercial fruit growing. It bruises very easily and stands no chance of getting from fruit farm to market and thence to the shops in an edible state. Eaten straight from the tree, however, there's no better variety, and so for the gardener it's virtually obligatory.

'Ashmead's Kernel' is another variety you'll almost certainly never find in the shops, yet it has one of the best flavours of all. Alas it's a russet, a type which, purely because of the dictates of fashion, is not so popular these days. This one was introduced as far back as 1700 but is still available from a few fruit specialists today. And if it's flavour you're after, there's not a modern variety to touch it.

## Fruit training

It's probably in terms of fruit-tree training and pruning that we can learn most from the past. Remember that the basic rule in our garden is that, in order to earn their place, even those plants grown to produce food must be attractive to look at too. And that has – often for different reasons – been the guiding rule in gardens throughout history.

*Fan-trained apple tree in the walled garden at Felbrigg Hall, Norfolk.*

The monks, for example, needed to be self-sufficient in food grown on their own monastery land. They also wanted to create an environment that was peaceful and beautiful and so conducive to prayer and contemplation. Beauty never took second place to efficiency, and so it should be in our gardens.

Their solution with fruit was the beginning of a long love affair with pruning and training which captured the imagination of many a gardener through the ages. The fruit arch was perhaps the beginning.

It's likely, I suppose, that the monastic cloisters were the inspiration behind fruit walks. What better way of providing a quiet, secluded and shady walk where one can turn one's thoughts to higher things than to use trees planted in a row on either side. It's a small, logical step to bend them over to the middle to provide shade and it's prudent to use fruit trees which will provide food as a bonus.

To achieve a symmetrical curve, the trees were tied in to a wooden framework as they grew and quite probably grafted at the top when they met. Medieval gardeners were enthusiastic grafters!

In later years, the fruit arch developed to include ornamental plants as well and was widely adopted in the great gardens of Europe. The fashion for young women to toast their skins golden brown is entirely modern. Before this century, what we would now consider a healthy and attractive colour was looked upon as very coarse and unladylike! So walking in the sunshine was not considered wise, lest our gently born lady develop a decidedly plebeian tan! The planted walk was the ideal answer.

These days, we may not be so sensitive about exposure to sunshine (though, who can tell what a further depletion of ozone will do?), but the fruit arch is still as attractive a way of growing apples and pears as ever it was (see p. 200).

From the fruit arch, all kinds of artistic shapes were developed. For some reason, the French seem to have been the leaders of the fashion for pruning and training trees which, like topiary, became something of an art form. Some methods of pruning were developed purely to produce trees with an artistic shape. There were goblets and wineglasses, palmettes and table-tops, all of which gave good crops of fruit, of course, but whose original intent seems to have been to delight the eye.

Perhaps the most important development from our point of view, was the training of trees fixed to walls. It had long been known that a stone or brick wall acted like a huge storage-heater, conserving the warmth of the sun and so reducing frost damage to sensitive flowers and hastening the ripening of fruit. Fans and espaliers were developed as much to spread out the branches to make the most of that reflected heat as to produce an attractive shape. Indeed, in Victorian times when both coal and labour were cheap and plentiful, a few of the wealthier landowners went to quite remarkable lengths to produce crops of peaches, nectarines and apricots. They built double walls around their kitchen gardens, with ducts and flues inside to carry heat from enormous boilers, just to ensure that their tender fruit was protected from frost! Not a technique I would recommend in modern times!

One thing those huge gardens were not short of was space, so I don't suppose it ever occurred to them that they had also invented a method of growing fruit that was ideally suited to tiny gardens.

These days, few of us can afford to build brick or stone walls around our gardens, though we can, of course, take advantage of the house walls to grow fruit. But, ironically enough, those fans and espaliers are the perfect means of growing a wide range of fruit without taking up valuable garden space.

Once again, old-fashioned methods have proved to be the perfect answer to a modern problem – albeit for a quite different reason.

One sure fact that has emerged from the fashion for training trees in all kinds of weird and wonderful shapes is that most fruit trees can be induced to grow into almost any shape you want. So the gardener has a great opportunity to exercise his imagination to produce a living sculpture. My own garden at Barnsdale now boasts a couple of what I call 'lollipop trees' – an allusion to their shape rather than the fruit they produce!

It was only relatively recently that methods of pruning and training were developed with the express intention of improving the health and cropping potential of the trees. Again, much of the inspiration came from France.

In about 1890, the head gardener at Wagnonville Agricultural College, one Louis Lorette, developed a system of summer pruning designed expressly to increase the efficiency of pear trees. This was the origin of the now universally popular 'cordon' system of growing and, as we shall see, the basis of pruning methods for most trained trees.

It was not until this century that the initiative finally crossed the Channel to East Malling in Kent. The fruit research station based there was set up to provide research into fruit growing for commercial growers. Until then, most commercial orchards were run on more-or-less amateur lines.

I suppose it's true to say that they started by adapting the methods of the big private gardens and applying them to the commercial situation. This led not only to newer methods of pruning and training but to the development of special rootstocks upon which trees are grafted in order to influence their size. Now the wheel has come full circle and we amateurs are adapting those commercial methods to fit our gardens. Many of them seem tailor-made.

# Chapter 2

# DESIGN AND PLANNING

##  DESIGN

The creation of a garden is just as much an art form as painting a picture or writing a concerto. The fact that it's something we can all be successful at does not devalue it as art one bit. And, since the essential essence of all art is that it's a personal expression of the artist, what on earth am I doing advising you on how to design your own garden?

However, even Michelangelo had to learn to use the tools. So look upon my advice as two things. Firstly, I hope to be able to suggest ways of achieving certain effects. There are many tricks of the trade that are simply the equivalent of learning to use the tools. Secondly, please realize that what I'm describing is *my* idea of how the ornamental kitchen garden should look.

Of course you'll want to change things here and there and to adapt my ideas to suit your own garden. If you are ever going to succeed in making a beautiful garden, you must have the confidence to go ahead with your own ideas rather than copying someone else's. After all, this is your garden we're talking about, you're going to live with it, and if it's beautiful in your eyes, then it jolly well *is* beautiful, whatever anyone else may think. So I hope you'll look upon my way as an inspiration but not a definitive blueprint.

**Membership qualifications**

The first and foremost rule of the ornamental kitchen garden is that every component within it must look beautiful. That may seem

a strange statement to make since surely the motivation of every garden designer is to create a thing of beauty. Agreed, but that's not always the first consideration of the kitchen gardener.

On the average allotment, for example, productivity is king. If a rickety structure of wood, corrugated iron and polythene is necessary to produce championship onions, then so be it. If the most convenient spot for the muck heap happens to mean it'll be the focal point of the garden, then no matter. The *sole* reason for the allotment is to grow as much produce as possible and aesthetics count for little.

But our garden needs to serve a dual function. It has to produce bumper crops of good food while at the same time looking marvellous. When you draw the bedroom curtains on a sunny summer morning, you want to look out on a garden full of flowers and foliage, that's buzzing with insects and alive with the song of birds. It beats the muck heap every time!

So, think about every feature carefully. Its position in the garden and the materials it's made of must be sympathetic with the garden as a whole. You'll notice, for example, that in my design I've used octagons for both the greenhouse and the rose arbour. Both, in fact, turn out to be quite functional items, but there's no reason why that should make them any the less beautiful. The shapes match and complement each other well, especially when viewed from the upstairs window.

The paths are made to blend in with the borders so well that after a year they virtually disappear under the wealth of spreading plant material dispersed between the slabs. Walking down the paths without crushing the plants out of existence is a time-consuming job, but that, in my view, is not a disadvantage since you are forced to slow down and so can enjoy your surroundings.

Even the compost bins, although hidden away behind the greenhouse, are made from *real* wood, treated to make them look attractive. No rusting corrugated iron for me!

Every item in the garden has to earn its place by adding something to the beauty of the whole. All my pots and containers are real, hand-thrown terracotta though I have to say they took a bit of saving for. Of course it's possible to force rhubarb under an old tin bucket but the real terracotta forcers look so much better that I actually leave mine in the garden even after they've done their job, because they gladden my eye. Certainly you may have to put up with plastic for the first few years if the budget's a bit tight. But you really will save a lot of money on fruit and vegetables, so you'll be able to treat yourself from time to time.

My cloches had to be hand-made to pass muster. For early vegetables, for ripening some of the later vegetable fruits and for winter protection, cloches are indispensable. But when I made the garden there was simply nothing available that looked at all beautiful. Having been spoilt by seeing some lovely old Victorian lantern cloches in a friend's garden, I simply couldn't bring myself to use a sheet of corrugated plastic! So I knocked up my own and they just about scrape in, I think!

Take care, too, when deciding on the plants you use. Most fruit trees and bushes can be made very attractive by training them into various shapes, and many types of vegetables and herbs are obtainable in more attractive forms. The variegated sage, for example, tastes just as good as the ordinary green one, the yellow beetroot will not disappoint you

and there's even a red Brussels sprout which adds a touch of class to an otherwise uninspiring vegetable!

## Requirements

The basic reason for designing this type of garden is to enable you to grow all your own vegetables and most of your fruit without having to resort to the expensive, stale, pesticide-ridden substitutes you find in the supermarkets. So space for growing plants is obviously the first requirement. Still, that doesn't mean that you have to sacrifice other features you would go for in the traditional design. Though there may not be space for the swimming pool, there's no reason at all to miss out on the patio, lawn, pool, seat in the shade, sandpit for the kids, etc.

So the first thing to do, before starting to draw, is to decide exactly what you want. Make a list in as much detail as possible to include, first of all, everything you *must* have. There has to be a place to put the dustbin, somewhere for the washing line, a place to store garden junk that may come in useful one day. (We all collect bits of wood, second-hand pots and seed trays, etc., that need storing.) There must be space for compost bins and, if you make your own sowing and potting compost, somewhere to mix it.

A second list should include all the features you *want*. This one is likely to be long and in all probability you'll eventually have to prune it down a bit, but put down everything you can think of in order of priority.

Finally make a third list of those features necessary to grow your garden organically. You must, for example, include a pool, and you will need space for compost and the storage of manure if you can get it. A greenhouse is highly desirable and you'll need more paths than the normal garden would use.

When you've made your lists, you'll probably be surprised at how many items feature in all three and at least in two. The patio, for example, may be on the 'wanted' list, but it will also be on the 'necessary' one because a hard space will be needed to house pots and boxes of plants waiting to be planted. The pool may also be considered a luxury, but it's also a necessity for every organic system that relies on wildlife to help with pest control.

## 🐿 THE DRAWING BOARD 🐿

With all your requirements in list form, all you have to do is to transfer them to a drawing, shuffle them around a bit and Bob's your uncle. Put like that, it all sounds pretty easy. In fact the arrangement of all the components into an attractive yet useful and convenient form is one of the most difficult parts of the project. But if you break your list down into its separate parts and address them one at a time, it becomes much easier. In any case, there are certain constraints which leave you few alternatives, so the decisions are not as difficult to make as they may at first appear.

The first job is to draw the outline of the garden on a sheet of paper, and for this you'll need to know a little about basic surveying. You'll also need a surveyor's tape, which you can hire, a clip-board (or a bit of hardboard and a bulldog clip), a pencil and preferably an assistant.

If the garden is exactly square or rectangular and completely empty, with the house sitting square in the plot, you have no problems. Simply measure the fences and, with a set square, draw them on a piece of paper. But of course, that's rarely the case. Nine times out of ten, though the site may *look* rectangular, the boundaries will not be at right angles to each other and the house will not sit square in the middle of the plot.

So the first job is to ascertain the exact position of the four corners (or there may be more on irregularly shaped plots). When you know these you can, of course, join them up to show the position of the fences. You find them with a technique known as 'triangulation'.

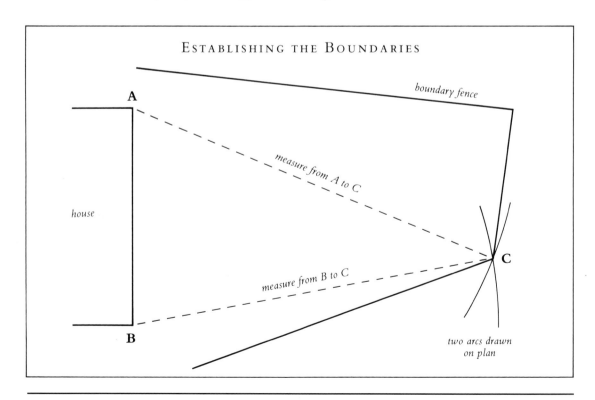

ESTABLISHING THE BOUNDARIES

A

boundary fence

measure from A to C

house

measure from B to C

B

C

two arcs drawn
on plan

Start by measuring the house and drawing it onto the master-plan. You can be certain that the angles will be right angles here, so it's just a straightforward case of measuring. Then you use the corners of the house as the fixed points from which to do your measuring.

Measure first from one corner of the house to the nearest corner of the garden. Draw a very rough plan on a sheet of paper on the clip-board, and mark in the measurement. Then measure from the opposite corner of the house to the *same* corner of the garden. Repeat the process for the other corners of the garden.

Equipped with all these measurements, you can then transfer the shape of the plot onto the master-plan, using a pair of compasses to locate exactly the corners of the plot in relation to the house. You'll have to draw to scale, of course, and the scale you use will depend on the size of the garden and the bit of paper you're using. Obviously it's easier to complete the drawing if the plan is as big as possible, so make the scale as large as you can. Try to make it as convenient as possible to avoid complicated mathematics. Working in metric measurements helps greatly here, since you can work comfortably in tenths, or decimal places – say 1 centimetre is equal to 1 metre. If, like me, you're an old reactionary and find it easier to work in feet and inches, the same principle applies but you'll need a more agile mathematical brain. Something like $\frac{1}{10}$ inch to 1 foot is not too difficult.

Once you've drawn in the boundaries, measure any other permanent features, like trees, manhole covers, etc., again using the triangulation method.

Now you're ready to start planning, but, before you do, there's one last job. Draw the master-plan in ink so that the boundaries and the shape of the house show up well, and then cover it with a piece of tracing paper. You'll find yourself doing lots of crossings off and rubbings out before you finally arrive at the design you want, and this will save you spoiling your master-plan.

 MY OWN GARDEN

My ornamental kitchen garden measures 30 × 50 ft (9 × 15 m). That's a bit bigger than the average estate house garden I know, but I make no excuses for allowing myself that luxury. I had to make a choice: do I make the plot quite small to reflect the average modern garden or do I allow myself a little more space so that I can demonstrate a wider variety of ideas? I decided on the latter and, even so, found myself frustrated by lack of space. And there's an important lesson to be learnt here.

I started out, as I've suggested, by drawing the boundaries on paper, listing my requirements and fitting in all the components. I must say that it looked a bit overcrowded on the drawing and, when I began to mark things out on the ground, it became quite obvious that I had let my enthusiasm run away with me! I simply couldn't fit it all in without creating a messy clutter. I simply had to cut my coat according to the cloth.

Trying to cram too much into a small space is a great mistake and something that's only too easy to do. Bear in mind that I *knew* the rules, but I still overdid it! It's important to remember that the smaller the space the simpler the design should be.

Having said that, it's certainly necessary to mask the square, claustrophobic effect of the three wooden fences most of us start out with. Those lines need to be softened and 'bent' to please the eye. But the way to do that is with plants. There you can, I think, afford to overdo it and, provided you can spare the time for a bit of clipping and training, the effect is always pleasing. But the first thing, of course, is to plan the basic layout.

**The patio**

In this garden, the back of the house faces south, so that's the obvious place to site the patio. There I'll be able to make the most of the sunny summer mornings to eat my breakfast in the company of the birds and the bees. I can put my barbecue in one corner so that it's handy when I want to entertain friends for lunch, and there will still be a corner where the evening sun will brighten a half-hour of pre-prandial relaxation.

But much more important than that, it'll be the ideal spot for my cold frame to catch all the available light in the spring to produce some short, sturdy seedlings. Don't ever feel guilty about allowing a reasonable space for paving, because in this sort of garden you'll always need plenty of hard surfaces for seedlings and plants awaiting their turn to be planted out in the borders.

Notice, too, that I have left a few slabs out near the fences, to allow the planting of permanent plants. This is most important if you are going to maximize the productive potential of your fences, since permanent plants will not do well in containers. It's especially important on the only south-facing wall, since it's here that you'll be able to grow exotic fruits like peaches, nectarines and apricots.

Because the paving slabs are square or rectangular, it's obviously easiest to make the patio in straight lines. The snag with that is that straight lines always look 'hard' and formal. What's more, by cutting across the garden with a straight line you just separate the patio from the rest of the garden and make the plot appear that much smaller.

I solved this problem with a circular lawn that appears to cut into the paving and so effectively links the patio with the rest of the garden. It won't have escaped you, of course, that this will necessitate cutting the paving slabs into a neat arc. It sounds difficult, but in fact it's easy to do with a special stone-cutting saw, which can be hired.

If your house doesn't face south, you may want to consider siting the paved area somewhere else. There's no doubt that, for the reasons I've mentioned, a sunny spot is much to be preferred.

The materials available for paving are many and varied. A trip to a couple of garden centres will produce quite a variety of choices. My own preference in this type of garden is for a natural stone like the marvellous old Yorkstone used to floor many an old building and for pavements. Second-hand slabs are still available and give a wonderful 'lived-in' look straight away. But alas, they're generally too expensive for anything but a tiny area. New slabs are out of the question. There are, however, several excellent imitations made from concrete but good enough to deceive all but the practised eye.

## The paths

Because of the particular way we're going to cultivate this garden, more paths are necessary than would be the case with traditional methods. Ideally, you should be able to reach right to the back of each border without treading on the soil at all. Or, if the beds are between two paths, you should be able to stretch to the middle. In fact, if the design is to be informal that's not always possible, but there are ways of managing, even in this case, without treading on the soil. All will become clear later.

The problem, of course, is that paths, like the patio, tend to look hard and 'man-made', while what we're really trying to achieve is as near a total coverage of plants as we can get. That, after all, is what gardening's all about. So, it's back to the good old compromise!

My paths were made with 18 inch (45 cm) square stepping-stones in the same paving I used for the patio. Generally it's wise not to mix the materials too much or, once again, you finish up with the 'cluttered' look. The slabs are spaced 3 inches (7.5 cm) apart, leaving plenty of space to plant spreading plants between. In a very short time they will grow to part-cover the slabs and to soften the edges. Walking down the paths will generally 'prune' the plants sufficiently to keep enough slab showing to enable you to use the paths, though even here, if you're growing your plants well, you may have to do a bit of cutting back from time to time.

Between the slabs I used pea-shingle to set them off and to increase the drainage around the plants. An inch or two of this material also makes an excellent weed inhibitor. It looks very attractive and, if the budget's tight, there's no reason why you shouldn't dispense with the slabs altogether and just use gravel. Naturally, you'll need to edge the paths with wooden boards to retain the gravel, but you'll cut the cost dramatically. The gravel can still be planted up in much the same way, keeping the plants to the edges and just trimming a little here and there if they get over-exuberant.

The central path is really quite different. I felt that this one needed to be a strong feature, giving shape and form to the whole garden. This time it's not hidden or even camouflaged by plants, but is intended to form a striking feature on its own. The materials need to stand out but should still be warm and sympathetic to the mass of planting that will surround it. So I chose red brick.

On the plan, the path curves from corner to corner, finishing in a hexagon of the same material. But, when the borders are planted and the garden is viewed from ground level, the path disappears behind plants and reappears in a most attractive way, which actually increases the sense of space. It gives you the feeling that, if you follow it, you just *could* come across the Wizard of Oz!

A glance at the plan will show that, unless you fill the garden with paths, you still can't quite reach the middle of all the borders without treading on the soil. The side paths are fine, since the two borders along the fences are just 2 feet (60 cm) wide and therefore easily reached. In the others, you need a two-pronged approach.

When you come to plant them up, put your permanent plants – the trees and shrubs in particular – in the centre of the borders. You'll need to attend to those no more than a couple of times a year, just to prune from time to time and perhaps to feed or mulch, so there won't be a lot of soil-trampling to do. Else-where, all you need is a strategically placed stepping-stone or two. I used logs set on end for mine and they all but disappear among the verdant growth in the summer. They need to be strategically placed, of course, and their position will certainly vary from year to year, planting to planting. So don't actually include them in the design. Better wait until you actu-ally come to plant and then put them in exactly where they're needed.

## The lawn

You may think twice about a lawn. This is the one unproductive area of the garden that can't be used for growing plants other than the grass itself and won't even come in useful for standing out plants awaiting planting. The best that can be said for it from a productive point of view is that the mowings will make excellent, constantly renewed compost and that it does make some wildlife feel more at home.

*Finished lawn and patio in Geoff Hamilton's garden at Barnsdale.*

# MY OWN GARDEN

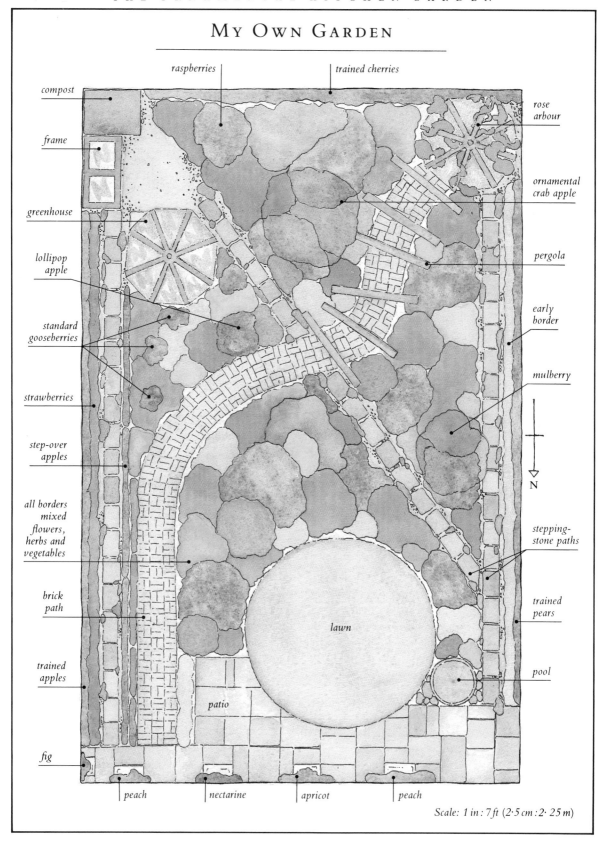

raspberries

trained cherries

compost

rose arbour

frame

ornamental crab apple

greenhouse

pergola

lollipop apple

early border

standard gooseberries

mulberry

strawberries

N

step-over apples

all borders mixed flowers, herbs and vegetables

stepping-stone paths

brick path

trained pears

lawn

trained apples

pool

fig

patio

peach

nectarine

apricot

peach

*Scale: 1 in : 7 ft (2·5 cm : 2· 25 m)*

I included mine because I like it. It makes an excellent foreground to the borders, it creates a certain feeling of space, and it's the kindest material of all for lazing about on and for kids to play on. If you are so inclined, a small lawn can also be used for agreeable leisure activities like clock golf or that well-known raiser of blood pressures and loser of friends, croquet!

Bear in mind, too, that it has to be cut at least once a week in summer and that even a tiny area will demand a mower and a pair of edging shears.

Another approach would be to make a wild flower lawn or to plant the area with ground-cover, and this is what I've done in the large garden plan on p. 43.

Lawns, of course, can be any shape you like. I've made mine circular because I feel that this semi-formal shape serves to link the formal patio area with the extreme informality of the rest of the garden. The one point to bear in mind when siting any grassed area is to put it in the sunshine if you can. Grass in shade will always have to struggle a little and will find it hard to compete with invasions of moss. This is particularly so on heavy or badly-drained soil. If you have to put it in shade, the best bet is to resign yourself to a less formal lawn which can be left longer and only cut about once a month.

## The pergola and rose arbour

In small gardens, there's often little scope for landscaping interesting contours. You might create small features like a rock-garden or raised beds for acid-loving plants but, unless the site has a natural slope, you are, in the main, stuck with working on the flat. And that's a most uninteresting prospect. The solution is to raise the perspective with plants.

Trees are obviously going to help, but in small gardens there's normally only space for one or two and small ones at that. Another way is to use climbing plants. Obviously the fences or walls are going to be used to full effect both for ornamental and productive climbers or wall plants. There's a wide range of fruiting plants, for example, that will greatly increase the productivity of the garden without taking up a lot of space and which will also look very attractive and serve to hide the squareness of a fenced plot. And these can be supplemented with free-standing features like a pergola or a rose arbour.

Both are quite simple for the competent handyman to build and you can buy kits of ready-cut and jointed timber which more or less do the job for you.

The pergola is simply a wooden archway straddling the path. I use mine for growing a number of ornamental climbers, interspersed with edible climbers like grape vines, runner beans and even marrows, cucumbers and squashes. If you choose attractive varieties of vegetables and fruit, they make a summer display every bit as good as the ornamental climbers and for a much longer period too. And, as you can imagine, bright yellow, rugby-ball sized squashes and striped marrows at eye level make quite a talking point!

The rose arbour is the main focal point of the garden. After only a year, it forms a flower-covered mound which makes an eye-catching feature, serving to invite the eye to the farthest corner of the garden, thus creating an illusion of space. Somehow it makes you want to follow that red-brick path to discover the shady delights within. Planted generously, it makes an entirely private little den in which you can retire with your book, however built-up it may be around you. These days I find that kind of therapy is much to be desired.

The arbour is octagonal in shape for practical as well as aesthetic reasons. It would probably be even more practical to make it square or rectangular and, if you feel the octagon is beyond your do-it-yourself capabilities, there's nothing to stop you taking the easier path. But there's no doubt that the eight-sided shape is much more exciting and it also provides more supports for climbers. It really isn't difficult to build, especially if you adapt one of the pergola kits you can buy in most garden centres. But from the design point of view, my main reason for using it was that it reflects so well the shape of the greenhouse, giving the whole layout a certain cohesion.

Inside the rose arbour sits my indulgence. Though you only catch tantalizing glimpses of it as you walk down the path, when you enter the arbour you're faced with the most beautiful seat I could find. It's an Edwin Lutyens design and it cost me a small fortune. But I've estimated that two years' profits from my home-grown fruit and vegetables should just about cover it!

## The greenhouse

A greenhouse should not be looked upon as an expensive luxury. If you aim to be near self-sufficient in vegetables, fruit and flowers, it's an essential piece of equipment. The alternative is to buy all your seedlings from the garden centre and it doesn't take an Albert Einstein to see how much more that's going to cost in the long run.

My own calculations show that, even at the most pessimistic, allowing for buying composts, fertilizers and containers in small quantities and heating the greenhouse, home-raised bedding plants and vegetable seedlings will cost a third of the price of buying them in. Add to that the fact that you'll be able to raise crops of tomatoes, cucumbers, peppers, aubergines, salads and even exotics like figs, grapes and oranges, and you'll realize that it soon becomes economic. And that says nothing of the creative enjoyment you'll derive from it. There's no satisfaction I know like raising a beautiful flower, a fine-tasting plate of vegetables or a bowl of delicious fruit right from scratch. It beats a meal in a restaurant any day and it'll cost you far less!

An octagonal greenhouse makes a very pleasant addition to the garden and has the other great advantage over a rectangular one, that it makes no difference which way you face it. In a small garden you can fit it in almost anywhere.

Greenhouses are available in aluminium, of course, but I chose cedar wood. That's a bit more expensive than metal but it blends in well with the rest of the garden while aluminium does tend to stand out on its own.

There is a school of thought that insists that aluminium greenhouses are to be preferred because they allow better light admission. This is a valid point, I think, only if you're going to be using the house for raising seedlings in winter, like the commercial grower would. Certainly at that time it's vital to make use of every available bit of light. But most amateur gardeners won't start sowing until February or even March when there's plenty of light available. By May, you'll need to be shading the glass, so all in all, I see little advantage in aluminium except the initial cost.

If you include a greenhouse in the garden, you'll need a cold frame too. After raising seedlings in a heated greenhouse they need to be acclimatized to the lower temperatures outside before planting out. The cold frame is ideal for the job. It's not too expensive to buy ready made, though it's very simple to make your own (see p. 63).

When it comes to siting it, I would suggest that you remain flexible. They are fairly portable things and can be moved around to make best use of the available sun. In the spring, for example, I would put it on my south-facing patio where the increased light will ensure strong, sturdy seedlings. In summer, it could be moved to the shadier part next to the compost heap, where plants like melons and cucumbers will relish the light shade.

## The pool

As I've previously suggested, an organic garden is not complete without a source of water for birds and insects. These, together with frogs, toads and perhaps small mammals, will use the pool and in return will go off and help control your pests.

A small garden can naturally only accommodate a small pool, but that doesn't matter. Provided you keep it topped up, even a tiny pool will suffice. Mine was made from a 2 foot (60 cm) diameter half-barrel and I sited it in the border so that plants would grow around it and into it to soften the rather hard edge. After only a few months it looked as if it had always been there.

Informal pools are also very easy to make, using a plastic or butyl liner (see p. 60). You can make them any shape and size you want, so they're easy to fit into the overall design. I've included an informal pool in the design for a large garden on p. 43.

## The utility area

Every garden must allow space for work. You'll need somewhere to mix composts or perhaps to set up your potting bench on sunny days. You'll need a certain amount of storage space for the bits of useful junk every gardener collects and you may need room for a water butt and, of course, the essential compost heaps.

I concreted a small triangular area behind the greenhouse where it won't be seen too easily. In fact, if everything is kept tidy, my home-made wooden compost bins and the cold frame don't look at all unsightly. If they really do offend your eye, it's not difficult to build a screen of trellis which, when covered with climbing plants, would hide the work area completely.

## Containers

In a small garden like this, everything, to earn its place, must be beautiful, so I took some care over the selection of containers. In the first year, I started out with plastic ones because they're cheap. Gradually, by saving

pennies and by dropping heavy hints at Christmas, I have replaced them with more attractive pots. Mind you, there are some quite good plastic containers available and I realize that I'm in danger of being branded a horticultural snob, but they're simply not a patch on good terracotta, stone or wood.

In summer, of course, when the containers are full to overflowing with flowering and fruiting plants, the pots themselves are hardly noticed. But in winter, when even close planting of bulbs, wallflowers, pansies or the like fails to hide the sides of the pots, the nature of the container itself is important. They should be looked on, like statuary, as decorative features in their own right, even when they're empty. I have even resorted to hand-thrown clay pots for growing my greenhouse tomatoes, melons, etc. for no better reason than that it does me good to look at them.

One word of warning. If you do decide on terracotta containers, do make sure that they're guaranteed frost-proof. It is possible to buy pots that are guaranteed for several years and, though you may pay a little more for them, they're well worth the extra. Avoid especially the very attractive clay pots from places like Spain and Mexico. They look lovely but won't last their first British winter.

*Container with white petunias, argyranthemum, begonias and blue lobelia mixed with helichrysum.*

## PLANNING THE PLANTING

Much of the planting of the ornamental kitchen garden is done with annuals at intervals throughout the season, but naturally trees, shrubs and herbaceous perennials have their place too. These will be permanent plantings of course or, with many of the herbaceous plants, at least semi-permanent, so their position needs careful planning at the design stage. Mind you, that doesn't mean that if you feel later on that you've made a mistake you have to grin and bear it for ever. Trees and shrubs will stand moving in their first or second year and herbaceous plants can be shifted at will any time. Indeed, most will need to be lifted, divided and replanted at two- or three-yearly intervals anyway. So have a stab at getting it right first time, of course, but don't get paranoid about it!

Start by choosing and planning the trees. The first point to bear in mind here is that they must be of a size that will suit the garden. There's a list of trees for small spaces on p. 121 to help you choose. Remember that trees will alter the growing conditions for some way around them so they'll materially affect what other planting you're able to do. When they grow to any size, they'll shade the soil beneath them and they'll compete with any other planting for water and nutrients.

That shouldn't put you off trees of course. There are loads of flowering plants that will relish the shade and several vegetables too, so

A TYPICAL BORDER
IN SUMMER

there will be plenty you can grow under trees. You'll have to pay extra attention to feeding the soil and you'll probably have to water artificially as well, but that shouldn't be a problem.

In this garden, the trees are there for other than purely aesthetic reasons and you should take this into account when choosing them. To begin with, of course, you may decide on a purely productive tree and so choose one that will bear fruit. When you come to think about it, if a nurseryman's catalogue offered a tree that bore masses of pink and white blossoms in spring, followed by bright red, yellow or muticoloured berries the size of your fist in late summer, you'd jump at it. And that, of course, exactly describes an apple tree!

The other factor to bear in mind is the value of the tree as an attractor of wildlife, birds in particular. Any tree will provide perching space and many will be valued for nesting too. Lots provide a hiding place for insects which will also attract birds and, if you choose something like one of the mountain ashes, you'll be providing a feast of berries in autumn and winter as well. Some gardeners resent the fact that birds strip trees of their berries, but there's little doubt that the advantages outweigh the disadvantages. The berries always last for quite a while into the autumn and the pleasure of watching the birds feeding more than makes up for their loss. After all, the garden is not just a static tableau to look at – it's a *living* thing. What's more, if you're

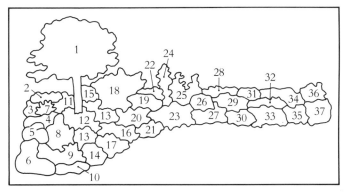

## KEY

1 Apple tree
2 Radish
3 Chives
4 *Genista pilosa* 'Lemon Spreader'
5 Lettuce
6 French marigold
7 Garlic
8 Lupin

9 Carrot
10 Lobelia
11 *Saponaria ocymoides*
12 Hosta

13 Potato
14 *Dianthus deltoides*
15 Beetroot
16 Petunia
17 *Bergenia stracheyi*
18 *Deutzia* 'Mont Rose'
19 *Rudbeckia fulgida* 'Goldsturm'
20 Rhubarb chard
21 *Limnanthes douglasii*
22 *Silene schafta*
23 French bean
24 Jerusalem artichoke

25 Bush tomato
26 Onion
27 Cerastium
28 *Begonia semperflorens*
29 Coreopsis
30 Parsley
31 Thyme
32 Courgette
33 Dwarf convolvulus
34 Impatiens
35 *Salvia* 'Tom Thumb'
36 Spinach
37 Golden sage

kind to the birds, they'll certainly repay their debt in pest control.

Flowering trees also serve to attract insects of which bees are particularly important. They, of course, play a vital role in the pollination of plants, including fruit trees. If you're unsure that you're getting good pollination of apples, for example, just plant one of a few varieties of flowering crab apple and the bees will do the rest.

When you position your chosen trees on the plan, take into account the position of the sun and where the shadows will be cast, and generally try to put them in the centre of the border. The edges, where you can reach from the paths, are best reserved for planting the vegetables and annual flowers to make access easier without treading on the soil.

Exactly the same rules apply when you choose and plant shrubs and roses. Avoid plants that are going to swamp the borders and aim to plant them near the middle of the borders.

Trees and shrubs, once planted, are best left where they are, but herbaceous perennials are more flexible. They can go nearer the edges and can be part of a two- or three-year rotation plan. In fact, in this type of garden, planting is so varied and haphazard that a traditionally planned rotation of vegetable crops is out of the question. The only rule I would strongly recommend is simply to avoid planting a crop where the same thing has recently grown. So when after two or three

years you come to lift and divide your herbaceous plants, you can replant in a different spot and use the soil they have come from, after revitalization, for vegetables or annuals.

These, of course, will be constantly changing, so there's no need to include them on the initial plan. I suppose that if you were really meticulous you might plan the planting areas each season. But such a complicated job could drive you mad, so the method I recommend is just to wait until a space becomes available where you've harvested a crop and then replant. This may mean holding a few plants in pots or boxes until the space becomes available, but it has the great advantage that every available inch of space is always being used. The garden looks fuller and better and it's much, much more productive.

*Flowers and vegetables waiting to be planted.*

## 🦎 THE LARGE GARDEN 🦎

You may feel that in a larger garden there's no need to grow flowers, fruit and vegetables all together in the same borders. After all, there's enough room to include all the ornamental features you may want while still leaving space for a traditional vegetable plot and perhaps a fruit garden too. Perfectly true, but don't forget the other distinct advantages of mixed planting.

A wide diversity of planting will encourage the build-up of a balanced community of wildlife – pests and predators – which ensures that no one single species becomes a problem. It's also possible to camouflage fruit and vegetable crops by mixed planting, so that the pests that locate their host plants by sight are frustrated. Furthermore, diseases that spread rapidly from plant to plant when they're grown in a block are much easier to contain when plants are more isolated. And finally, it's a method that looks great and is simple and fun to do.

The basic design principles are just the same as those described for a small garden, though there are one or two extra difficulties – and space for some additional features.

The first 'problem' in my example is that the garden slopes up away from the house. Many gardens present this kind of difficulty and I felt it would be cheating to make life too easy! In fact, a slope can be seen as an advantage because it enables you to create an interesting variation of levels. I don't believe in just leaving the slopes as they are as that makes for uncomfortable gardening.

It's much better to terrace the garden into a series of plateaux, linked by steps and steep banks, but you need to be a little bit subtle. If you simply build a number of walls straight across from side to side, you effectively cut the garden into strips. This inevitably has a fore-shortening effect and looks very boring indeed. What I've done here is to make the terraces in a kind of zig-zag pattern to avoid these straight lines.

Note that the paved area includes a drain and soakaway. When the garden slopes up from the house, that's most essential if the patio is not to become a swimming pool after the first shower!

The next problem is a couple of established trees. Obviously it would be a sin to take them out, so they have to be incorporated into the design. Under the one nearest the house I've used grass but, unlike the rest of the lawn, this will be allowed to grow long and will only be cut twice a year. The grass can be planted with a selection of wild flowers to make an attractive floral 'meadow' which will also contribute to the attraction of birds and insects. Even a tiny wild-flower meadow will be filled with the flutter of butterflies and the buzz of bees and hoverflies in summer (see p. 66).

I've put a seat under the other one and this is surrounded by ground-cover planting of things like crane's-bills (*Geranium*) and barrenworts (*Epimedium*), which will thrive in dry shade.

Because the garden is large, it obviously costs a lot more to build. So instead of using expensive materials like paving stepping-stones or brick paviors, I've economized. The steps from the patio have to be made of stone to match the paving, but the others are made with railway sleepers. They're quite easy to obtain through the classified columns of the farming magazines and they're much cheaper and easier to install. The paths are made with gravel to cut costs too. If you wish, you can of course add the stepping-stones later.

Here there's also space for a fruit arch which is a marvellous way to grow a selection of apples and pears to give you continuity of picking. The arches are available in plastic-covered metal, and after a couple of years when the trees have grown to meet in the middle they look superb (see p. 202).

There's also room for a larger pool, so here you could raise a colony of frogs, which are the most effective slug controllers I know.

# PLAN FOR A SMALL GARDEN

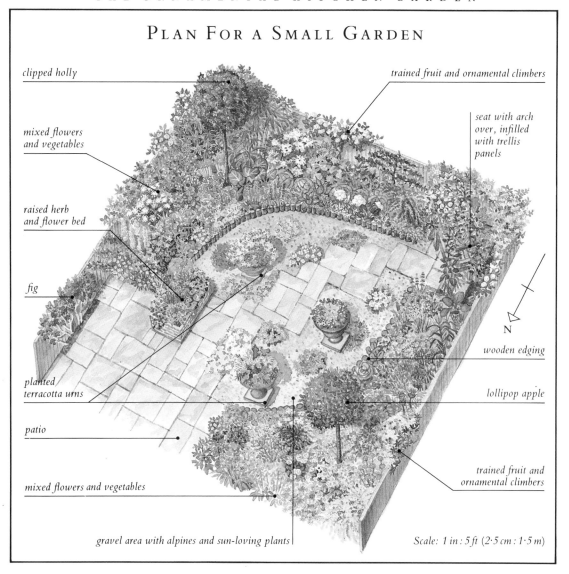

clipped holly

trained fruit and ornamental climbers

mixed flowers
and vegetables

seat with arch
over, infilled
with trellis
panels

raised herb
and flower bed

fig

N

wooden edging

planted
terracotta urns

lollipop apple

patio

mixed flowers and vegetables

trained fruit and
ornamental climbers

gravel area with alpines and sun-loving plants

Scale: 1 in : 5 ft (2·5 cm : 1·5 m)

This one is made with a butyl-rubber liner and includes an artificial bog garden to increase the range of plants you can grow. If you plant the back of the pool to provide a bit of cover, you'll be able to sit in the arbour and watch a great variety of birds who'll surely come for a bath and a drink. I would do without ornamental fish though, because they'll eat frog spawn and some of the insects which come for a drink.

The raised bed near the house could be made with brick or stone, or again, railway sleepers, and can be used for a variety of purposes. If your soil is limy, you may decide to fill it with an acid soil and grow ericaceous plants like rhododendrons, heathers, pieris, etc. Alternatively, if you're of a culinary bent, you could make it a herb garden where the herbs will be almost within reach of the kitchen window.

The work area is somewhat larger than the one in the small garden, so here you could fit in a larger, rectangular greenhouse. In a bigger garden you'll certainly need to raise more plants. You'll also need more space for compost of course, so I've allowed for four bins instead of two. In this type of garden you simply can't make too much compost.

# PLAN FOR A LARGE GARDEN

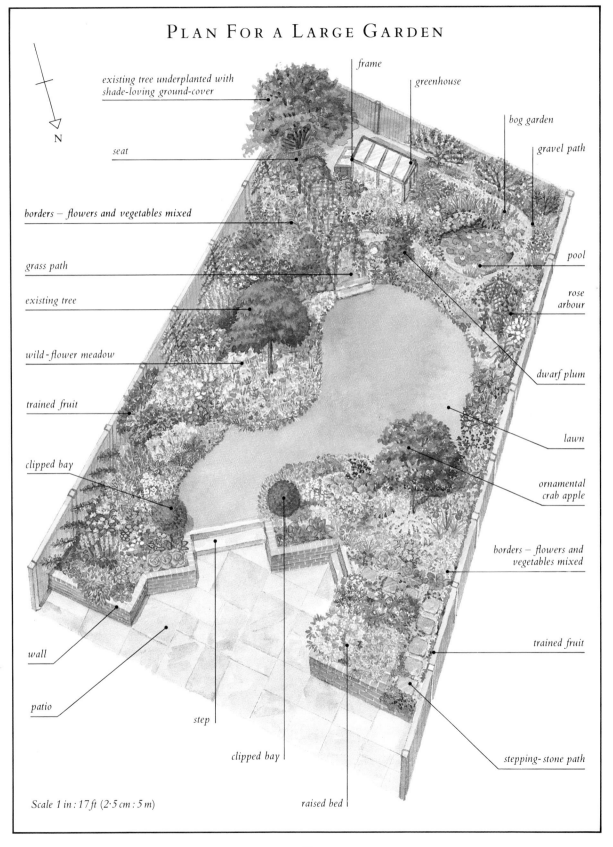

N

existing tree underplanted with
shade-loving ground-cover

seat

borders – flowers and vegetables mixed

grass path

existing tree

wild-flower meadow

trained fruit

clipped bay

wall

patio

frame

greenhouse

bog garden

gravel path

pool

rose
arbour

dwarf plum

lawn

ornamental
crab apple

borders – flowers and
vegetables mixed

trained fruit

stepping-stone path

step

clipped bay

raised bed

Scale 1 in : 17 ft (2·5 cm : 5 m)

## 🌿 PLANNING THE FORMAL GARDEN 🌿

Medieval gardens were always very formal in design, growing vegetables, herbs and flowers together in rectangular and circular beds. It's a style that fits modern gardens quite well, particularly when space is so limited that informal designs become difficult.

My own formal garden developed from a plot of 'deep-beds' which I have found to be an excellent way to grow vegetables, increasing yields per square yard by at least a hundred per cent. The method of making them is described on p. 75.

It's important with these formal designs that the geometric style of the beds should be clearly defined since the informal nature of the planting and the very formal shapes of the beds make a very pleasing contrast.

To achieve this, the beds should be edged with a permanent material. If you can lay

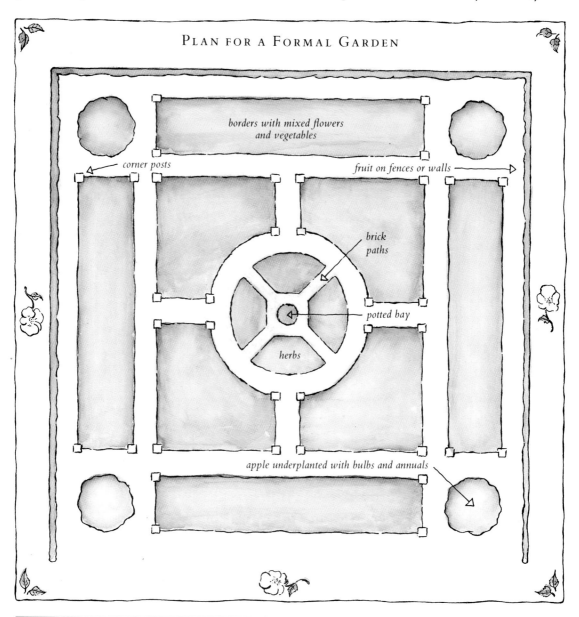

PLAN FOR A FORMAL GARDEN

*borders with mixed flowers and vegetables*

*corner posts*

*fruit on fences or walls*

*brick paths*

*potted bay*

*herbs*

*apple underplanted with bulbs and annuals*

## TWO SIMPLE DESIGNS FOR A HERB GARDEN

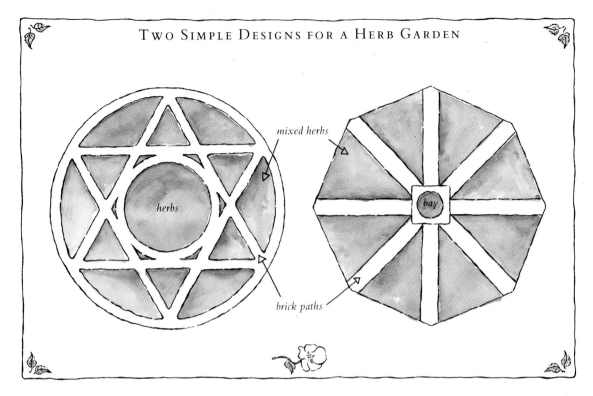

*mixed herbs*

*herbs*

*bay*

*brick paths*

hands on some Victorian edging tiles or even engineering bricks, you can make a very decorative edging indeed. But the easiest and certainly the cheapest way is to use wood. Mine was 4 × 1 in (10 × 2.5 cm) timber stained green and supported on wooden pegs. Just to embellish the corners a little, I put in some posts with a decorative acorn on the top of each and, though originally intended purely for decoration, I discovered that they were useful too. They enable me to pull the hose round the garden without any danger of it crushing the plants in the beds (see p. 69).

The paths are made simply and cheaply by spreading a couple of inches of pea-shingle between the beds.

Though the beds are strictly formal, the planting within should be fairly informal. I use annual flowers like marigolds, petunias and cosmos in among the vegetables, for the dual purpose of attracting insect predators and giving a lift to the spirits.

The herb garden is made in an octagonal shape and again edged with timber. The cart-

wheel shape is a traditional one for herbs, with the 'spokes' in this case being made with brick paviors to facilitate access. It's important in this and any other small herb garden to avoid tall or rampant-growing varieties. One plant of lovage or angelica, for example, would swamp the lot, so stick to lower-growing plants like thyme, marjoram, dill, sage and parsley.

The fertility in this garden is maintained with horse manure, which is pretty widely available though rather expensive. In order to make the most of it, I use it twice. I buy it fresh and stack it in my hotbed, which enables me to produce very early crops cheaply when prices are high in the shops. Then, after a year, when the manure has rotted down, I dig it into the garden. You'll find the hotbed details on p. 64.

Don't forget to include a bed for the permanent crops like rhubarb, asparagus and seakale and, if you have walls or fences round the garden, to use them to grow trained fruit trees (see p. 202).

## KNOTS AND PARTERRES

Knot gardens and parterres were popular in this country and in France as far back as the fifteenth century. In a formal setting they still make a delightful feature even in modern gardens. You can make something very complicated as a feature in its own right or you can stick to a simpler design and use it to make a formal structure for growing herbs. If you do decide to grow herbs within the edgings,

you'll have to make sure you don't use anything too rampant and you'll certainly have to do some cutting back from time to time to prevent the herbs growing into the hedging plants and spoiling them.

The standard plant for making a knot is box, but there are alternatives. Indeed, many knot gardens and parterres use a variety of different coloured plants like thymes, lavender and cotton lavender (*Santolina*) to make an attractive contrast.

*The knot garden at Hatfield House in Hertfordshire.*

## A SIMPLE PARTERRE

*all beds with mixed flowers and vegetables*

*gravel paths*

*box edging*

The snag with box is that it's expensive. But if you have patience, you can easily take cuttings to reduce the costs. I made a fair sized knot all from one plant which cost 50p to buy. In the first year the number of cuttings available is small, but from then on you can take cuttings from the cuttings, so you soon have enough. It took five years from scratch for mine (see p. 150).

There are numerous designs you can use, and it's fun to sit down with a piece of paper, a pair of compasses and a set square and design your own. The one illustrated here is simple enough to incorporate into even a small garden, but it can, of course, be made to any size. Details of how to build a parterre are on pp. 70–1.

# Chapter 3

## CONSTRUCTION AND CULTIVATION

### 🌼 MAKING A CLEAN START 🌼

By the time you've finished planning, your enthusiasm will be running high. You'll be tempted to rush out and get at it just as soon as the weather allows. Before you do, it'll pay to mark out with canes the shape of your paths and borders and the position of the patio and greenhouse, etc. Then wander around and try to visualize how it'll look. It takes a bit of imagination of course and you'll still need to be flexible when you come to actually start building, but it could save you a bit of unnecessary work.

It always pays to start clean, so the first job will probably be to clear up and remove piles of builder's rubbish. If there's a lot of it, hire a skip and get rid of it all, right away. It'll make life a lot easier and you'll feel a sight better when you've done it! The same goes for weeds, and here I have to admit to being unashamedly non-organic.

If your plot is infested with a pernicious weed like bindweed, ground elder or couch-grass, it's absolutely essential to get rid of every scrap of it before you start. If you're in a hurry to get going, there's only one way to do it – weedkiller. Yes, I know that's a dirty word in our language, but this is the one and only concession that I think can be allowed. Spray the lot with glyphosate, a couple of times if necessary, and from then on never let a drop of chemical pass the gate.

If you simply can't bring yourself to be that philistine, you'll have to sacrifice the first season and cover the lot with black polythene. If you exclude the light for a year, you should get rid of even bindweed and couch-grass and you don't actually have to waste the year. You could cut small slits in the polythene and plant potatoes through it. That way you'll still kill the weeds but the potatoes will grow through the slits and give you a fair crop. But you must make sure that no weeds find their way through the slits, or you'll be back where you started.

The other alternative is to work at it slowly, pulling or hoeing the weeds as soon as they appear. But it's a long and arduous task and you never really win in the end.

With the site clean, construction can start. Begin with the 'hard' landscaping – the patio, paths, pergola, etc. These features will set not only the position of the lawn and the borders, but the levels too, so you'll have to get them done first. They're also the messiest jobs, so it's good to get them out of the way before you start cultivations.

## ❧ LAYING A PATIO ❧

Making a good job of laying a patio is not as difficult as it looks, but it's vital to take lots of time and trouble over getting it just right. If a border looks wrong when it's finished or a bit of turf dies, if a few plants fail to survive or you decide you've planted a tree in the wrong place – well it's not the end of the world and it's easy to put right. But if the patio's badly done, it could spell disaster.

You must be meticulous with your initial levelling, especially if, as is generally the case, the paving joins the house wall. Get the slope wrong and you could find water seeping into the sitting room.

It's important to use adequate foundations, especially if the house is new. If it is, the footings will have been dug out with an over-sized machine and refilled. That soil will *always* sink, however firm it may seem at first. So putting down a bit of hardcore and laying the slabs on sand will simply not do. It'll result in the paving sinking unevenly and tipping and tilting all over the place. That looks awful and is very dangerous indeed. The good news is that it's not a job that takes a lot of skill and it's not nearly as back-breaking as it seems at first sight.

### Setting out

Start by marking out the shape of the paved area with strong pegs. If you have a young family, it's a good idea to paint the pegs white and to warn them of the danger of tripping over them. Make the area a couple of inches bigger overall, to allow a margin of error.

*The finished patio. Laid in a random pattern, the slabs look attractive and provide a useful surface.*

Then cut a number of levelling pegs about 1 foot (30 cm) long and mark a clear line on each, $2\frac{1}{2}$ inches (6.5 cm) from the top – you'll see why later. Bang in the first one near the wall of the house. The top of it represents the finished level of the paving and should come at least two courses of bricks below the damp-proof course. This generally consists of a slightly thicker layer of mortar between the bricks, but sometimes, on older houses particularly, it's a course of blue engineering bricks.

To level the rest of the pegs and the slabs, you'll need a straight-edge 8–9 feet (2.5–3 m) long, and a spirit-level. You'll be able to hire both those. Now put a row of pegs 8–9 feet (2.5–3 m) apart along the house wall in a line, setting each one level with the first peg. The second row of pegs should be 3–4 feet (90–120 cm) away from the wall, but these must be a little lower than the first row to allow the paving to slope away from the house. To ensure an even slope, put a $\frac{1}{2}$ inch (1 cm) piece of wood on the first of the new row of pegs and level as before. Remove the wood and the peg will be $\frac{1}{2}$ inch (1 cm) lower. Then set the second row level with that peg. If the patio is wide you may need a third row which should be exactly the same distance apart and again, $\frac{1}{2}$ inch (1 cm) lower.

## The base

With all the pegs in position, you should now dig out to about 6 inches (15 cm) below the top of the pegs. That leaves enough room for a good, solid base.

The base is made by mixing 8 parts of ballast with 1 part of cement. You'll find it an easy job if you don't add any water at all. Just mix it dry and spread it out over the area so that it finishes at the line you've marked on the pegs. Then go over it all, treading it down firmly, and add a little more to again bring it up to the line. In a very short time, water from below and of course rain from above will wet the mixture enough to weld it into a solid block. You can start laying the slabs straight away.

## Laying the slabs

You may decide to work out a pattern of slabs first of all and to stick to that. I prefer to make

LAYING A PATIO

**1** *Start by setting out level pegs, so that the tops are at the proposed surface level of the paving.*

**2** *Dig out the soil as necessary to allow 6 inches (15 cm) below the top of the pegs.*

**3** *Make the base with a mix of 8 parts of ballast to 1 part of cement. Spread so that it comes to about 2 inches (5 cm) below the top of the pegs. Tread it down firmly.*

a completely random effect by laying the slabs as they come. It means you have to think a couple of slabs ahead of yourself all the time, to avoid long 'tramlines' between slabs, but the finished, informal effect is much more in keeping with this type of garden.

The slabs are set on a mortar made by mixing 3 parts of builders' sand with 1 part of cement, mixed so that it's fairly dry. If you make it too wet it'll slump with the weight of the slabs. Set each slab on five small heaps of mortar to bring them at least 2 inches (5 cm) above the finished level and then tap them down level. Do this with the handle of a 3 lb (1.4 kg) club-hammer to avoid damaging the slabs. You'll ruin the hammer handle but they're easily replaced.

Level the slab against the tops of the pegs using the straight-edge and spirit-level, checking carefully both ways. It's important to get every slab just right and if it's not, or if it rocks when you push down one corner, it's worth while lifting it and starting again.

The second slab is set flush with the first, without allowing space for mortar between. In my view they look a lot better that way but the main reason is that these small spaces allow water to percolate between the slabs so the patio will quickly dry out after rain.

Then continue laying the remainder of the slabs in just the same way. Make sure that when you see a long line developing between slabs that you 'break' it by laying a slab across it. Naturally, you shouldn't walk on the slabs for at least a couple of days and preferably a week, to give them a chance to set solid.

In my designs, I've allowed for beds against the walls of the house and the side fences. This is essential in small gardens where you need to make maximum use of every available inch of space, including the walls. Climbing plants and especially trained fruit trees will not do well in pots so it's important to allow room to plant them directly into the soil. The way to manage that is to put the base in so that it covers the whole area but to leave out slabs where you want the beds to be. Later, it's no problem to chip out the dry cement base with a cold chisel and remove it. Then the soil underneath can be dug, manure or compost incorporated and good soil put on top to bring it slightly above the level of the paving. Then your wall plants will reward you with prolific crops.

**4** *The slabs are laid on five piles of mortar, one at each corner and one in the middle.*

**5** *Set the slabs carefully on the top. Each slab should butt up closely to its neighbour.*

**6** *Tap the slabs down firmly with the handle of a hammer, checking regularly with the straight-edge for level.*

## SCREE PATHS

Paths are a bit of a problem. In a small ornamental kitchen garden cultivated on the 'modified deep-bed style' (see p. 75) they're absolutely necessary so that all the cultivations can be done without trampling down the soil. But they do take up quite a lot of space.

To make matters worse, it's a fact that narrow paths tend to actually reduce the apparent size of the garden, giving it a mean, 'pinched' look, while a wide sweep has a noble, expansive air. Yet no gardener worth his salt wants to fill his small plot with concrete, gravel or paving slabs – plants are the thing and as much space as possible must be saved for them. The scree path solves all the problems perfectly.

Start by marking out the path with a couple of garden lines. I made mine 2 feet 6 inches (75 cm) wide, but there's no reason why it should not be wider. Don't make it a lot narrower though, or you'll lose it under a tangle of plants!

Dig out slightly wider than the lines to make sure you have room to work, going down no more than 4–5 inches (10–12 cm).

You'll then need to make a wooden edging to retain the gravel. Use 3 × 1 inch (7.5 × 2.5 cm) timber and ideally buy it pressure-treated with preservative. That way it'll literally last a lifetime.

The edging is simply nailed into pegs driven into the ground on the *outside* of the path. Set them so that they finish a little lower than the edging boards. Eventually they'll be covered with soil and you won't see them.

As you nail the boards onto the pegs, check regularly with a spirit-level to ensure that both sides are level.

The slabs are laid on a good, free-draining compost. Make it up by mixing about 3 parts of the soil you dug out with 1 of sphagnum peat or ground coconut fibre and 2 parts of coarse grit.

Dump the compost between the edging boards and rake it out roughly. Then go over it all, treading it down, just as if you were preparing for a lawn (see p. 64).

The slabs are just laid on the top and tapped down with the handle of a club-hammer. Obviously, you'll need to adjust the compost bed before you lay each one, taking a little off or adding some to bring it to the right level. The tops should come just below the level of the top of the edging boards, so you can check

LAYING A SCREE PATH

**1** *Start by putting in the edging boards. Use 3 × 1 inch (7.5 × 2.5 cm) timber nailed to pegs made from the same material.*

**2** *Dig out to leave 3 inches (7.5 cm) and fill with a compost made from equal parts soil, peat and coarse grit. Tread the compost down and level.*

**3** *Make sure each slab is exactly the same distance from the edging board by using a small piece of wood as a spacer.*

by placing a piece of wood across. I also keep a long straight-edge handy and check each slab against those I've already laid, to be quite sure.

Make sure, too, that each slab is exactly the same distance from the edging boards with exactly the same spacing between each one. The easy way is to keep a piece of wood handy to use as a spacer when you position each slab.

The next step is to fill between the slabs with the same coarse grit or pea-shingle used for making the compost, and then comes the exciting part.

The plants should be chosen carefully, bearing in mind that they may take a fair amount of wear and tear from careless feet. There are many alpine plants that are suitable and these are simply planted between the slabs. Eventually they'll spread to cover and soften the edges of the slabs. Indeed, you may have to do a bit of judicial clipping back from time to time after the first season.

It should be said that there is a strong likelihood that the slabs will sink a little at first, and of course they never do so evenly. In fact a little sinkage serves to make the path look less formal and rigid, but you may find you need to lift the odd one or two and to push a

*The plants beside the scree path will spread to obscure the hard edges of the slabs, making an attractive planted walkway.*

little compost underneath. However, after six months or so, the plant roots will have stabilized them and they'll move no more.

Because the ornamental kitchen garden is so closely planted, a lot of trimming, training and tying is necessary and the scree path is no exception. Most of the alpine plants you'll be using will be sun-lovers so it's essential to prevent plants from the borders flopping over to cover them. So, keep an eye on them, especially in summer when growth is fast, and clip back the plants in the borders as necessary. For a selection of plants suitable for the scree path, see p. 153.

**4** *Set the slabs on top and tap them down level.*

**5** *Brush more of the coarse grit between the slabs to make an attractive finish and to protect the plants against wet.*

**6** *Plant between and alongside the slabs with spreading alpine plants. Choose plants that will put up with a little damage from feet.*

## ❧ BRICK PATHS ☙

Brick paviors are marvellous for paths because they provide a soft, informal look and they're obtainable in some very warm colours. I chose a traditional deep red which looks great wet or dry. They do tend to look a bit municipal when they're first put down. But, if you lay them as I've suggested, they'll move very, very slightly, which will not be enough to make the path dangerous but just right to give that less formal look. What's more, the joints become mossed after a short while to add that final touch of maturity.

But you *must* make sure you use proper paviors. Bricks intended for wall building are much too soft and will flake after the first frost. Most garden centres or builders' merchants will be able to supply a range.

The paviors are set in sand but, unless the base of the path is very well consolidated, you'll need to put down some concrete first. Do this in exactly the way described for the base of the patio (see p. 50).

The first job is to provide an edging to ensure that the sand doesn't work out from underneath the bricks at a later stage. You can do this with $3 \times 1$ inch ($7.5 \times 2.5$ cm) timber in the way described for the scree path (see p. 52). Before you do it, lay out a few bricks loose on the ground to roughly the width you want the path. Allow a space of about $\frac{1}{4}$ inch (6 mm) between them and then measure the width exactly. If you set your edging to that width, you'll save yourself a lot of cutting.

With the edging installed and the dry concrete base laid, you can now make the sand-bed. Use sharp sand rather than the orange-coloured builders' sand to make the bed for brick-laying. Spread it out roughly almost to the top of the boards and then tread it down firmly. Go over the whole area with your weight on your heels, paying special attention to the edges, so that the base is really firm.

It's important now to get the top of the sand-bed absolutely level. This is done with a home-made scraper, which is simply a length of wood a little wider than the path, with two notches cut in the ends. The notches should be $1\frac{1}{2}$ inches (4 cm) deep, so that when you rest the ends on the timber edging the scraper rests $1\frac{1}{2}$ inches (4 cm) below the edging. When you set out the bricks, you'll find they stand

LAYING A BRICK PATH

**1** *The wooden edging is supported on stout pegs. Cut a marker board first to measure the correct width. Check with a spirit-level that the edging boards are dead level both sides.*

**2** *If the path is curved, you will need to make a series of saw-cuts in the edging boards.*

**3** *Put down 2 inches (5 cm) of dry concrete and then cover with a layer of sand. Consolidate it by treading. Cut a scraper board to give the correct depth of sand and use it to level the surface.*

slightly proud of the edging, allowing just enough to bed them down level when you come to consolidate them.

Scrape the sand level and then lay the bricks. There are all kinds of patterns you can use, but make sure you leave at least $\frac{1}{4}$ inch (6 mm) between the joints. On the straight part of the path, the way to do that is to have a piece of $\frac{1}{4}$ inch (6 mm) plywood handy to put between the bricks as you set them out. On the curved part, you'll find that you need wider gaps occasionally, so here just set them by eye, making them as uniform as possible.

Though it's not absolutely necessary, I would suggest just tapping the bricks down a little with the handle of a 3 lb (1.4 kg) hammer. This beds them in just enough to ensure that they stay put while you work.

When you've laid a few rows, throw a couple of shovelfuls of dry, sharp sand over the top and brush it in to fill all the cracks.

The final bashing down is done with a stout board across the width of the path. This is thumped with a large baulk of timber like a 3 × 3 inch (7.5 × 7.5 cm) fencing post. The bricks will settle down evenly to the level of the wooden edging and the sand will settle

down between the joints to hold them firm.

When the whole path is finished, brush a few more shovelfuls of sharp sand over the path just to top up the spaces between the bricks. The path will immediately look good, can be used straight away and will leave you with a great feeling of satisfaction.

Of course, the edges of the path will look rather stark and hard to start with and you can alleviate this in two ways.

I quite like the look of a gently curving path, so, if your taste tends towards the formal, one way is actually to accentuate it by edging it with a formal hedge. For this job you could use box but, if you do, make quite sure you buy the right one. There are many different forms, several of which will grow much too tall. The best is the 'edging box' (*Buxus sempervirens* 'Suffruticosa'). It's an expensive plant but easy to propagate yourself if you have the patience (see p. 150).

Lavender also makes a good dwarf hedge for edging paths and again you must ensure you buy the right variety. A dwarf, compact one is the order of the day and one of the best is *Lavandula angustifolia* 'Munstead'. Another alternative is to use rosemary.

**4** *Lay out the special brick paviors in a pre-determined pattern, leaving about $\frac{1}{4}$ inch (6 mm) between them. To settle the bricks in slightly, tap them down with the hammer handle.*

**5** *Using a soft broom, fill between the bricks with very dry sharp sand.*

**6** *Put a strong board across the bricks and, with a fencing post or something similar, hammer them down level with the edging.*

## 🦡 THE ROSE ARBOUR 🦡

Like everything else in the garden, the rose arbour only earns its place by being both attractive and useful. It passes the test with flying colours.

In the new garden it gives immediate impact by providing instant height. Of course it's designed to attract the eye even when unclothed, but within only months of planting it will bring foliage and flower colour onto a higher plane.

The addition of a bench makes it a marvellous place to sit in spring and summer. A surround of lush foliage and sweetly perfumed flowers plus the buzzing of the myriad insects they'll attract makes it just about perfect for an hour or two of relaxation. But in this garden even that's not enough to earn its keep.

So, as well as supporting the purely ornamental plants, the arbour is used as a climbing frame for fruit and vegetables too. And you'll be surprised how attractive this can look.

Grown on the ground, marrows, for example, are hardly worth a second glance. The fruits are generally hidden among the large leaves and soon become dirty and splashed with mud. But when they're grown upright as climbers, the bright green, yellow or gaily striped skins shine out from the foliage as bright and as gay as a beach umbrella. What's more, they're safe from marauding slugs and, because they remain clean and dry, they escape fungus problems too.

If it's more Bacchanalian pleasures you're after, you could stretch out on your cushioned bench on sunny autumn afternoons and pick your own grapes, straight from vine to mouth. Need I go on?

Mind you, there's a bit of work to do first.

The paving base of the arbour is octagonal and made with bricks to match the brick path. In my own garden, the arbour was made at the end of the brick path but it could equally well be free-standing.

Start by marking out a 4 foot (120 cm) diameter circle, but when you've done it, make sure you leave the central peg and the string because you're going to need it again shortly. Then cut eight pieces of the 3 × 1 inch (7.5 × 2.5 cm) edging board 3 feet (90 cm) long. These are fixed to pegs in the way described for the brick path (see p. 54). The bricks are laid on a sand bed in exactly the same way except that you'll need to do some cutting, but they're not difficult to cut with a brick bolster (like a wide cold chisel) and club-hammer.

### MAKING A ROSE ARBOUR

**1** *Make an octagon, using 3 foot (90 cm) long wooden edgings, fill with sand, level and then mark it out in sections.*

**2** *Set the bricks as described for the path. They can easily be cut to fit with a brick bolster and hammer.*

**3** *Set fencing posts at each of the points of the octagons. Check carefully that each one is level both ways.*

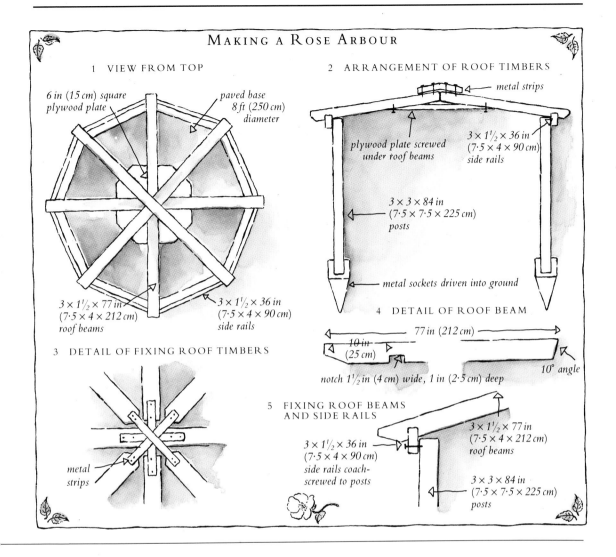

## MAKING A ROSE ARBOUR

**1 VIEW FROM TOP**

6 in (15 cm) square plywood plate

paved base 8 ft (250 cm) diameter

$3 \times 1\frac{1}{2} \times 77$ in ($7.5 \times 4 \times 212$ cm) roof beams

$3 \times 1\frac{1}{2} \times 36$ in ($7.5 \times 4 \times 90$ cm) side rails

**2 ARRANGEMENT OF ROOF TIMBERS**

metal strips

plywood plate screwed under roof beams

$3 \times 1\frac{1}{2} \times 36$ in ($7.5 \times 4 \times 90$ cm) side rails

$3 \times 3 \times 84$ in ($7.5 \times 7.5 \times 225$ cm) posts

metal sockets driven into ground

**4 DETAIL OF ROOF BEAM**

77 in (212 cm)

10 in (25 cm)

10° angle

notch $1\frac{1}{2}$ in (4 cm) wide, 1 in (2.5 cm) deep

**3 DETAIL OF FIXING ROOF TIMBERS**

metal strips

**5 FIXING ROOF BEAMS AND SIDE RAILS**

$3 \times 1\frac{1}{2} \times 36$ in ($7.5 \times 4 \times 90$ cm) side rails coach-screwed to posts

$3 \times 1\frac{1}{2} \times 77$ in ($7.5 \times 4 \times 212$ cm) roof beams

$3 \times 3 \times 84$ in ($7.5 \times 7.5 \times 225$ cm) posts

**4** *Join them at the tops with $3 \times 3$ inch ($7.5 \times 7.5$ cm) beams which should again be levelled and firmly fixed with coach-screws.*

**5** *The top beams are then cut to shape and fixed by nailing them on to the cross-members.*

**6** *To make sure they're rock solid, screw a plywood plate on to the central joint of the beams.*

Start by laying the first row against one of the edging boards. Then, if you stretch the string from the centre to the end of the board, you'll see where you have to cut. In fact the easiest way is to have a string from the centre to each end of the edging board so that you can see instantly where the bricks have to be cut.

When all the bricks are laid, you'll finish up with a brick octagon with eight lines radiating out from the middle. It looks very attractive, but inevitably you'll finish with a hole in the middle. To fill this I pinched an idea from that great Victorian architect Edwin Lutyens. I saw it at Hestercombe House in Somerset, in a garden designed by him in partnership with Gertrude Jekyll.

You may have to hunt around for a series of clay pots which will fit one inside the other, starting with one about 6 inches (15 cm) in diameter and finishing with a tiny 'thimble pot' about $1\frac{1}{2}$ inches (4 cm) across. Put them all inside each other and sink them in the centre on a bed of sand. Then fill between them with sand to finish off a very attractive pattern of concentric circles (see p. 20). With the paved base completed, the positions for the posts are marked. To save time and trouble, they can be fixed into special metal spikes which are simply driven into the ground, one at each of the eight points of the octagon.

To tell you the truth, I'm not very keen on these spikes for fencing (for which they're really designed), because there's such a lot of wind resistance on a fence panel that they often loosen in the soil. But for the much more open structure of a rose arbour they're ideal.

Drive them in so that the bottom of the socket is level with the top of the paving and then slot in eight 7 foot (2 m) fencing posts. Level the tops of them with a spirit-level.

The beams that make up the roof are made from $3 \times 1\frac{1}{2}$ inch (7.5 × 4 cm) timber and they're fixed to side rails of the same material. When you buy the timber it's worth while asking for it to be pressure-treated with a preserv-ative. Most timber merchants will be able to supply it and, though it'll cost a bit more, it virtually guarantees a lifetime's freedom from rot. If you want to save some money, buy second-hand floor-joists from the demolition contractor. They're generally $3 \times 2$ inch (7.5 × 5 cm) and make a really strong job.

Cut the side rails to 3 feet (90 cm) long and fix them to the posts with coach-screws. They should project 1 inch (2.5 cm) over the top of the post to take the top beams.

These are cut to shape with a 10 degree angle at the end that goes to the centre. This will give the slope of the roof and also ensures that the whole structure remains rock solid. Ideally, use a proper carpenter's bevel square to mark the angles but, if you haven't got one, you'll manage quite well with an ordinary school protractor.

The notch cut out of the other end fits over the top of the side rail and can be secured with a nail.

When the first two beams are in position, fix them together in the middle with a metal strap. You should be able to buy these from a builders' merchant but, if not, you'll have to make your own from a cocoa tin. If you do that, give them a coat of paint before fixing to ensure that they don't rust. Fix them with a couple of screws per beam and get someone to support the beams while you do it.

The rest of the beams are fixed in the same way. Once you've got the first four in position to form a cross, you'll need to bevel the ends of the others to fit.

If your cutting has been accurate, the roof beams will lock together and hold without any fixing at the top at all. But I feel a lot safer with those metal strips in place and, as a bit of 'belt and braces' insurance, I screwed a circle of outdoor-quality plywood to the bottom as well. That's pure pessimism but makes for a bit more peace of mind when you're sitting underneath enjoying your grapes!

For a selection of plants for the arbour, see p. 163.

## GARDEN POOLS

Gardeners are often put off any kind of water feature because of the well-publicized problems. Concrete pools often leak, while almost any area of water is likely to become bright green or sludge brown within weeks of installation. Well, those problems certainly can crop up but are equally certainly very easy to avoid. The one and only factor that may make you think twice is a small child in the family. It cannot be denied that almost any size or depth of water is dangerous to tiny children and a risk hardly worth taking.

That aside, a pool in the ornamental kitchen garden is more or less essential. It provides a magnetic attraction for wildlife which helps control pests. And it adds another interest to your gardening, as it enables you to grow a whole new range of plants.

In a small garden the pool, to be in proportion, must be small too, and this can often lead to problems with green algae. However, it is possible to keep even an area as small as 2 feet (60 cm) across crystal clear. The water must be kept as cool as possible, so either avoid placing the pool in full sun or plant round it to provide a little shade. Make it as deep as possible and cover the surface of the water with plants in summer, again to provide shade.

### A barrel pool

The pool in my own garden is tiny. It was made by cutting a 2 foot (60 cm) diameter wooden barrel in half and sinking it in the ground. It really is as easy as that. It's essential, of course, to ensure that it sits dead level in its hole so that the water comes right to the rim all round. That's simply a matter of levelling both ways with a spirit-level.

To make the pool as attractive to wildlife as possible, put a layer of soil in the bottom to plant the aquatic plants, but include one 'marginal' plant growing in a large pot. This

should be rested on bricks to bring the top of the pot level with the edge of the barrel. Then put a few large stones in the pot so that they overlap the edges a little and form a small 'jetty'. This is important to allow wildlife to climb out of the water if they go in for a dip. It also provides a place for birds to come for a drink and to have a 'bath' – and that's certainly worth watching!

A few more pebbles around the pool finish it off, and once the surrounding plants grow to cover the edges it blends into the scheme well. You will find, of course, that the water is anything but clear to start with, but you shouldn't be tempted to clean it out and start again. The algae that make the water green live on mineral salts and sunlight. Once the salts are exhausted and the water is shaded a little, they'll disappear.

### A larger pool

The best way to make a bigger pool is with a butyl-rubber liner. It's by no means the cheapest material but should last a lifetime without problems. You'll also need a special fibre sheet to line the hole before putting in the butyl rubber, to ensure that no sharp stones work their way up to puncture the sheet. When

*A pool looks good and attracts wildlife.*

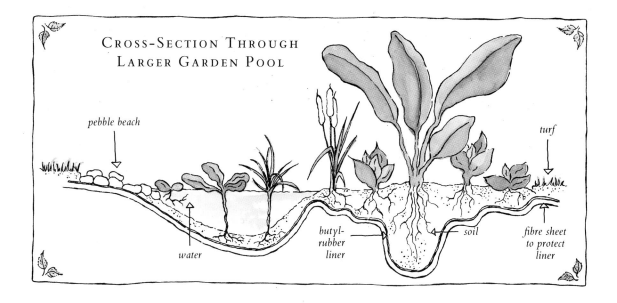

CROSS-SECTION THROUGH LARGER GARDEN POOL

pebble beach

turf

water

butyl-rubber liner

soil

fibre sheet to protect liner

ordering, allow for the size of the hole, plus twice the proposed depth, plus 1 foot (30 cm) to allow for anchorage.

Start by marking out the pool area with canes and, if it's in the lawn, remove the turf to 1 foot (30 cm) wider all round to allow for anchorage of the sheeting.

To avoid showing areas of butyl rubber round the top of the pool, you'll need to make it dead level round the edge, so put in some pegs and level them with the spirit-level. The soil should then be cut away or replaced to finish level with the tops of the pegs.

When digging the hole, make sure that at least one side slopes very gently. This will provide a 'beach' to allow wildlife to enter the pool and, of course, to get out again. There's no need to excavate deeper than about $2\frac{1}{2}$ feet (75 cm) at the deepest point.

Place the fibre liner over the hole so that it

## MAKING A BARREL POOL

**1** *Set the pool so that the top is more or less at soil level and then level all round with a spirit-level.*

**2** *Fill the tub with water and, when it has swollen enough to become watertight, put a shallow layer of soil in the bottom.*

**3** *Plant some oxygenating weed into the soil at the bottom and then set a brick or two on top of the soil.*

hangs loosely inside and hold down the edges with bricks. Then stretch the liner over it and hold with plenty of bricks round the edges.

Filling with water will force the liner and the fibre mat downwards to take up the contours of the hole. As it sinks, you may have to reposition the bricks to allow it to move and you'll also have to fold and tuck the liner here and there to make a neat finish.

Turn off the water when it reaches the rim and cut the liner and the fibre mat to leave 6 inches (15 cm) all round for anchorage. This can be covered with soil and turfed to hide the edge.

Ideally, the liner should then be covered with a thin layer of soil, sloping up to nothing at the 'beach' end and this part is finished off with large pebbles to make an ideal breeding area for water life and to provide easy access for land-based wildlife.

The aquatic plants, oxygenating weed and marginal plants can then be planted directly in the soil for a much more natural effect.

## The bog garden

An area of boggy soil adjacent to the pool makes a marvellous place to grow yet another collection of plants that may not be otherwise possible. There's a fine range that like a soil that is constantly moist – things like primulas, kingcups, globe flowers, musks and many more. It's not at all difficult to provide ideal conditions.

When you have dug the hole for the pool, simply dig another hole alongside, allowing a wall of soil between. When you have levelled the rim of the pool all round, remove another couple of inches of soil from the dividing wall to allow a constant supply of water to seep in. Then, if the hole for the bog garden is arranged so that there are different depths of soil, you'll be able to grow everything from the small kingcups (*Caltha palustris*) to enormous *Gunnera manicata*, which looks like giant rhubarb.

After putting in the liner, the bog garden is then refilled with soil and can be planted. With an increase in the area of evaporation, you'll find that the water level of the pool drops faster than normal and, of course, if it gets lower than 2 inches (5 cm), the bog will start to dry out. So you'll have to make sure water is added from time to time as necessary.

You'll find details of plants suitable for the pool and the bog garden on p. 165.

**4** *Plant a pot with a marginal plant and lower it on to the bricks so that the top of the soil is 2 inches (5 cm) below the water.*

**5** *Fill around the pool and on top of the pot with large pebbles to hide the edge of the barrel.*

**6** *When the plants have grown around the pool, it makes an attractive watering hole for wildlife.*

## ✿ PERGOLAS ✿

Like the arbour, the pergola adds instant height to the garden and provides a place for climbing plants to flourish. It too can be used to grow flowering plants, vegetables and climbing fruits and it makes a pleasantly shady spot in summer.

Traditionally, pergolas were made with brick columns and hefty overhead timbers – fine for large gardens but much too heavy for a small plot. It's obviously important to keep any structure like this to scale so in a small garden it's better to use timber posts.

You can buy ready made-up kits to make a pergola and there's little to be saved by making your own unless you prefer a different design or can get hold of suitable second-hand timber. Whichever you decide to use, make sure you mount the posts in metal sockets as recommended for the arbour. This is a sure-fire way of preventing rotting at the base. One thing you should never do is to use rustic poles driven into the ground. Larch or pine poles which are often sold at garden centres will last no more than a few years. When the pergola is covered with established plants, it's very difficult to replace rotten poles.

Use 3 × 3 inch × 7 foot (7.5 × 7.5 × 225 cm) posts and try to get them pressure-treated with preservative. It's well worth the slightly higher cost. Set the posts in their metal sockets 7–9 feet (2–3 m) apart on either side of the path. Where the path curves, it will be necessary to vary the distance between the posts so that the cross-members are always at right angles to the line of the path.

Join the posts at the top with 3 × 1½ inch (7.5 × 4 cm) rails which can be screwed or coach-screwed into the posts.

Most pergola kits supply cross-members which have been half-jointed so that they simply drop over the top of the rails, and then it's just a case of drilling and screwing to fix them securely. But this does have the slight disadvantage of setting for you the width of the pergola. In my own garden, this pre-setting was too wide, so I made my own in much the same design as the kit. If, however, you don't fancy yourself as a woodworker, there's a much easier way.

Cut the cross-members as shown, but instead of cutting out half-joints (which is the difficult bit), simply place the cross-members on top of the side rails and hold them on with metal angle-brackets.

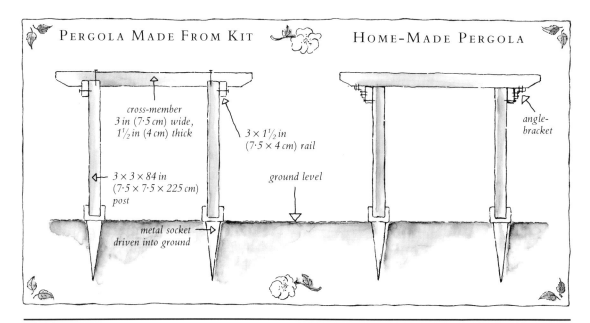

PERGOLA MADE FROM KIT

HOME-MADE PERGOLA

*cross-member 3 in (7·5 cm) wide, 1½ in (4 cm) thick*

*3 × 1½ in (7·5 × 4 cm) rail*

*3 × 3 × 84 in (7·5 × 7·5 × 225 cm) post*

*ground level*

*metal socket driven into ground*

*angle-bracket*

## ✿ MAKING A COLD FRAME ✿

A cold frame is much more than a mere luxury in the ornamental kitchen garden. It should be in use and highly productive all year.

It starts the season as a vital means of acclimatizing greenhouse-grown flower and vegetable plants to the cooler temperatures outside. This 'weaning' is essential if plants are not to suffer a shock and a subsequent delay in growth. Then it'll be planted up with aubergines, courgettes, melons and tomatoes, and in the autumn it could raise young plants of cauliflower, cabbages, etc., or grow crops of carrots, lettuce and spinach for the earliest harvests of the following year.

If you add a little heat, it can double as a propagator for seeds and cuttings or for growing very early vegetables.

### Making the frame

The easiest and most attractive way to make your own cold frame is with wood. It's easy to work, attractive and cheap, especially if you buy it second-hand. Floorboards are ideal and these are generally readily available from a demolition contractor.

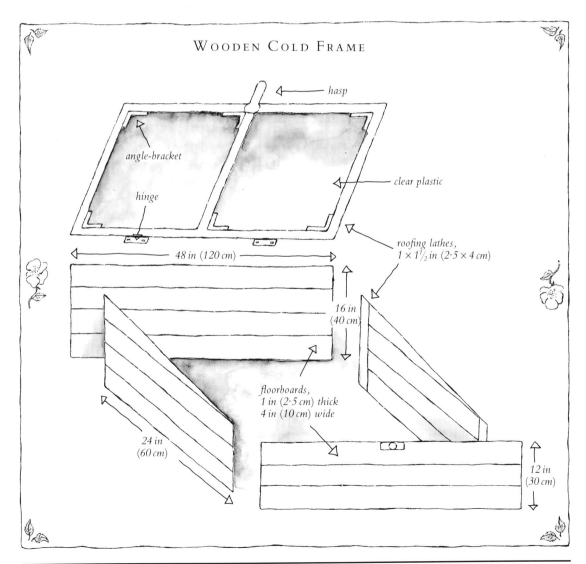

WOODEN COLD FRAME

hasp

angle-bracket

hinge

clear plastic

48 in (120 cm)

roofing lathes,
1 × 1½ in (2·5 × 4 cm)

16 in
(40 cm)

floorboards,
1 in (2·5 cm) thick
4 in (10 cm) wide

24 in
(60 cm)

12 in
(30 cm)

The boards are held together with $1 \times 1\frac{1}{2}$ inch (2.5 × 4 cm) roofing laths which have the advantage of being both cheap and ready pressure-treated with preservative.

There are several alternatives for the top. You can make a frame using roofing laths held together with metal angle-brackets and covered with rigid PVC. This is then hinged to the back of the box. Alternatively use corrugated plastic which is flexible enough to allow you to nail through it, making the job much easier. The snag is that it's white rather than clear and, though it lets in enough light, it doesn't look very attractive.

Ideally, use polycarbonate sheeting. It's clear, attractive and immensely strong. In fact with this material there's no need to make a frame at all. Just cut the sheet to size and fix the hinges with thin bolts. Being twin-walled it remains perfectly rigid.

### Heating

If you decide to heat the frame, there are several possible alternatives. You could buy an electric heating mat, which sits on a piece of polystyrene on the base of the frame and is covered with strong polythene and then a piece of capillary matting. Alternatively, there are tubular heaters especially made for cold frames.

Another way is to provide free heat with a hotbed. This is simply a pile of fresh horse manure stacked about 3 feet (1 m) high and covered with a 6 inch (15 cm) layer of soil. You can just make a neat pile of it but, if you can manage it, it's much better to build a wooden structure to contain it. I found someone who would cut railway sleepers down the middle to make boards of an ideal thickness at a quarter of the price of new timber. You'll need to arrange the container so that the boards can be progressively removed because the heap will sink to about a third of its original height by the end of the season.

## 🦎 THE LAWN 🦎

Lawns are much easier work and a thousand times more satisfying if you start off on the right foot. If you buy weed-infested turf, or fail to prepare the ground properly, or sow an unsuitable seed mixture, you're just piling up heartache for yourself. Get it right from the outset and you may even find time to lie on it a bit!

### Preparation

Once you've grown your grass, you'll never be able to get underneath it again, so it's worth preparing the soil really well beforehand. Most of the perennial weeds will disappear once you start mowing regularly anyway, though any that grow too close to the ground to be decapitated by the mower, like dandelions, daisies and buttercups, will have to go. In this case, digging over and removing all signs of roots will do, since the really pernicious stuff like ground elder and even couch-grass will succumb to the mower.

If you're starting the lawn from seed, annual weeds could be a problem, so get rid of them with a 'stale seedbed'. This is a good old traditional way of preparing a seedbed. Simply dig the soil over and roughly level it. Then leave it for a week or two, during which time the weed seeds that are present in the soil will germinate. Hoe them off, finally level and then sow the grass immediately. That way it'll have a good head start on the weeds and will get well established without competition.

If your soil is really heavy, you'll have a drainage problem. You'll often be advised to put in land drains on really heavy soil, but the problem is where on earth do you drain it to. In the absence of a suitable ditch, I would suggest another method. When you dig over the land, work in a quantity of coarse grit. The ideal stuff is the kind of pea-shingle used when they tar-spray roads – you can buy it at the builders' merchants. The heavier the soil, the more grit you should use, from about a barrowload every 3 sq yd (2.5 sq m) upwards. Cover that with an equal quantity of mushroom compost or manure and dig it in.

Single digging will normally be sufficient for a lawn, unless you are blessed with a hard layer of soil beneath the topsoil, in which case it will have to be broken by double digging.

Roughly level with the back of a fork, just to take out the local lumps and bumps, and then, when the surface is dry enough not to stick to your boots, consolidate by treading.

The final levelling is the difficult bit, so take some time over it. Stand back every now and then, get your head as near the ground as possible and squint across the surface. You'll soon pick out the high and low areas.

### Seed or turf?

If the lawn will get a lot of wear, there's no point in buying the finest turf or the best seed mixture. It will soon be colonized by coarser grass and weeds. Indeed, only go for the finest grasses if you're prepared to cut the lawn at least every other day in season and not to use it too much either.

You can now buy excellent cultivated turf. It's quite a bit more expensive but cuts out all the previous uncertainty and risk of buying poor, weed-infested stuff. You'll be able to specify the grade of grass you need and it'll be guaranteed evenly cut and weed-free. The great advantage with turf, of course, is that it makes an instant effect, but it's many times more expensive than seed.

If you decide on seed, my recommendation would be one of the newer rye-grass mixtures. The plant breeders have now come up with some excellent, hard-wearing varieties that are quite fine enough for even the fussy lawn owner. When ordering, calculate to sow at 1 oz per sq yd (30 gm per sq m).

*To distribute seed use two pots. Twist the inside one to align the holes to give optimum delivery.*

*To rake the seed in without disturbing the levels, the best tool is a lawn rake.*

##  A WILD-FLOWER MEADOW

Fine grass will never do very well in shady areas, especially under trees. The trees will compete for light, water and nutrients and they'll always win, so be realistic and don't even try. It's certainly possible to grow grass under trees but to be successful it must be allowed to grow much longer than the lawn and it should be cut less frequently. The ideal solution in the larger ornamental kitchen garden is a wild-flower meadow.

Though I must say that I can find no evidence that adult insects have any preferences for particular flowers from which to take pollen or nectar, when it comes to *breeding* it's quite a different matter. Insects seem to be much more fussy when they're looking for egg-laying sites because their young are adapted to feed on quite specific plants. To attract native insects to breed in the garden, what you need are native plants.

Of course, there are other good reasons for growing native species. With the increase in chemical farming and the loss of truly wild habitats, wild flowers are disappearing. So the provision of an alternative home in the garden will certainly help towards their conservation. What is also important for the gardener to realize is that many of our native species are extremely attractive.

### Sowing

You can buy special grass/wild flower mixtures from some specialist seedsmen and there's quite a wide choice. Make sure you choose a mixture of flowers that will suit your particular situation and soil because there are mixtures for clay or sand, acid or limy soils and others for wet areas or shady places, even coastal and woodland areas.

Or you can buy grass seed and mix it at a ratio of about 1 oz (30 gm) of mixed flower seed to 1 lb (450 gm) of grass seed.

Prepare the soil just as you would for a lawn (see p. 64) but add no fertilizer. Wild flowers prefer the kind of poor soil they'd get in their natural habitat. Sow at a rate of about 1 oz per square yard (30 gm per sq m) and rake in, just as you would for a lawn.

### Maintenance

In the first year, the grass should be cut every 6–8 weeks to make sure the wild flowers are not completely swamped by the grass. In subsequent years, cut in October when all the wild flowers have finished blooming and dropped their seed. This will ensure that the annuals survive and that the perennials spread. After cutting, it's important that all the cuttings should be raked up and removed.

You'll find that the flower population changes a little over the years. Those species that are not particularly well suited to the conditions will become weaker and could eventually die out altogether, while those that thrive will take their place. But you'll still maintain a wide diversity which will give plenty of flower over a long period, so it's best just to let nature take its course.

### Planting

If you have an existing lawn, the best bet is to grow the plants in small pots and plant them out when they're well established. Though I have seen wild flowers establish themselves from seed simply scattered onto the surface of an existing meadow, it's a bit hit-or-miss and a lot of expensive seed could be wasted.

Sow the seed in seed trays in March and germinate them in the cold frame or even outside. Pot them into 3 inch (7.5 cm) pots when they're big enough to handle and plant them out when the roots fill the pot.

The best varieties for your situation will depend on where you live and the nature of your soil, so get hold of a good specialist seedsman's catalogue and use its recommendations for your particular conditions.

##  BUILDING THE FORMAL GARDEN

If you decide to make your garden entirely formal you'll need to start by making a good resolution. The essence of this type of garden is clean lines and a neat, well-manicured appearance. So you need to be especially tidy-minded and meticulous in your garden 'housekeeping'. Mind you, though the actual layout of the beds and the paths is geometric, there's no need to be formal in the planting. You can still mix flowers, fruit and vegetables together to create the same kind of effect as the more informal approach.

### The walls

Start with the walls or fences. Just as in the informal garden, they can be used to grow all kinds of fruit and flowers, but the emphasis here will be on fruit trained into formal shapes. There will be fans and espaliers and perhaps a few cordons too. The method of growing trees and bushes into these shapes is covered in Chapters 8 and 9, but the first job is to provide some support for them. The best and cheapest way is with galvanized wires. Make sure you use wire strong enough to last a lifetime. Replacing broken wires behind established trees is an awkward and time-consuming job. Generally gauge 12 wire is fine.

On wooden fences, they can simply be fixed to the posts with staples, setting them about 1 foot (30 cm) apart. If you have an old wall, use galvanized steel vine-eyes. These are wedge-shaped tags made from specially hard-ened steel and can be driven into old lime mortar quite easily. Walls made with modern mortar are much harder and will need to be drilled and fitted with plugs and screw-eyes.

The horizontal wires are ideal for fruit trees and bushes, but if you want to intersperse them with ornamental climbers that have a twining habit, like clematis, you'll have to provide some vertical wires too. Use thin-gauge wire for this job and simply cut it into lengths to fit and twist it round the horizontal wires to make a square mesh.

### Paths

The paths can be made with paving or brick as previously described (see pp. 52–5) but planted paths like the scree path are not suitable here where the emphasis is on clean, formal lines. Alternatively, use gravel.

Gravel paths can be laid straight onto beaten earth where the drainage is adequate. Ideally, the base should be cambered first so that it slopes up to the middle, allowing water to run to the sides. If you have hardcore available (and on a new building site most gardens will contain more than their fair share!), dig a shallow trench along each side of the path, fill

*Mixed beds in a formal garden. The gravel paths have wooden edging and decorative corner posts.*

it with hardcore and then cover with gravel. This will ensure dry paths even in the heaviest rain. Cover the beaten soil with about 2 inches (5 cm) of pea-shingle and rake it level. Of course it's likely that the path will sink unevenly as the soil settles, but all you have to do to rectify unevenness is to rake on a little more gravel.

## Borders

The borders are laid out in very formal fashion, so naturally they must be edged to keep them neat. If your design only incorporates straight lines, the edging can be done with timber quite easily. Use 4 × 1 inch (10 × 2.5 cm) softwood, which ideally should be pressure-treated with preservative. In my own garden I painted the boards with a matt green wood preservative and this was contrasted with bright red posts at every corner.

The 2 foot (60 cm) long posts were cut from 2 × 2 inch (5 × 5 cm) softwood and had a 3 inch (7.5 cm) square of timber screwed to the top. Before fixing it onto the post a screw is inserted through the centre of the square to provide a fixing for the top ball. In fact I bought small wooden 'acorns' for the tops of the posts and I must say they looked attractive and saved a lot of time pulling the hose round the garden.

The balls and squares are removed before hammering the posts into the ground to avoid damage. Set the posts at each corner so that the timber edging comes to the centre of the post. Drive them into the ground so that there's exactly 5 inches (12.5 cm) of post above the level of the boards, which means that there will be 15 inches (37.5 cm) in the ground.

The edging boards are fixed first to posts driven into the ground on the border side of the edging boards and set a little below the top so that they will later be covered with soil and will not be seen – exactly as described for making the scree path (see p. 52). Again, make sure the boards are dead level, using a spirit-level. When they're in position, they can be screwed through to the corner posts to make the whole thing rigid. Then screw back the squares and balls.

If you want to include curves in the design, timber, as you can imagine, becomes much

## FIXING WIRES

**1** *On older walls, where the mortar is reasonably soft, the easiest way to fix wires is to hammer in vine-eyes. These are hardened metal tags with a hole to take the wire.*

**2** *For plants like roses, which are tied in, horizontal wires are sufficient, but for twiners like clematis you'll need to twist vertical wires on to them to make a mesh.*

**3** *On wooden fences, strain the wires taut using a length of wood as a lever against the post and fix them with large staples.*

more difficult to use. If the curves are shallow, bend the timber by making a series of saw-cuts on the inside of the curve as described for the brick path (see p. 54). If they are more pronounced, and particularly for small diameter circles, this won't work.

An easier way would be to use either Victorian edging tiles, which can still (quite rarely) be found, though I have to say, at a price. There are one or two modern manufacturers but the tiles are still very expensive.

Alternatively use bricks, which can be set on edge at an angle to make a quite attractive finish. If you decide to do it this way, try to get hold of brick paviors or engineering bricks which will not crumble when they freeze.

It is also possible to use timber but only with a very complicated procedure. Buy $\frac{1}{8}$ inch (3 mm) exterior quality plywood and cut it into 4 inch (10 cm) strips. Bend it round pegs banged into the ground in the shape and size you require and then coat the outer surface with waterproof glue. Glue on another strip, starting on the opposite side so that the joins do not coincide, and finally four more, to make a circular piece of homemade plywood $\frac{3}{4}$ inch (2 cm) thick.

## Planting

The planting in this type of garden can be more formal than in the other designs, using perhaps one type of plant per bed and perhaps even edging the beds with a low hedge of something like box or lavender. Certainly flowers should be included for the reasons I've previously expressed and they can either be mixed with the vegetables and fruit or be confined to a separate bed on their own.

The free-standing trees will look most attractive if they're trained in a very formal shape. Here you could use something like clipped, half-standard holly or, if your garden is warm enough, bay. Alternatively, to be more productive, you could have some fun with a few 'lollipop' apple trees (see p. 207).

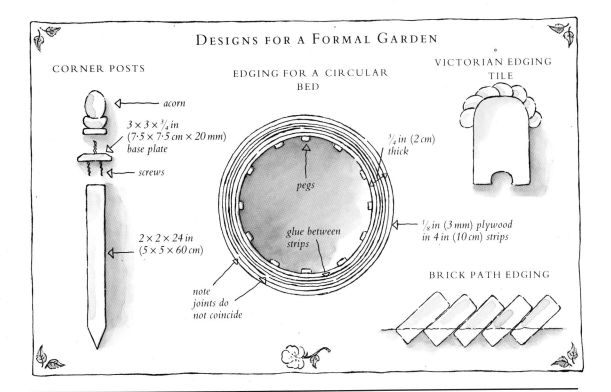

DESIGNS FOR A FORMAL GARDEN

CORNER POSTS

acorn

$3 \times 3 \times \frac{3}{4}$ in
$(7 \cdot 5 \times 7 \cdot 5 \, cm \times 20 \, mm)$
base plate

screws

$2 \times 2 \times 24$ in
$(5 \times 5 \times 60 \, cm)$

EDGING FOR A CIRCULAR BED

pegs

glue between strips

note joints do not coincide

$\frac{3}{4}$ in (2 cm) thick

$\frac{1}{8}$ in (3 mm) plywood in 4 in (10 cm) strips

VICTORIAN EDGING TILE

BRICK PATH EDGING

## MAKING KNOTS AND PARTERRES

The formal style of knot gardens and parterres is an ancient one but it fits very well with modern gardens. It's especially used these days as a decorative way to grow herbs but there's no reason why the pattern of low hedges should not be used for flowers and vegetables too. Indeed, the best of all worlds is to mix all three types of plants, giving each one a separate 'compartment' in the scheme.

The great gardens at Villandry are a perfect example of the technique, though on the grand scale of course. In a modern semi, you'd have to pull your horns in just a bit!

### The design

The first step should be to draw the design to scale on a sheet of graph paper. Ancient knots were often extremely complicated, resembling the designs on Persian and Indian carpets in their complexity. That's fine if you have plenty of room and plenty of time to do the trimming, but in small gardens, especially where you intend to use the design to contain herbs, flowers or vegetables, it's best to keep it simple.

Prepare the area first by digging, removing perennial weeds and incorporating manure or compost. Then tread it down firmly with your feet and rake it level.

Transfer the design to the land, using a series of garden lines for straight lines and scratching into the soil for circles or curves. It's not a bad idea to mark out the layout with sand, especially if you can't get all the planting done straight away, since scratched lines can get washed away.

### Planting

Certainly the best plant to use for formal knots and parterres is the common box (*Buxus sempervirens*) which, though expensive, is quite easily raised from cuttings (see p. 150). Make sure you buy the right variety, since there are some that will grow tall and with quite a loose habit of growth. The one used for centuries for edging is 'Suffruticosa' and this remains the best.

### MAKING A KNOT GARDEN

**1** *Mark out the outside shape of the knot garden first with lines. With a square or rectangular shape it's easy to check that the sides are exactly at right angles to one another by measuring from corner to corner and adjusting if necessary.*

**2** *Find the centre of the square by putting a couple of lines from corner to corner. The cane in the middle should remain there throughout the setting out since it determines most of the future measurements.*

**3** *Make a string with a loop in each end and the exact length of the required radius of the centre circle. Then fill a wine bottle with sharp sand and use it to mark out the centre circle.*

Plant with a trowel about 6–9 inches (15–23 cm) apart along the lines you have marked out. If you have raised your own plants from cuttings, growing them on in the open ground, and you wish to plant them 'bare-rooted', the best time for this is September or April. Container-grown plants can of course be planted at any time. It's a good idea, even when you have enough plants for the complete garden, to keep a few extras going in a corner somewhere. Occasionally, and especially in colder areas, the odd plant may die, quite suddenly and for no apparent reason, so it's good to have a few to fill any gaps.

There are, as you would imagine, other plants you could use. Lavender, cotton lavender and rosemary are old favourites, but they do tend to become rather bare at the base and can look untidy after a few years.

Once the hedging is planted, you can plant or sow the compartments straight away, though it's a good idea not to overdo it in the first year to give the box a chance to become established. In any case, you'll have to be careful not to grow plants which will rapidly outgrow their space and flop over the hedging.

## Maintenance

Trim the sides of the hedge with shears right from the start, as soon as they begin to grow wider than required. You may not need to trim the tops until the second year when they are as high as you want them. The best time to do the job is July and August.

The art of trimming, like any hedge-cutting, is to keep the tops and the sides as even as possible and the 'corners' straight and sharp. You can stretch a line at the required height for the top of the hedge to give you a guide, but there's no substitute for a good eye and a lot of time. Keep standing back and squinting along the line of the hedge to check how you're doing and try not to take off too much at a time.

It's most important to feed the hedging every year. This is a job that's often neglected and results in odd plants dying out, spoiling the look of the hedge. A dressing of blood, fish and bone meal in February will suffice and the plants will, of course, also be able to take advantage of the manure and compost used within the compartments.

**4** *The box plants are put in 6–9 inches (15–23 cm) apart along the lines marked by the sand and strings. If you've taken the cuttings over a long period, as I did, the plants will be of different sizes.*

**5** *When all the edgings are in position the shape of the knot garden can be seen. Now dig over the areas in between the hedging where you may have trodden, firm the path areas by treading, and cover them with pea shingle.*

**6** *Finally, plant herbs within the areas marked by the box. Make sure that you choose types which will neither grow too tall and overpower the scheme nor will run, like mint, and choke out the rest.*

## ❧ COMPOST BINS ❧

Bulky organic matter is the very basis of fertility in the ornamental kitchen garden and garden compost should make up a large part of it. It's an excellent soil conditioner, improving both drainage and water-holding capacity, it provides a home for millions of beneficial micro-organisms and it contains a fair bit of plant food too. What's more, it's a jolly good way to get rid of all your vegetable rubbish from the garden and the kitchen and it's more or less free.

To make good compost you need at least two containers – one to fill up while the other one is maturing. There are plenty available at garden centres but most of them have the big disadvantage that they are designed with too many air spaces. It has long been known that the bacteria which rot down vegetable matter to make good compost need air. So containers have been made with large spaces between the boards or, in the case of plastic containers, with plenty of holes in the sides. Not only is that amount of air quite unnecessary, it's actually counter-productive.

To make really good compost and to ensure that weed seeds and pathogens are destroyed, it's best to create a really hot heap. The only way to do that is to insulate the contents from the outside air and that means a closed container. The best bet, and certainly by far the cheapest, is to make your own. It's quite easy.

My design utilizes floorboards which you can buy from any timber merchant but are much cheaper bought second-hand from a demolition contractor. The $3 \times 1$ inch (7.5 × 2.5 cm) timber for the corner posts can also be bought from the demolition yard much cheaper than new wood.

Notice that there are no gaps between the boards, just a space right at the bottom for air, and that the container has a lid. Don't try to do without the lid which will keep out the rain and keep in the heat, but if you feel that

a wooden one is an unnecessary expense, a piece of old carpet will do just as well.

You can, of course, make single containers but, since two will be needed, you might as well save the cost of an extra 'wall' by making a double heap if you have a space for it.

Just about everything that will rot down can go on the compost heap: all your weeds and vegetable waste, grass cuttings, fresh vegetable waste from the kitchen, even cotton or woollen clothes. Avoid cooked food which attracts rats, roots of pernicious weeds like docks, couch-grass and ground elder, any plant material that's diseased and any weeds that are actually seeding.

The aim is to provide for plenty of air through the heap or the waste will be rotted down by a different set of bacteria and it will turn into a slimy mess. You must have seen large piles of grass which compress and become smelly and putrid: certainly no good for soil improvement.

The way to achieve plenty of air circulation, without sacrificing the all-important heat which builds up in the heap and accelerates

*Two wooden compost containers, with a wire and post container for leaf mould beside them.*

## COMPOST BIN

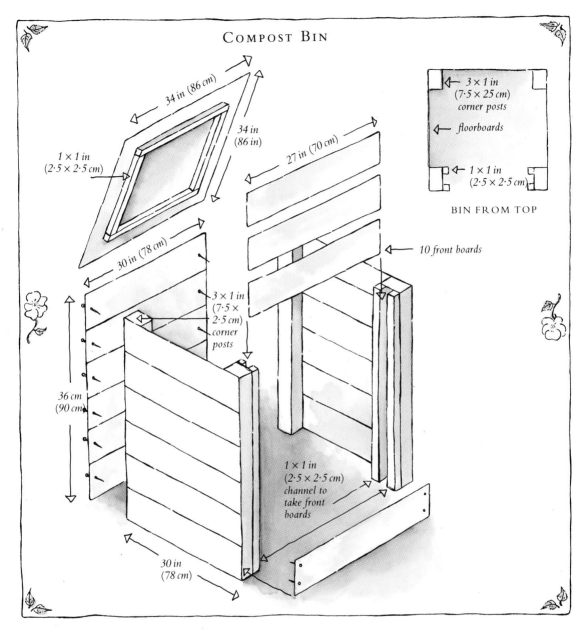

34 in (86 cm)

34 in (86 in)

1 × 1 in (2·5 × 2·5 cm)

30 in (78 cm)

27 in (70 cm)

3 × 1 in (7·5 × 25 cm) corner posts

floorboards

1 × 1 in (2·5 × 2·5 cm)

BIN FROM TOP

10 front boards

3 × 1 in (7·5 × 2·5 cm) corner posts

36 cm (90 cm)

1 × 1 in (2·5 × 2·5 cm) channel to take front boards

30 in (78 cm)

rotting, is to mix your materials thoroughly. I keep a couple of bags of fresh horse manure handy to mix in with smaller, finer materials like grass cuttings to ensure that they don't compress and exclude all the air. The manure also provides enough nitrogen for the bacteria to use as fuel in the rotting process.

But don't be misled into thinking that you can just put the waste in the bin and forget it. The makers of compost accelerators would love you to believe that, because it makes compost-making sound so easy. It isn't true. To make really good compost in a reasonable time it's *essential* to turn the heap at least twice in its life. Just dig the compost out of the heap, piling it up in front of the container, and then throw it back in again. When you do, shake out any compressed material and you'll make the finest, crumbliest, sweetest-smelling soil conditioner imaginable.

## 🌿 CLOCHES 🌿

There are two ways of increasing yields of vegetables in a small garden. One is to grow in highly fertile soil which is deeply cultivated and never trodden on and the other is to lengthen the growing season at both ends. You need to produce the earliest crops possible and then to keep them going well into the autumn and early winter. Obviously the greenhouse is going to be a valuable aid, but you can add to that by using cloches outside.

Cloches have been used for centuries to warm up the soil and to increase the air temperature around plants, thus enabling them to be harvested earlier. They have the added advantage of keeping plants generally free from the attention of pests and diseases and the battering effects of the weather too, so quality is always higher.

Even during the height of the summer they can be used to protect some of the more tender crops like tomatoes, peppers and aubergines (though great care is needed to avoid *too* high a temperature). In the autumn they come into use again. They are then handy to finish off ripening crops like tomatoes and to wring the last drop of productivity from the year with late crops of lettuce, carrots, etc.

In the ornamental kitchen garden, however, modern cloches are not really suitable. First of all, they're designed for growing in long rows, so they're the wrong shape. And then it has to be said that they are made to be functional rather than pretty!

What is needed is the old-fashioned bell cloche (the original, of course, from which the name is derived) or, even better, the Victorian lantern cloche. Both enhance the look of the garden and both are the right shape too.

Unfortunately, neither cloche seems to be readily available now, but a reasonably attractive alternative is not difficult to make.

### The modern lantern cloche

The design for this cloche is based on the Victorian lantern cloche, but there the resemblance ends. It's made from the most modern of materials – rigid PVC, which is readily available from do-it-yourself shops.

Cut it to shape with a special tool which you can also buy very cheaply when you get the PVC. The pieces are stuck together with impact adhesive and held firmly with special outdoor quality waterproof tape. It's generally recommended for repairing glass and you can buy it at the garden centre.

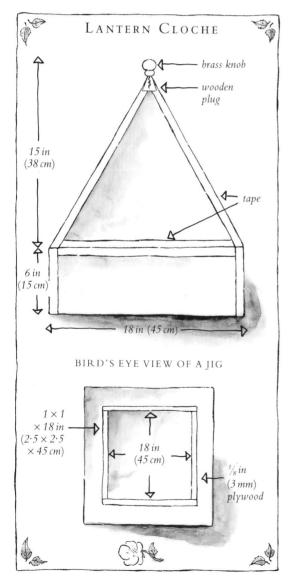

LANTERN CLOCHE

brass knob

wooden plug

tape

15 in (38 cm)

6 in (15 cm)

18 in (45 cm)

BIRD'S EYE VIEW OF A JIG

1 × 1 × 18 in (2·5 × 2·5 × 45 cm)

18 in (45 cm)

⅛ in (3 mm) plywood

*Home-made lantern cloche.*

Fitting it together is a bit of a fiddle and I found the best way was to make up a 'jig' which is simply a flat board with four pieces of wood nailed on so that the cut pieces of plastic fit exactly into them.

To finish off the cloche it needs a handle so that it can be picked up easily with one hand. The simplest and most attractive way is to use a brass drawer-knob which is pushed through the top of the cloche and screwed into a wooden block inside.

## CULTIVATION

I'm often asked why it is that gardeners have to go to all the trouble to dig, manure, fertilize, lime, water, etc. to produce their crops when nature, the architect of it all, does none of these things and yet still produces perfectly good plants. Well the answer is that nature *does* do much the same things through falling leaves, rotting vegetation, animal manure, etc., but at a lower rate. The fact is that we expect to get 10 times more from the soil than nature ever intended, so we organic gardeners must certainly learn from nature's example and do the same things – only more so.

In the ornamental kitchen garden, we take it even a stage further. Here we're growing

more, closer together and with greater frequency than most traditional gardeners would do. The competition between plants for food and water is terrific and the gardener must make sure that none of them ever go short. That means a soil constantly in superb condition and a far greater input than is normal.

## The deep-bed method

The deep-bed method of growing is something that has been developed over many years and I have experimented with it for about twenty years. Basically the method entails deep-digging to two spades deep initially and a regular input of manure, compost or one of the alternative sources of bulky organic matter.

Plants are grown in narrow beds so that all the work can be done from the paths and the soil is never compacted. So, even though subsequent cultivations consist only of single digging, the plants' roots can penetrate deeply. That lessens the amount of competition from plants growing close together. Instead of spreading outwards, roots can reach down.

Because of the high fertility and deep soil, plants can be grown closer together too. Over the years I have found that this method always doubles yields per square yard and often trebles them.

The borders in the ornamental kitchen garden are simply an extension of the deep-bed method. The only difference is that the beds are less formal in shape and that they grow not only vegetables but flowers as well.

## Double digging

The much publicized trend in agriculture these days is to reduce deep cultivations to a minimum and this is not just to save money. Deep ploughing or, in our case digging, is bound to disturb the subterranean life and will certainly upset the natural balance below the surface. However, there's no doubt either that a deep soil will allow more root room, allowing plants to bring up nutrients from lower levels, and will improve the aeration and drainage of heavy soils. So my conclusion is that the soil should be deeply dug just once. After that initial effort, single digging should suffice for at least 10 years and maybe more.

Generally it will be enough to incorporate only bulky organic matter – manure, spent-mushroom compost or garden compost. But on very heavy soils you can make a permanent improvement by adding coarse grit. Use really coarse material about $\frac{1}{8}$–$\frac{1}{4}$ inch (3–6 mm) in diameter. Never use sand which could make matters worse. Spread about a 2 inch (5 cm) layer over the soil before digging and incorporate it as you go.

Note that the organic matter is distributed throughout all levels of the soil and not just in the bottom of the trench as is often recommended. The addition of the organic matter and the deep digging will have the effect of raising the soil level at least 6 inches (15 cm) above the level of the paths. This in itself will improve local drainage and aeration of the top layer and so dry out and warm up the soil, making an ideal medium for the healthy growth of plant roots.

## Single digging

The only time you're allowed to tread on the borders is when you dig, either between crops or at the end of the season. Note that the organic matter is again incorporated throughout all levels but this time by spreading it up the sloping bank of the trench in front of you. This puts it right in the root zone where plants can make immediate use of it.

Once the borders are planted with permanent plants, you have to be careful not to disturb their roots too much, of course. For this reason, some areas will be left for the growing of annuals and vegetables while the trees and shrubs, the herbaceous plants and the permanent vegetables and fruit should remain undisturbed.

## Between crops

Single digging is normally done in the autumn or spring, between seasons but, in order to maintain the very high level of fertility necessary, some revitalization is always needed

## DOUBLE DIGGING

**1** *Mark out a 2 foot (60 cm) trench and dig out the topsoil to a spade's depth. Break up the bottom with a fork. Avoid turning over this lower level.*

**2** *Fork in a liberal dressing of well-rotted manure, garden compost, spent mushroom compost or one of the suggested alternative soil conditioners.*

**3** *Mark out another trench and throw the soil forward to fill the first. At the halfway stage, put in another layer of organic matter and then continue digging.*

between crops. When you have lifted one crop and before you plant or sow the next, spread a shallow layer of manure or compost over the area, add a light dusting of blood, fish and bone meal and lightly fork it in.

## Weeding

One of the advantages of growing plants close together is that there's very little room for weeds. Needless to say, you will have to do a bit and you should make sure you never allow them to grow large enough to compete with the plants, but you'll find that in the loose soil they can be pulled by hand very easily. There's rarely even need, or space, to use a hoe, let alone a weedkiller!

## Mulching

At the end of each season, all the permanent plants will benefit from spreading a 2 inch (5 cm) layer of compost or manure around them to add nutrients and to conserve moisture. No extra feeding is necessary since they'll get all they need when you feed the annuals and vegetables.

*Mulching at the end of the season.*

## Extra feeding

The only extra feeding I do, and I'm not convinced that this is absolutely necessary, is to spray the whole garden once a fortnight in the growing season with seaweed extract. This adds necessary trace elements which all plants need and it also helps with pest and disease control. There's no doubt that the plants' health improves, making them more able to shrug off pest and disease attack, and I also believe that the coating of alginate from the seaweed protects the foliage from fungus spores and possibly insects too (see p. 241).

## BETWEEN CROPS

**1** *It's essential to maintain a high state of fertility so, as soon as a crop is harvested, enrich the soil with a dressing of garden compost or manure.*

**2** *Though the constant addition of organic matter will go a long way to maintaining the nutrient level, it's as well to make sure by adding organic fertilizer too.*

**3** *These ingredients, worked in regularly, will improve drainage and the capacity to hold water and nutrients, as well as encouraging biological activity.*

## 🦎 PLANTING AND SOWING 🦎

Planting and sowing the ornamental kitchen garden is a pretty random exercise. Or at least it's meant to look that way. In fact, a certain amount of planning is necessary.

Details of planting and sowing methods, dates and distances apart etc., are to be found in the relevant chapters, but first it's necessary to describe the overall approach.

### Planting the permanent plants

Start by planting the permanent plants. Now I'm not suggesting that you get all the trees, shrubs and herbaceous plants in during the first season – indeed I would recommend that you take several years over it. Planting a garden is never a thing to rush. It's much better to take time to learn about plants, to look at other gardens and to plan a succession of colour and an attractive variety of foliage and flower. But if you're going to put in permanent plants during the season, it's best to get the job done before the main sowing and planting time for vegetables and annuals. In any case, autumn and spring are much the best times for planting trees, shrubs, roses, herbaceous perennials and fruit trees and bushes.

Begin with the trees, and when you do, bear in mind the effect they'll have on other plants. Trees always cast shade and will provide permanent competition for light, water and nutrients. These are not factors that are impossible to cope with, of course, but they need to be taken into account. Trained

## A TYPICAL FLOWER AND VEGETABLE BORDER PLAN

Malus 'John Downie'

trees on the fences will have no effect on light conditions, for example, so in a small garden you may decide to settle for those and to keep the rest of the garden in full sun. Or, if your garden faces south, you may prefer to plant a free-standing tree or two near the house so that the shade is cast only over the patio. But don't be frightened of creating shaded areas. Some of the best ornamental plants are shade lovers and there are plenty of fruit and vegetables that will produce good yields in the shade. They will often do so a little later than similar plants in the sun, so you could achieve a longer period of harvesting.

Taller shrubs, herbaceous plants and fruit bushes should go towards the middle of the borders. Because of the informal design of the beds, there will be some areas that can't be reached by leaning over from the paths, so they'll be awkward for our method of vegetable growing. So that's the place to put those plants that will need very little attention during the year. You'll need to think long and hard before planting the shrubs and fruit bushes because they really need to get their roots down and get established without disturbance. Herbaceous perennials, on the other hand, in the main actually thrive on being lifted, split up and moved so, if you feel after the first season that you've made a mistake, there's nothing to stop you simply digging the plant up and moving it.

After planting the middles, this then leaves you with those areas that are 4 feet (120 cm) or less from the paths. Certainly you'll want to put some lower growing herbaceous plants

| KEY | | |
|---|---|---|
| 1 Petunia | 11 *Hydrangea hortensis* | 31 *Iris germanica* |
| 2 Lobelia | 12 Cabbage | 32 Hosta |
| 3 Beetroot | 13 Lobelia | 33 *Carex pendula* |
| 4 Salad onion | 14 Turnip | 34 Annual convolvulus |
| 5 Lettuce | 15 *Hypericum androsaemum* | 35 *Begonia semperflorens* |
| 6 *Helleborus orientalis* | 16 *Geranium* 'Johnson's Blue' | 36 French bean |
| 7 *Bergenia* 'Ballawley' | 17 *Euphorbia robbiae* | 37 Garlic chives |
| 8 Geranium (annual) | 18 French marigold | 38 Bedding dahlia |
| 9 *Limnanthes douglasii* | 19 Rhubarb | 39 Cauliflower |
| 10 *Mahonia* 'Charity' | 20 *Dicentra formosa* | 40 Calendula |
| | 21 Spinach | 41 Cosmos |
| | 22 Lettuce | 42 Floribunda rose |
| | 23 Annual salvia | 43 Carrot |
| | 24 Ruby chard | 44 *Skimmia rubella* |
| | 25 *Ajuga* 'Burgundy Glow' | 45 Globe artichoke |
| | 26 *Heuchera tiarelloides* | 46 *Potentilla* 'Gibson's Scarlet' |
| | 27 Parsley | 47 Tagetes |
| | 28 Fennel | 48 Lettuce |
| | 29 Phacelia | 49 Radish |
| | 30 Courgette | 50 *Saponaria ocymoides* |
| | | 51 Potato |
| | | 52 Thyme |
| | | 53 Allysum |
| | | 54 Onion |

and shrubs in here too, but you must leave room for annuals and vegetables. The idea is to plant the permanent plants so that you leave a number of bays of different sizes for annuals and vegetables.

## Annuals and vegetables

This is where the ornamental kitchen garden system differs dramatically from traditional methods. The annuals are not here grown formally in regimented rows or blocks but in very informal drifts, and again enough space must be left for the vegetables, which are also grown informally. Forget all about the traditional method of sowing in long, straight rows with paths in between. That's not only much too formal for our cottage garden effect, but it's a criminal waste of space too!

Here the crops are grown in patches of irregular shape, though, with a few exceptions, still in rows within the patches. Imagine, for example, that you have an oval-shaped area in which you wish to grow carrots. With a stick, you would simply draw a series of shallow drills about 2 inches (5 cm) apart. There's no need to use a garden line because you're not worried about getting them *exactly*

right, but you should draw all the drills first, before sowing. Then you can see clearly that they're the right distance apart. Then sow the seeds within all the drills and cover them by brushing over the top with the flat of your hand. Tap down lightly with your hand or the back of a rake and the job's done.

When the seedlings are large enough, thin them in the rows to 2 inches (5 cm) apart also. If you work it out, you'll find that the area of that small patch produces many more carrots in the space available than a couple of traditional rows with the obligatory 1 foot (30 cm) access row between them.

You can use exactly the same system for plants like beetroot, lettuce, turnips, etc., whether sowing direct or planting out, but as you would expect, there are one or two exceptions. Radish, salad onions, round-rooted carrots, etc. can simply be sown broadcast and selectively thinned as you start to harvest, taking out the biggest and leaving the smaller ones to grow on.

All you have to do with potatoes is plant two or three tubers with a trowel, setting them about 1 foot (30 cm) apart. Larger plants like the marvellous globe artichoke are planted singly and look terrific rising from the

SOWING AND PLANTING

**1** *To prepare an area, first spread a little compost.*

**2** *Lightly fork over the area with a small border fork and rake it level and fairly fine.*

**3** *Scratch a series of shallow drills in the soil. A short stick is the best implement.*

flower border in noble splendour. All these variations are explained under their relevant headings in Chapter 7.

## Keeping the continuity

If you're going to be anywhere near self-sufficient in a small garden, it's essential to keep a regular continuity of harvesting. The day a patch is cleared it must be sown or planted with something else. And while it's impossible to plan a rotation of crops in this garden, it's wise to ensure that you don't follow one crop with the same thing or something similar.

However, it has to be admitted that keeping a regular harvest of every vegetable you want is a lot easier said than done! You're bound to get caught out from time to time, especially in the early years, until you get used to the system. But there's one way to make things a lot easier.

Make use of your greenhouse and cold frame early in the season, and your patio later on, to raise a number of plants in pots and boxes – a kind of 'holding area' until a patch of soil becomes vacant. That way, just as soon as you've got a space, you can plant it up with vegetables that are already part-grown and so save several weeks of waiting.

## Trimming and pruning

Finally you should be warned that this type of gardening is *not* labour-saving. If you are going to make what amounts to three gardens in the space of one, you'll have to put in more time than most traditional gardeners. While there's very little weeding to do, you'll *have* to keep an eagle eye on your charges and be ruthless with the knife or secateurs. Pruning, trimming and tying are constant tasks.

The first mistake I made in my own ornamental kitchen garden provides a good lesson. Alongside my scree path, which was burgeoning with alpines, I planted a row of strawberries. Alas, I was not vigilant enough, the strawberries grew lush and vigorous and their leaves swamped the alpines. Most alpines need full sunshine of course, so at the beginning of the next season I found myself replanting quite a few. I moved the strawberries further back and made quite sure the following season that I trimmed back any foliage rash enough to stray from its allotted space. So be warned!

**4** *If the soil is dry, always water* before *sowing to avoid the soil forming a crust.*

**5** *Sow the seed thinly. The best way is to take it in pinches between finger and thumb. Cover the drills with* dry *soil and firm by patting it down with your hand.*

**6** *Use the same technique when planting, setting the plants in blocks rather than rows.*

# WINTER PLANTS

**Autumn Cherry** *Prunus subhirtella* 'Autumnalis Rosea'
A small tree which flowers inter-mittently throughout the winter until late March. 15ft (4.5m)

**Pieris** *Pieris japonica* 'Variegata'
A slow-growing, medium-sized shrub with prettily variegated leaves and white flowers. Needs an acid soil. 6ft (2m)

**Hardy Cyclamen** *Cyclamen hederifolium*
This produces a rounded tuber from which arise attractively marked leaves and red/purple, pink or white flowers. 6ft (15cm)

**Snowdrop** *Galanthus nivalis*
One of the first bulbs to flower in winter. Excellent under trees or shrubs. 8ft (20cm)

**Daffodil** *Narcissus* spp.
There are several daffodils both large and small which provide a welcome splash of colour in late winter. 4–24in (10–60cm)

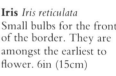

**Scorzonera** *Scorzonera hispanica*
A gourmet root vegetable which produces black roots, white when peeled. Can be left in the ground over winter. 15ft (40cm)

**Iris** *Iris reticulata*
Small bulbs for the front of the border. They are amongst the earliest to flower. 6in (15cm)

**Brussels Sprouts** *Brassica oleracea gemmifera*
Members of the cabbage family which form one of the main winter greens in colder areas. They are entirely hardy. 2–3ft (60–90cm)

**Chicory** *Cichorium intybus*
One of the best winter salads. Roots can be lifted for forcing as required throughout the winter. 4ft (1.25m)

**Mahonia** *Mahonia* 'Charity'
A shrub with attractive evergreen foliage and yellow flowers in late winter and spring. 8–10ft (2.5–3.5m)

**Carrot** *Daucus carota sativus*
Well-known root vegetable with attractive feathery foliage which goes well in the flower borders. 1ft (30m)

**Potato** *Solanum tuberosum*
A staple food in northern hemisphere countries. The tubers will store right through winter until a new crop is ready. 2½ft (75cm)

**Leek** *Allium porrum*
A very hardy winter vegetable with a mild onion flavour. Will stand in the coldest weather until spring. 2ft (60cm)

**Savoy** *Brassica oleracea bullata*
A winter hardy cabbage with attractive, often bluish, crinkly leaves and a fine flavour. 18in (45cm)

**Apple** *Malus domestica*
The main winter standby in northern hemisphere gardens. Some varieties will store in cool conditions until the spring.

**Twisted Hazel** *Corylus avellana* 'Contorta'
A large shrub with interestingly twisted stems and catkins in late winter. 8ft (2.5m)

**Lungwort**
*Pulmonaria longifolia*
A useful herbaceous perennial which flowers early and has the bonus of attractively spotted leaves. 1ft (30cm)

**Viburnum**
*Viburnum bodnantense* 'Dawn'
A large shrub producing rounded heads of fragrant flowers intermittently throughout the winter. 10ft (3.5m)

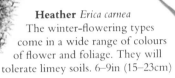

**Heather** *Erica carnea*
The winter-flowering types come in a wide range of colours of flower and foliage. They will tolerate limey soils. 6–9in (15–23cm)

**Stinking Hellebore** *Helleborus foetidus*
A herbaceous perennial with attractively toothed foliage and large spikes of yellow/green flowers. 1½ft (45cm)

**Salsify**
*Tragopogon porrifolius*
A winter root with a fine, delicate flavour much like scorzonera, but the root lacks the black skin. 15in (40cm)

**Parsnip** *Pastinaca sativa*
A very hardy winter root with a fine flavour. Better after a touch of frost. Susceptible to carrot-fly. 2ft (60cm)

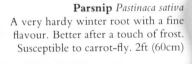

**Laurustinus**
*Viburnum tinus* 'Eve Price'
Rounded shrub with glossy evergreen leaves and white clusters of flowers in winter and spring. 10ft (3.5m)

**Jerusalem Artichoke**
*Helianthus tuberosus*
A valuable winter root which can be left in and dug as required. 10ft (3.5m)

**Witch Hazel** *Hamamelis spp.*
Distinctive spreading shrubs which produce in late winter spidery flowers of yellow to coppery red. 8ft (2.5m)

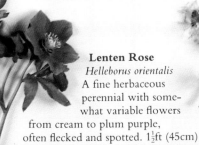

**Lenten Rose**
*Helleborus orientalis*
A fine herbaceous perennial with somewhat variable flowers from cream to plum purple, often flecked and spotted. 1½ft (45cm)

# JANUARY

## 🦎 OUTSIDE 🦎

◆ Jobs for the winter months tend to merge since they are generally carried out over a long period depending on the weather and other seasonal commitments. So the digging, planting, pruning, etc., begun in November should continue until March, though the earlier it's done the better.

◆ Buy in manure if you can and stack it ready for use later. I would delay buying fresh horse manure until March when it can be used to make a hotbed while it's rotting down. Using it twice makes it half the price!

◆ In bad weather, make sure you have everything to hand for the beginning of the season. Check all the tools, make and repair equipment as necessary, add a lick of paint to machines etc.

◆ Check the garden centre for bargains. At this time of year they sometimes sell off cheaply, items unsold from Christmas and will also often give quite good discounts for large orders of things like fertilizer and composts. Remember that it always pays to buy the biggest bags possible, even if this constitutes the whole season's supply.

◆ Plant new crowns of rhubarb, preparing the soil well with manure or compost beforehand.

◆ If you have hedges in the garden, clean out the bottoms thoroughly and mulch them with a thick layer of rotted manure or compost.

◆ If you haven't already done so, cover a few areas with polythene to keep the soil dry and to warm it up for the earliest start to the season.

◆ Bonfires are not advised unless you have diseased material to dispose of. If you have piled up the bonfire for a week or more, check for hibernating hedgehogs before you light it.

◆ If the soil is frozen solid, there's not much planting that can be done, but it's a good time to wheel out the manure to where it will be needed. The frozen ground will make the job much easier and it should be left in heaps where it's to be spread.

◆ In a spell of mild weather, take hardwood cuttings of willows. Shoots about 1 foot (30 cm) long, buried 9 inches (23 cm) deep in a sand-lined trench, will soon root.

◆ If you want to win a few prizes at the village show, buy some seed of a large strain of onion and sow them in a heated propagator to grow on to large bulbs. The kitchen gardener should bear in mind that these large bulbs don't keep as well.

## 🦎 INSIDE 🦎

◆ Towards the end of the month, start off a small amount of 'Tom Thumb' lettuce and radish 'Robino' in pots. The radish can be left to grow on in their pots for the earliest picking, while the lettuce should be transplanted into $3\frac{1}{2}$ inch (9 cm) pots and grown to maturity, again for the earliest crop.

◆ Make sure you have ordered all your seeds and that you have seed trays, pots and compost to hand for an early start in the greenhouse.

◆ Give the greenhouse and frame a thorough cleaning with disinfectant.

◆ Check all fruit and vegetables in store and remove any showing signs of rotting.

◆ Put grease-bands on the staging legs in the greenhouse to prevent adult vine weevils crawling up.

# FEBRUARY

## 🦎 OUTSIDE 🦎

◆ If you haven't finished the digging and mulching, try to get it done as soon as possible while there's still some frost about to break down the clods and to help kill soil pests.

◆ Early in the month, put out cloches where you wish to grow early vegetables. This will keep the soil dry and warm it up ready for sowing and planting. There's little point in sowing until the soil has reached a temperature of 45°F (7°C).

◆ This is a good time to winter-prune fruit trees provided the weather is not too hard. At this time of year it's a case of removing dead, diseased or crossing branches completely.

◆ Some weeds could still be seeding, even at this time of year, so check the borders and clean the ground thoroughly.

◆ Test the soil for lime and add it now if necessary, just scattering it over the surface to allow the rain to take it in. Aim for a pH of 6.5.

◆ Feed fruit trees and bushes with a light dressing of rock potash.

◆ Plant Jerusalem artichokes.

◆ Cover early strawberries with cloches and bring potted plants into the greenhouse.

◆ Towards the end of the month, when cloches have been down for about a fortnight, sow broad beans, cabbage, carrots, cauli-flower, lettuce, early peas, salad onions, spinach and turnips. Plant out the same crops either under cloches or in the cold frame if you have raised them in the greenhouse.

◆ Plant onion sets and shallots outside if the weather is favourable. There's no rush for these things and it's often better to wait.

◆ Prune deciduous shrubs that flower later in the year, like the butterfly bush (*Buddleia davidii*). Prune hypericums right back to the ground if infected with rust disease last year.

◆ Cover peach trees to prevent peach leaf curl fungus settling and protect early flowers from frost with light netting or spun poly-propylene fleece.

◆ Prune late flowering clematis hard back to within 6 inches (15 cm) of the ground.

◆ Prune autumn-fruiting raspberries to ground level. Shred the prunings through an electric shredder for use as a mulch.

◆ Protect black currant buds from bird damage with cotton or fine netting.

◆ Feed spring cabbage with dried blood.

## 🦎 INSIDE 🦎

◆ Set up potato tubers in a light, cool but frost-free place to start the sprouts growing.

◆ Sow alpines in pots and put them in the cold frame.

◆ Sow begonias and geraniums in a propa-gator in the heated greenhouse or on the win-dowsill.

◆ Pick over rooted cuttings, removing any leaves showing signs of fungus attack.

◆ Sow seeds of broad beans, cabbage, carrots, cauliflower, celeriac, celery, early lettuce, onions, early peas, salad onions, spinach and turnips.

◆ Sow some French beans, setting 3 to a 5 inch (12.5 cm) pot to grow on to harvesting in the greenhouse.

◆ Sow some hardy annuals in modules and germinate them in the cold frame.

◆ Start to take cuttings of chrysanthemums and fuchsias.

◆ Sow globe artichokes in 3 inch (7.5 cm) pots for planting outside to crop this year.

◆ Tie up rods of grape vines.

# EARLY SPRING PLANTS

**Skimmia** *Skimmia japonica* 'Kew Green'
A small, dome-shaped shrub
with greenish-white, heavily
scented flowers. 3ft (90cm)

**Flowering Currant**
*Ribes sanguineum*
An easily grown shrub
for the middle of the
border. 7ft (2.25m)

**Viburnum**
*Viburnum carlesii*
A rounded shrub with downy
leaves. The flowers are pink in
bud and very fragrant. 8ft (2.5m)

**Flowering Almond**
*Prunus dulcis*
The almonds are among
the best spring-flowering
trees but prone to peach
leaf curl. 20ft (6m)

**Forsythia**
*Forsythia* 'Lynwood'
A superb cultivar of this
popular shrub. The flowers
are unusually big and it is
very reliable. 8ft (2.5m)

**Wood Spurge** *Euphorbia
amygdaloides* 'Purpurea'
A superb perennial with
mahogany leaves and yellow
flowers in spring. Grow in sun
or shade. 1ft (30cm)

**Tulip**
There are many forms
of this bulbous plant
that are excellent for this
type of garden. The
dwarf forms are
particularly suitable.
9in (23cm)

**Drumstick
Primula**
*Primula denticulata*
A reliable flowerer
available in several
colours ranging from
lavender to carmine
and white. 1ft (30cm)

**Lettuce** *Lactuca sativa*
The earliest lettuces can be
grown in pots in the greenhouse. Use a small variety.
6in (15cm)

**Elephant's
Ears** *Bergenia*
'Bressingham
White'
An evergreen pe
ennial for shade o
full sun. 18in (45cm

**Spurge** *Euphorbia characias*
A fine herbaceous perennial
for the centre of the
border. Good winter
foliage and long-
lasting flowers.
4ft (1.25m)

**Cauliflower**
*Brassica oleracea* 'Purple Cape'
One of the most useful and
attractive of winter and spring
vegetables. 2ft (60cm)

**Polyanthus** *Primula polyantha*
Popular spring bedding plants which are available in a wide variety of colours, often double- or even triple-coloured. Lift and split after flowering.
10in (25cm)

**Flowering Cherry**
*Prunus* 'Accolade'
A small, spreading tree, unfailingly producing masses of pendulous clusters of blossom in early spring. One of the best of all cherries. 20ft (6m)

**Grape Hyacinth**
*Muscari armeniacum*
A small, clump-forming bulb for the front of the border. Available in other shades of blue. 9in (23cm)

**Flowering Quince**
*Chaenomeles speciosa*
A spreading shrub with generally red flowers followed by large, yellow, edible fruits. 7ft (2.25m)

**Pieris** *Pieris* 'Forest Flame'
A lovely small shrub with red young leaves and white flowers. Needs an acid soil. 7ft (2.25m)

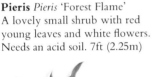

**Magnolia** *Magnolia stellata*
A small variety with star-shaped flowers in early spring. It prefers full sun. 8ft (2.5m)

**Radish** *Raphanus sativus*
The quickest-maturing and therefore earliest of all vegetables, it can be forced in the greenhouse or frame. 6in (15cm)

**Daffodil** *Narcissus* spp.
There are dozens of daffodils suitable for this garden. Plant them near spreading perennials to hide the foliage after flowering. 4–24in (10–60cm)

**Spring Cabbage**
*Brassica oleracea*
The spring varieties are invaluable to help fill the 'hungry gap' from April to May. 18in (45cm)

# MARCH

###  OUTSIDE

- Lift, split and transplant snowdrops.
- Early in the month, sow parsnips outside and plant Jerusalem artichokes and rhubarb.
- Plant early potatoes, sow beetroot and make another sowing under cloches of all the vegetables suggested for sowing under cloches in February.
- Plant perennial herbs.
- Sow sweet peas or transplant outdoors seedlings raised from an autumn sowing in the greenhouse, having first hardened them off in the cold frame.
- Towards the end of the month, you may be able to plant out the hardy annuals raised last month in the frame. You should also be able to sow outside if the soil is dry enough. If the soil is still wet and cold, it's best to delay both planting and sowing until next month.
- Prune roses, cutting out dead, diseased and crossing branches and cutting back to a plump, outward-facing bud to leave shoots between 2–4 inches (5–10 cm) long.
- Try to complete the planting of bare-rooted deciduous trees and shrubs and all fruit trees and bushes by the end of the month.
- Prune the Smoke Tree (*Cotinus coggygria*) to encourage larger leaves.
- Plant herbaceous plants and, if the weather is favourable, lift, divide and replant old clumps.
- Towards the end of the month, make a seedbed and sow short rows of autumn and winter cabbage, sprouting broccoli, Brussels sprouts, cauliflower, kale and leeks for planting out later.
- Check the scree path and replace any alpines that have suffered from careless feet.
- Hard prune dogwoods and willows grown for bark colour to produce colourful new stems for next winter.
- Rake the lawn to remove old thatch and, once it starts growing, begin to mow. The cuttings, of course, go on the compost heap.
- If compost containers are full you may have to empty the one that's most rotted and pile the contents in a corner to make room.
- Lay turf lawns except when the soil is frozen.
- Trim winter-flowering heathers with shears as they go out of flower.
- Plant out globe artichokes towards the end of the month.
- Plant asparagus crowns in well-prepared soil. If drainage is poor, make a raised bed and mix in plenty of compost and coarse grit. Mulch established plants with garden compost.
- Plant gladioli towards the end of the month.
- Lift, divide and replant chives, garlic chives and sorrel.
- Graft apples and pears.
- Put down some tiles, slates or boards to trap slugs and turn them over each morning to expose the slugs to the birds. Keep the hoe going to expose their eggs and young too.
- Plant lilies outside if the weather is favourable. If it isn't, pot and plant out later.

## ❦ INSIDE ❧

◆ Take cuttings of dahlias, fuchsias and geraniums.

◆ Sow cucumbers, melons and tomatoes for growing in the cool greenhouse.

◆ Sow some more half-hardy annuals for planting outside later.

◆ Check fruit growing in pots in the greenhouse and repot if necessary.

◆ Begin feeding potted plants with a liquid fertilizer.

◆ Check all plants under cloches regularly. On sunny days, even though the temperatures may be low outside, plants under small cloches in particular are prone to scorching, so they may need ventilating.

◆ Make further sowings of salad crops under cloches.

◆ Take cuttings of special varieties of lupins and delphiniums.

◆ Surround susceptible crops like lettuce and any seedlings under cloches with lime, soot or calcified seaweed to deter slugs.

◆ Sow seeds of perennials for flowering this year.

◆ Sow tender perennials like salvias, eccremocarpus, rhodochiton, etc. in gentle heat for flowering this year.

◆ Take cuttings of heathers.

# LATE SPRING PLANTS

**Flowering Gooseberry**
*Ribes speciosum*
An attractive shrub best grown against the fence or wall in colder areas. 10ft (3.5m)

**Clematis**
*Clematis montana*
A small-flowered species which makes very rampant growth. Ideal for covering an unsightly feature. 20ft (6m)

**Honeysuckle** *Lonicera syringantha*
A shrubby, densely branched honeysuckle with soft lilac flowers producing a powerful perfume. 6ft (2m)

**Carrot** *Daucus carota sativus*
This variety, 'Rondo', is excellent for early crops and particularly suited to growing in modules. 6in (15cm)

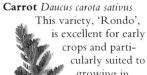

**Avens** *Geum coccineum*
'Mrs Bradshaw'
A hardy perennial for the front of the border, available in several colours. 18in (45cm)

**Barberry**
*Berberis thunbergii* 'Aurea'
A good small shrub for the front of the border, grown for its outstanding golden foliage. 1ft (30cm)

**French Marigold**
*Tagetes patula*
A popular bedding plant which can be forced early and grown under cloches with early vegetables. 10in (25cm)

**Parsley**
*Petroselinum hortense*
An invaluable herb which can be forced under cloches to produce the earliest crops. 9in (23cm)

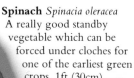

**Spinach** *Spinacia oleracea*
A really good standby vegetable which can be forced under cloches for one of the earliest green crops. 1ft (30cm)

**Rhododendron hybrid**
There are dozens of small rhododendron hybrids but they like an acid soil so must be given special provision in this garden. 2ft (60cm) upwards

**Granny's Bonnets** *Aquilegia vulgaris* 'Nora Barlow'
A traditional cottage garden perennial which comes more or less true from seed. 2ft 6in (75cm)

### Japanese Snowball
*Viburnum plicatum* 'Mariesii'
A hardy shrub for the middle of the
border. It grows in layers to form
an attractive mound of white in late
spring. 10ft (3.5m)

**Flowering Thorn** *Crataegus
oxyacantha* 'Paul's Scarlet'
A small tree with double red
flowers in spring followed by
red berries. 20ft (6m)

### False Acacia
*Robinia pseudoacacia* 'Frisia'
A small tree grown for its
outstanding golden foliage.
Suffers from die-back a little.
20ft (6m)

**Whitebeam** *Sorbus aria*
A medium tree with young leaves, greyish
at first. Red berries in autumn. 25ft (8m)

**Rosemary** *Rosmarinus officinalis*
A popular herb forming a small shrub
with aromatic foliage and blue flowers.
2ft (60cm)

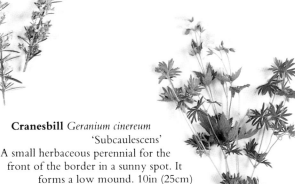

### Creeping
### Blue Blossom
*Ceanothus thyrsiflorus* 'Repens'
A vigorous, mound-forming
shrub with glossy evergreen
leaves and masses of flowers.
4ft (1.25m)

**Cranesbill** *Geranium cinereum*
'Subcaulescens'
A small herbaceous perennial for the
front of the border in a sunny spot. It
forms a low mound. 10in (25cm)

**Turnip** *Brassica rapa*
The variety 'Milan
Purple Top' is ideal for
forcing under cloches for
the earliest crops.
1ft (30cm)

**Geranium** *Pelargonium hortorum*
Well-known half-hardy annual useful
in the greenhouse until June when it can
go outside. 18in
(45cm)

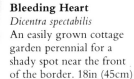

### Bleeding Heart
*Dicentra spectabilis*
An easily grown cottage
garden perennial for a
shady spot near the front
of the border. 18in (45cm)

### Knotweed
*Polygonum affine*
A first-rate carpeter
for the front of the
border. Brown-
tinted leaves in
winter. 9in (23cm)

# APRIL

## ⚘ OUTSIDE ⚘

◆ Sow a maincrop variety of beetroot, broad bean, carrot, Florence fennel, kohl rabi, lettuce, onion, pea, radish, salad onion, salsify, scorzonera, spinach, summer cabbage, summer cauliflower, Swiss chard and turnip.

◆ Towards the end of the month sow French beans.

◆ Continue to plant early varieties of potatoes for a succession of harvesting.

◆ Trim back heathers when they finish flowering.

◆ Thin out seedlings sown previously and transplant where applicable.

◆ As bulbs go out of flower, pinch off the seed-heads to avoid a waste of energy and to encourage instead a build-up of the bulb for next year's flowering. However, some bulbs, such as snowdrops, can be left to seed to increase stock.

◆ Continue planting acidanthera, crocosmia, galtonia, gladioli, nerine and ornithogalum.

◆ This is a good month to plant evergreens, especially those that have been lifted from the field and root-wrapped in hessian.

◆ Prune cherries and plums. This mainly involves cutting out dead, diseased, crossing or overcrowded branches.

◆ Plant out sweet peas.

◆ Plant onions raised in the greenhouse or frame.

◆ Towards the end of the month, chrysanthemums can be planted out.

◆ Mow the lawn regularly.

◆ Take cuttings of conifers.

◆ Finish lifting, dividing and replanting herbaceous perennials early in the month.

◆ This can be a dry month so check all plantings regularly and water if necessary.

◆ Weeds will be growing strongly this month, so make weeding a regular job. It's much easier if you catch them young.

◆ Continue turfing and sow new lawns.

◆ Mulch with manure or compost around rhubarb.

◆ Prune forsythia, flowering currant and other spring-flowering deciduous shrubs as soon as flowering has finished.

◆ Remove weak shoots from herbaceous perennials like delphiniums, echinops, heleniums, lupins, Michaelmas daisies and phlox.

◆ Sow hardy annuals outside.

◆ Sow dill, hyssop, marjoram, parsley, rue and thyme.

◆ Plant aquatic plants in the pool and remove early signs of blanket weed.

◆ Plant asparagus crowns.

◆ During the day, take off cloches protecting strawberries to allow pollinating insects to get in.

## INSIDE

◆ Ventilate the greenhouse as often as possible and keep the floor and staging damped down to maintain humidity. Close the ventilators at night.

◆ Sow sweet corn and tomatoes for planting outside.

◆ Continue to repot plants as required.

◆ Continue sowing half-hardy annuals for planting outside and to provide pot plants for the house.

◆ Take dahlia cuttings. If you want new varieties, buy tubers and pot them up. They will produce several shoots, some of which can be taken as cuttings. Leave a few on and plant out the tuber as well.

◆ Continue sowing all the salad crops, plus spinach, Swiss chard, etc., and pot them up when they are ready. These will provide 'instant' plants when a space becomes available outside. Harden off any already in pots.

◆ Take cuttings of conifers and heathers.

◆ Early in the month, sow leeks in the greenhouse or on the windowsill.

◆ Plant tomatoes in pots or in the borders and pot up aubergines, cucumbers and peppers.

◆ Whitefly can be a problem from now on, so use yellow cards or buy in some predators.

◆ Towards the end of the month, some half-hardy annuals and perennials can be moved to the cold frame for hardening off. Cover the frames if frost is threatened.

# EARLY SUMMER PLANTS

**Chilean Glory Flower**
*Eccremocarpus scaber*
Hardy in most years, this vigorous climber produces masses of seed which germinates freely, so it's easy to keep going. 15ft (4.5m)

**Maple** *Acer pseudoplatanus* 'Simon-Louis Freres'
One variety in a wide selection of excellent foliage trees. 30ft (9m)

**Mountain Ash** *Sorbus* spp.
Small trees with white flowers and berries of various colours depending on variety. 20ft (6m)

**Cape Marigold**
*Osteospermum* spp.
A group of half-hardy perennials which are quite simple to propagate from cuttings and so are easy to keep going.
2ft (60cm)

**Petunia**
*Petunia hybrida*
A group of half-hardy annuals producing a succession of flowers over a long period in summer. 9in (23cm)

**Pansy** *Viola* spp.
Short-lived perennials best treated as annuals. They come in a wide range of colours. 6in (15cm)

**Oriental Poppy**
*Papaver orientale*
Perennials for the middle of the border, available in a range of colours. They tend to flop after flowering. 2ft (60cm)

**Monkshood**
*Aconitum napellus*
Herbaceous perennials for the middle of the border. They have interestingly hooded flowers. 3ft 6in (1.1m)

**Fennel** *Foeniculum vulgare*
A very decorative and useful perennial herb with a mild aniseed flavour and attractive yellow flowers. 5ft (1.5m)

**Potato** *Solanum tuberosum*
Early potatoes are worth growing for an improved, fresh flavour. 2ft (60cm)

**Lilac** *Syringa vulgaris*
Well-known hardy
shrubs for the middle
of the border, available
in a wide range of
colours and superbly
scented. Avoid suckers by buying
micro-propagated plants. 12ft (4m)

**Laburnum** *Laburnum anagyroides* 'Vossii'
A medium-sized tree with
bright yellow, pendulous
flowers. Note that
the seeds are
poisonous.
25ft (8m)

**Begonia**
*Begonia semperflorens*
A succulent-looking,
half-hardy annual in a range
of pinks, reds and white. The
leaves are often bronze-red too,
depending on variety. 6in (15cm)

**Fuchsia**
There are many var-
ieties of this hardy or
half-hardy shrub.
Check to establish
hardiness and treat
the half-hardies as
summer bedding. 2ft
(60cm)

**Daisy Bush**
*Olearia scilloniensis*
A hardy shrub which, even
when young, is covered in a
mass of pink and white
flowers from late spring to
mid-summer. 7ft (2.25m)

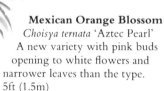

**Mexican Orange Blossom**
*Choisya ternata* 'Aztec Pearl'
A new variety with pink buds
opening to white flowers and
narrower leaves than the type.
5ft (1.5m)

**Lupin** *Lupinus polyphyllus*
Hybrid herbaceous
perennials with attractive
foliage and spikes of
flowers in a wide
range of colours.
3ft 6 in (1.1m)

**Spurge** *Euphorbia griffithii* 'Fireglow'
A slow-spreading, hardy
perennial with attractive
foliage and bright red
bracts in early summer.
May need controlling
occasionally. 4ft (1.25m)

**Plantain Lily** *Hosta* spp.
Generally shade-loving plants grown
for their attractive foliage and spikes
of lavender flowers. Unfortunately
they are very prone to slug damage
but well worth persevering with.
1–3ft (30–90cm)

**Jamaica Primrose**
*Argyranthemum frutescens*
A half-hardy perennial easily
rooted from cuttings so not
difficult to keep going. 3ft (90cm)

# MAY

### 🐦 OUTSIDE 🐦

◆ Continue successional sowings of salads, chicory, kohl rabi, peas and spinach.

◆ Sow swedes.

◆ Early in the month, plant cucumbers, French beans, runner beans and squashes under cloches.

◆ Pinch out the tops of broad beans if they are attacked by blackfly.

◆ Put a protective screen around carrots against carrot fly.

◆ Put out codling moth traps.

◆ Earth up potatoes and, if the shoots are threatened by frost, draw a little soil right over them or cover them with spun poly-propylene fleece.

◆ Plant leeks and all the members of the cabbage family sown in the seedbed.

◆ Plant out chrysanthemums.

◆ Continue to sow and turf new lawns but be prepared to water.

◆ Plant self-blanching celery.

◆ Tie in the new growth of briar fruits as they grow. Beware of letting them go too far, as it then becomes an almost impossible job.

◆ Stake tall herbaceous plants before they grow too big.

◆ Thin out excessive growth of aquatic plants and continue to remove blanket weed and excess duckweed.

◆ Take cuttings of mint and rosemary.

◆ Ventilate cold frames more generously, opening them during the day at the beginning of the month and then at night as well towards the end, to acclimatize half-hardy plants to the lower temperatures outside.

◆ Tuck straw under strawberries as the fruit begins to swell.

◆ Prune early spring-flowering shrubs like *Kerria japonica* and *Spiraea arguta*.

◆ Sow courgettes, cucumbers, runner beans and sweet corn outside. At the end of the month, gardeners in warmer areas might want to risk planting out these plants together with tomatoes that have been raised inside. In colder areas it's always best to wait until the beginning of next month. The same applies to half-hardy annual and perennial bedding plants.

◆ Watch for signs of apple and pear scab and remove infected leaves.

◆ Thin out hardy annuals sown earlier and keep a regular eye on recently sown vegetables so that you thin them when they are just big enough to handle.

◆ Continue to mow regularly and be prepared to water the lawn from now on. Remove weeds with a knife, or put a tiny pinch of salt in the centre of each weed rosette to kill it.

◆ Sow hardy perennials and biennials in a seedbed outside.

◆ Prune early-flowering clematis, cutting it back to fill its allotted space.

◆ Lift, divide and replant polyanthus.

◆ Lift bulbs that are looking untidy and heel them into a corner to continue building up their bulbs.

◆ After hardening off, plant out hardy perennials raised in the greenhouse.

◆ Trim alpines in the scree path if they are spreading beyond their required space.

◆ Tie in climbers regularly and clip back any plants that are getting out of hand.

◆ Continue hand-weeding regularly.

## ❦ INSIDE ❦

◆ Keep the greenhouse well ventilated and damped down. You will probably need to shade the glass this month. Certainly young seedlings should be protected from hot sun.

◆ Towards the end of the month, if you have room, plant up tubs and baskets with half-hardy flowers and vegetables but keep them inside until early in June.

◆ Remove side-shoots from tomatoes as they appear and start feeding with a liquid fertilizer at every watering.

◆ Pot on peppers into their final pots.

◆ Start to feed aubergines, cucumbers, melons and peppers growing in pots.

◆ Sow pot plants for the house for flowering in autumn and winter. These include calceolarias, cinerarias and primulas.

◆ Start to take softwood cuttings of shrubs.

◆ If plants in pots and boxes waiting to be planted out begin to look yellow, give them a liquid feed.

◆ Start to summer-prune grape vines.

# MIDSUMMER PLANTS

**False Acacia** *Robinia pseudoacacia* 'Frisia'
An outstanding small tree with golden foliage. It
tends to suffer from die-back when young so buy
only container-grown plants. 20ft (6m)

**Chilean Glory Flower** *Eccremocarpus scaber*
This excellent climber will last well into late
summer when it sets prolific seed. It may die back
in the winter but will generally shoot again in
spring. 15ft (4.5m)

**Giant Bellflower**
*Campanula latifolia*
A striking perennial
for the middle or
back of the border.
It flowers for
a long period and
will seed itself prolifically. 4ft (1.25m)

**Senecio** *Senecio greyi*
A popular and attractive shrub for
near the front of the border, this has
evergreen leaves of silvery grey. It's
hardy, wind-resistant and ideal for
chalky soils and seaside gardens.
3ft (90cm)

**Ornamental Onion** *Allium* spp.
Decorative onions like the small *Allium cernuum*
and the taller *A. christophii* make excellent border
plants for a sunny spot and many can be cut and
dried for use in the house. 1–2ft (30–60cm)

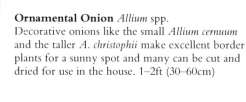

**Fig** *Ficus carica*
Figs can be grown against a
south- or west-facing fence
where they look most attractive and are quite prolific.
Alternatively, they can be
grown as standards in pots.
5–20ft (1.5–6m)

**Cabbage** *Brassica oleracea*
Summer cabbages are easy to grow
either started off in the greenhouse or
sown direct. They make very attractive
plants in the borders grown in groups
of two or three. 1ft (30cm)

**Sweet Pea** *Lathyrus odoratus*
Hardy annual climbers available in a wide range of
colours and mostly sweetly scented. 10ft (3.5m)

**Masterwort** *Astratia carniolica* 'Rubra'
A hardy perennial with curiously shaped flowers that are very delicate in structure. Excellent for cutting. 2ft (60cm)

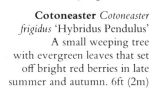

**Gum Tree**
*Eucalyptus gunnii*
A moderate to very hardy tree with greyish peeling bark. Can be kept as a shrub by regular pruning in late winter.
100ft (30m)

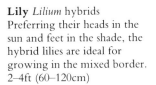

**Lily** *Lilium* hybrids
Preferring their heads in the sun and feet in the shade, the hybrid lilies are ideal for growing in the mixed border.
2–4ft (60–120cm)

**Cotoneaster** *Cotoneaster frigidus* 'Hybridus Pendulus'
A small weeping tree with evergreen leaves that set off bright red berries in late summer and autumn. 6ft (2m)

**Sweet William**
*Dianthus barbatus*
A short-lived perennial best grown as a biennial. It is available in a wide range of flower colours, and some dwarf varieties.
6–24in (15–60cm)

**Marjoram** *Origanum majorana*
A popular herb for a sunny spot and a rich soil. Used widely in the kitchen, it is also a good butterfly and bee attractor.
1ft (30cm)

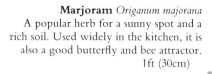

**Rose Campion**
*Lychnis coronaria*
A hardy perennial that's often considered difficult to place because of its bright magenta flowers. It prefers a sunny spot. 2ft (60cm)

**Thyme** *Thymus* spp.
There are many different species and varieties of thyme including coloured-leaved varieties and some with very aromatic foliage. They are excellent for growing in paths and between paving as well as in the borders and can, of course, be put to a variety of uses in the kitchen.
4–6in (10–15cm)

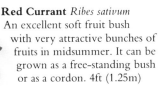

**Swiss Chard, Rhubarb Chard and Spinach**
*Beta vulgaris cycla, Spinacea oleracea*
All these leaf vegetables look very attractive in the borders, the spinach with fresh green leaves and the chards with bright silver and red stems.
1½ft (45cm)

**Red Currant** *Ribes sativum*
An excellent soft fruit bush with very attractive bunches of fruits in midsummer. It can be grown as a free-standing bush or as a cordon. 4ft (1.25m)

**Potato** *Solanum tuberosum*
Second early and maincrop potatoes should be considered if space allows. They'll store much longer than the early varieties, generally until late spring. 3ft (90cm)

# JUNE

### OUTSIDE

◆ In the first week of the month, plant out half-hardy annuals and perennials and all of the half-hardy vegetables – courgettes, cucumbers, marrows, runner beans, squashes, sweet corn, etc.

◆ Early in the month, put out planted tubs and hanging baskets. Baskets will need watering every day and both tubs and baskets should be fed with liquid fertilizer once a week.

◆ Continue sowing radish and spinach but, from now on, put them in a shady spot to prevent them running to seed prematurely.

◆ Peg down runners of strawberries to make new plants for potting up and forcing in the greenhouse.

◆ This is the main month for taking soft-wood cuttings of shrubs.

◆ You'll need to keep the sprinkler going from now until the autumn, both on the lawn and the borders, so check that you have a licence if it's needed.

◆ Keep an eye open for greenfly. If you see their eggs on the underside of leaves, rub them off. Caterpillars can be controlled with the bacterium *Bacillus thuringiensis*.

◆ Continue successional sowings of beetroot, carrots, chicory, endive, lettuce, swedes and turnips.

◆ Trim back brooms that have finished flowering, avoiding cutting into the old wood.

◆ Continue to trim and tie herbaceous plants and climbers to ensure that none get out of hand.

◆ Sow chicory for forcing for winter salads.

◆ Net fruit trees and bushes against birds.

◆ Divide and replant rhizomes of flag irises (*Iris germanica*).

◆ When herbaceous plants have finished flowering, cut off the old flower spikes and put them on the compost heap or through the shredder, unless, of course, you wish to save seed.

◆ Turn the compost heap to accelerate rotting.

◆ Sow spinach beet for use in the autumn.

◆ Pick the first gooseberries for cooking, leave the rest to ripen for dessert use.

◆ Plant corms of *Anemone coronaria* 'de Caen' for autumn flowering.

◆ Take stem cuttings of pinks.

◆ Tie in climbing plants regularly.

◆ Transplant to nursery rows seedlings of perennials and biennials sown last month.

◆ Propagate climbers by layering.

◆ Top up the pool and bog garden in dry weather.

◆ Protect newly planted cabbages, cauliflowers, Brussels sprouts, etc. from cabbage root fly.

◆ Harvest and store shallots and continue to harvest early potatoes.

◆ Continue tying in and pinching out wall-trained fruit.

◆ Stake gladioli as the spikes begin to form.

◆ Remove flower spikes if they form on rhubarb.

◆ Continue hand-weeding but look out for self-sown seedlings and leave them if they're in the right place.

## 🜨 INSIDE 🜨

◆ Ventilate freely, all night if necessary, and keep the atmosphere humid by damping down. You will almost certainly need to shade the greenhouse now.

◆ Prick out seedlings of calceolaria, cinerarias and primula sown earlier.

◆ Trim cucumbers and continue to feed them regularly.

◆ Put greenhouse pot plants like azaleas, pelargoniums and solanum outside for the summer.

◆ Pinch back vines regularly.

◆ Continue to feed fruit in pots and support growing fruit to avoid breaking stems.

◆ Sow more half-hardy annuals and salad vegetables for potting up later as replacements in the borders.

# MIDSUMMER PLANTS

**Honeysuckle**
*Lonicera periclymenum*
Vigorous climbers giving a long
period of flowering but liable to take
over completely. Need regular trimming. 30ft (9m)

**Carnations and Pinks**
*Dianthus* spp.
Superb perennials for the front of
the border. They flower for a long
period and fill the
garden with perfume.
9–24in (23–60cm)

**Cinquefoil**
*Potentilla fruticosa*
Hardy and easy-to-grow
shrubs for a sunny spot.
Available in several colours.
4ft (1.25m)

**Marigold**
*Calendula officinalis*
Easily grown hardy annuals
for the front of the border.
They seed freely so will
always be with you after the
first sowing. 12in (30cm)

**Borage** *Borago officinalis*
An attractive herb for the
middle of the border.
It seeds itself freely and
is always welcome
wherever it comes up.
2ft (60cm)

**Rhubarb**
*Rheum rhaponticum*
An indispensible veg
etable/fruit. Very
decorative and the
first fruit of the
season. Can also be
forced. 3ft (90cm)

**Lavender** *Lavandula angustifolia*
A superb shrubby herb with
aromatic flowers and foliage.
Available in blues, pink and white.
2ft (60cm)

**Lettuce** *Lactuca sativa*
A popular salad vegetable that
can be successionally sown to
produce heads more or less all
the year round.
6–12in (15–30cm)

**Canterbury Bell**
*Campanula medium*
A stately biennial for the
middle of the border
producing superb spikes
of bell-like flowers in a
range of colours.
3ft (90cm)

**Smoke Bush**
*Cotinus coggygria*
A fine shrub with foliage in
grey-green to deep purple,
depending on variety.
10ft (3m)

**Miniature Marguerite**
*Chrysanthemum paludosum*
A hardy annual which can
be sown direct and produces
a succession of flowers right
through the summer.
1ft (30cm)

**Globe Flower** *Trollius europaeus*
A moisture lover most at home
in the bog garden or at the pool
edge where it will flower for a
very long period in summer.
2½ft (90cm)

**Spiraea** *Spiraea bumalda* 'Anthony Waterer'
A shrub forming a small domed bush with carmine
red flowers. Can be pruned hard to keep it compact.
4ft (1.25m)

**Broad Bean** *Vicia faba major*
The first bean to crop
and very valuable for
that and its unique
flavour. A good soil
improver too. 1–3ft
(30–90cm)

**Jacob's Ladder** *Polemonium caeruleum*
Popular cottage garden perennials
which seed freely
throughout the
borders. Attrac-
tive foliage and
flowers of dark
blue, light blue or
white. 2ft (60cm)

**Gooseberry** *Ribes grossularia*
A popular fruiting bush which
can also be grown as a cordon against the
fence or wall. One of the earliest fruits.
3ft (90cm)

**Salad Onion**
*Allium cepa*
A useful salad
crop which can be
produced more or
less all the year
round. 1ft (30m)

**Penstemon**
Long-flowering hardy perennials for near
the front of the border. Available in reds,
purples, pinks and blues as well as white.
1–3ft (30–90cm)

**Globe Artichoke**
*Cynara scolymus*
Worth growing just for its
superb foliage but with the
bonus of delicately flav-
oured, much sought after
and expensive flower heads.
5ft (1.5m)

**Beetroot** *Beta vulgaris*
A succession of this
popular root vegetable
can be obtained by pro-
tected growing and
storage of roots in
winter. Very dec-
orative foliage.
1ft (30cm)

**Primula**
*Primula vialii*
A bright perennial
with flowers like red
hot pokers. Best in
cool, moist shade.
1ft (30cm)

# JULY

### ❧ OUTSIDE ❧

◆ Pinch out the growing points of upright tomatoes when they have made three flower trusses. Put straw under bush tomatoes to keep the fruit clean and raise it above slug level.

◆ Many herbs will now be ready for picking and drying.

◆ Continue with successional sowings of salads and, early in the month, sow the root vegetables needed for winter storage.

◆ Disbud chrysanthemums and dahlias if you require large blooms.

◆ Look at alpines in the scree path. If they are going bare in the middles, mound them up with a little fine compost at the centre of each plant to encourage rooting and further growth.

◆ Plant *Nerine bowdenii* against south-facing walls or fences.

◆ Harvest globe artichokes while the heads are still small.

◆ Remove flower spikes from herbaceous plants unless you intend to save seed.

◆ Prune summer-flowering deciduous shrubs, cutting out a proportion of the old wood to encourage further new growth.

◆ Lift shallots and dry them before storing in nets.

◆ Thin out excess growth of oxygenating weed in the pool.

◆ Dead-head roses and annual bedding to encourage further flowering.

◆ Towards the end of the month, start to sow some early varieties of vegetables for quick maturing.

◆ Sow a clump or two of broad beans for the tops which make a delicious alternative to cabbage in autumn, while the roots supply nitrogen to the soil.

◆ Cut off the old leaves of strawberries and transfer all debris to the compost heap.

◆ Take cuttings of hydrangeas.

◆ Layer border carnations.

◆ Transplant perennial and biennial seedlings to wider spacings.

◆ Collect and sow seeds of primulas using a soilless compost. Leave them outside, protected from birds and cats with wire netting.

◆ Check other perennials regularly for ripening seed and collect it before it falls.

◆ Take half-ripe cuttings of shrubs like berberis, camellia, ceanothus, choisya, cytisus, escallonia, genista, hebe, hypericum, kolkwitzia, lavatera, lonicera, potentilla, pyracantha, spiraea, syringa, viburnum, weigela.

◆ Sow Chinese cabbage, French beans, spring cabbage, Swiss chard and rhubarb chard.

◆ Water and feed regularly all container plants, especially those in hanging baskets.

◆ Pinch out the growing points of runner beans when they reach the tops of their canes.

◆ Cut back straggly growth on arabis, aubrieta, pansies and violas.

◆ Plant bulbs of amaryllis, colchicum, hardy cyclamen and other autumn-flowering types.

◆ Complete planting of Brussels sprouts, cabbage, cauliflower and other members of the cabbage family.

◆ Harvest and prune raspberries.

◆ Summer-prune pears.

## 🦎 INSIDE 🦎

◆ Full ventilation should be given on hot days and at nights. Damp down paths and stagings often.

◆ Continue removing side-shoots of tomatoes and trimming cucumbers. Feed aubergines and peppers. Remove lower leaves of tomatoes only when they go brown or yellow.

◆ Take cuttings of Regal pelargoniums.

◆ Avoid splashing water from the floor onto tomato fruits, which might spread botrytis in the form of 'halo blight'.

◆ Sow annuals for autumn pot plants, together with calceolaria, cineraria, coleus and exacum.

# MIDSUMMER PLANTS

**Norway Maple**
*Acer platanoides* 'Crimson King'
One of a number of superb
foliage trees in this group. They
are available in various leaf
colours, some of which are bi-
coloured. 30ft (9m)

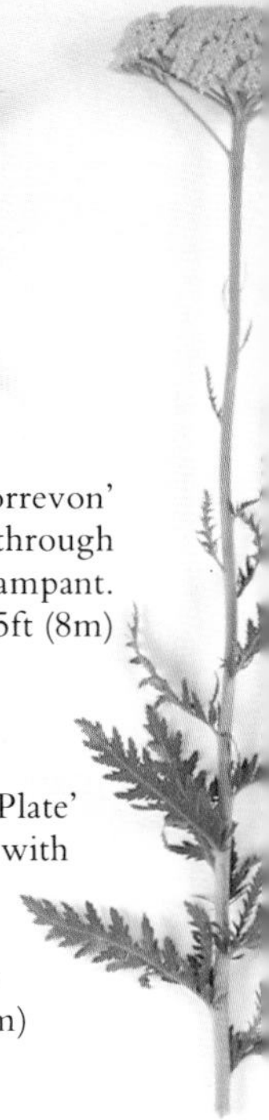

**Cranesbill** *Geranium* spp.
Hardy perennials, many of
which are excellent for dry shade
under trees where a few other
plants will grow well.
1–2½ft (30–75cm)

**Pansy** *Viola* spp.
There are dozens of varieties of
this versatile group, which flower
at different times to give a display
right through the year. 8in (20cm)

**Clematis** *Clematis viticella* 'Madame Julia Correvon'
This group of climbers is ideal for growing through
trees and over shrubs since they're not too rampant.
Cut right back in the autumn. 25ft (8m)

**Yarrow** *Achillea
filipendulina* 'Gold Plate'
A hardy perennial with
grey, toothed
leaves and bright
heads of flowers in
summer. 4ft (1.25m)

**Poached Egg Flower**
*Limnanthes douglasii*
A bright annual which is an excellent
hoverfly attractor. It seeds itself freely
each year. 6in (15cm)

**Delphinium**
Tall, stately herbaceous
perennials available in
many shades of blue, pink
and white. Easy to raise
from seed. 4–8ft (1.25–2.5m)

**Carrot**
*Daucus carota sativus*
Carrots can be sown in
succession right through
the summer. The foliage is
very attractive. 1ft (30cm)

**Kohlrabi**
*Brassica oleracea gongyloides*
An attractive vegetable for
the front of the border. It
can be cooked like a turnip
or in soups. 1½ft (45cm)

**Honey Locust** *Gleditsia triacanthos* 'Sunburst'
A striking small tree with bright golden foliage.
It tends to leaf a little late. 20ft (6m)

**Weeping Pear**
*Pyrus salicifolia* 'Pendula'
A fine small tree with an
attractive weeping habit and
downy grey leaves. 20ft (6m)

**Cinquefoil** *Potentilla atrosanguinea*
Herbaceous perennial with a
spreading habit, available
in many colours.
$1\frac{1}{2}$ft (45cm)

**Red Raripila
Spearmint**
*Mentha raripila
rubra*
A herb with a
sweet spearmint
flavour and
purple flowers.
2ft (60cm)

**Apple Mint**
*Mentha
suaveolens*
One of the
most popular
cooking herbs
with fresh,
green, hairy
leaves.
2ft (60cm)

**Rose** *Rosa* spp.
All types of rose species and
hybrids are suitable for this
garden, ranging from
miniatures to climbers.
1–20ft (30cm–6m)

**Water Iris** *Iris laevigata*
Tall stately perennials for the
bog garden or the edge of the
pool. Available in several
colours. $1\frac{1}{2}$–$2\frac{1}{2}$ft (45–75cm)

**Strawberry** *Fragaria* spp.
The strawberries are amongst the most
prolific and rewarding fruits and have
attractive flowers, foliage and fruit.
1ft (30cm)

**Cauliflower**
*Brassica oleracea botrytis*
The summer cauliflowers
are easy to raise from direct
sowing or in the greenhouse
to give a long succession.
$1\frac{1}{2}$ft (45cm)

**Anthemis**
*Anthemis cupaniana*
Mat-forming herbaceous
perennials with attractive
grey foliage. They can be
invasive. 1ft (30cm)

**St John's Wort** *Hypericum* spp.
There are several of these attractive
and floriferous plants suitable for most
positions. 6in–7ft (15cm–2.25m)

# AUGUST

### 🦎 OUTSIDE 🦎

◆ Once raspberries have been harvested, prune out the old canes and tie in strong new growths. The old canes make excellent material for shredding.

◆ Autumn-fruiting raspberries don't need tying to wires but in windy gardens it's as well to support the fully grown canes with a string tied to posts around the rows.

◆ Take clematis cuttings.

◆ Take cuttings of alpines, especially those plants like *Euryops acraeus* and the aubrietas which have a short life.

◆ Water regularly if you are confident of being able to apply enough to reach right down to the roots. If not, it's probably best not to start.

◆ Sow a patch or two of lettuce using a mildew-resistant variety like 'Avondefiance'.

◆ Prune cordon gooseberries and red currants.

◆ Trim conifer hedges and cut out the tops of any that have reached 3 feet (1 m) more than the required height.

◆ Sow new lawns but be prepared to water if necessary.

◆ If potatoes show the brown spots typical of blight, cut off the tops immediately and harvest the crop. Check also for the blackening at the bottom of the stem that indicates an attack by the disease blackleg and take similar action. The old haulms should be destroyed or carted away.

◆ If summer bedding plants have gone out of flower, remove them and fill the space either from your reserve of standby pots or by sowing biennials like wallflowers or forget-me-nots *in situ*. When they come through, just thin them out.

◆ After briars finish fruiting, remove the fruited wood and tie in new shoots in their place.

◆ Sow Japanese onions, winter-hardy salad onions and winter radish.

◆ Sow spring cabbage in a seedbed.

◆ Harvest early varieties of apple which don't store well. Eat fresh. Support heavily laden branches with wooden props.

◆ At the end of the month, protect autumn-fruiting raspberries and strawberries from birds.

◆ Allow a few French beans to ripen and go hard before harvesting and store them in air-tight jars for winter use.

◆ Plant daffodils and narcissi.

◆ Continue to feed flowering plants in pots but switch to a high-nitrogen liquid fertilizer to encourage more leaf growth and a slightly longer season.

◆ Cut the flowers of gladioli but leave the foliage to help build next year's corm.

◆ Take half-ripe cuttings of shrubs and shrubby herbs.

◆ Take cuttings of geraniums and fuchsias.

◆ Plant strawberries for fruiting next season.

◆ Remove faded flowers from roses, annuals and herbaceous perennials to prolong their flowering, unless you wish to save seed.

◆ Prune rambler roses after flowering.

◆ Begin to divide and transplant perennials.

◆ Start summer-pruning trained fruit trees, beginning with the pears.

◆ Early in the month, plant autumn-flowering bulbs like autumn-flowering crocus, colchicum and sternbergia.

◆ Check herbaceous perennials regularly for ripening seed and harvest it before it falls.

◆ Cut, dry and store herbs.

◆ Pot up rooted strawberry runners but leave them outside until next February.

## ❧ INSIDE ❧

◆ Maintain continual day and night ventilation and damp down paths and staging regularly.

◆ Harvest aubergines, cucumbers, melons, peppers and tomatoes regularly and remove all old or diseased leaves. Continue feeding at every watering.

◆ For pot plants for the house, sow calceolarias, cyclamen, primulas and schizanthus together with a selection of half-hardy annuals. Pot up prepared hyacinths for Christmas flowering.

◆ Sow winter lettuce for growing in the cold or slightly heated greenhouse.

◆ Repot cyclamen corms which have been resting.

◆ At the end of the month, lift a few annuals like begonias and impatiens from the garden, cut them back and pot them on. They'll make new growth quite soon to grow into pot plants for the house.

# LATE SUMMER PLANTS

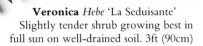

**Veronica** *Hebe* 'La Seduisante'
Slightly tender shrub growing best in
full sun on well-drained soil. 3ft (90cm)

**Apple** *Malus sylvestris*
A popular and widely grown tree fruit for
sun or part shade. Prefers a well-drained
soil but will tolerate heavier land. Height
and spread controlled by training.

**Yellow Flax** *Linum* 'Gemmel's Hybrid'
A hardy perennial for full sun and retentive
soil. It produces a succession of flowers all
summer. 1ft (30cm)

**Fuschia** *Fuschia* 'Tom Thumb'
A very free-flowing dwarf shrub
for a sunny spot on any soil.
1–1½ft (30–45cm)

**Morning Glory** *Ipomoea rubro-caerulea*
A half-hardy climber for a sunny spot
in any soil. Will grow through shrubs
or with climbing vegetables. 12ft (4m)

**Gladiolus** *Gladiolus* hybrid
A half-hardy corm, used for summer
bedding and cut flowers. Available
in a variety of colours, it likes a sunny
spot in any well-drained soil.

**Aubergine, Egg Plant**
*Solanum melongena*
A tender vegetable giving good
crops under glass or against a
warm wall outside. 3ft (90cm)

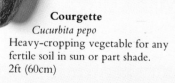

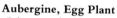

**Courgette**
*Cucurbita pepo*
Heavy-cropping vegetable for any
fertile soil in sun or part shade.
2ft (60cm)

**Red Lettuce** *Lactuca sativa*
An attractive lettuce that can be used
on a cut-and-come-again basis right
through the summer. Any soil or
position. 8in (20cm)

**Grape** *Vitis vinifera*
A climbing plant which can be grown as a standard in the greenhouse or, in warmer areas, outside. Produces red or white fruits for dessert or wine-making according to variety. 30ft (9m)

**Coyote Willow** *Salix exigua*
A large shrub or small tree. Will tolerate shade but must have a retentive soil. It bears slender catkins in spring. 15ft (4.5m)

**Mallow** *Lavatera* 'Barnsley'
A shrubby hardy perennial for a sunny spot on most soils. Long flowering period. 4–5ft (1.25–1.5m)

**Tomato** *Lycopersicon lycopersicum*
A productive and decorative vegetable fruit for a sunny position. It can be grown as a bush or climber, inside or out, depending on variety. $1\frac{1}{2}$–4ft (45–120cm)

**Nasturtium** *Tropaeolum majus*
An easy hardy annual for a sunny spot on poor soil. Flowers all summer. The seeds are edible. 1ft (30cm)

**Parsley** *Petroselinum crispum*
A well-known herb ideal for edging paths. Grows in any fertile soil in sun or part shade. 9in (23cm)

**Sweet Corn** *Zea mays*
Newer varieties allow this superb vegetable to be grown even in cooler areas. It needs a sunny spot and fertile soil. 4ft (120cm)

**Climbing French Beans** *Phaseolus vulgaris*
These purple-podded beans can be grown up canes or a pergola or look attractive grown through shrubs. They need a retentive soil but will tolerate some shade. 10ft (3.5m)

**Rosemary** *Rosmarinus officinalis*
A shrubby herb for a sunny spot in well-drained soil. Can be kept more compact by regular picking. 3–4 ft (90–120cm)

**Nutmeg Tree** *Leycesteria formosa*
A medium-sized shrub which thrives in any good soil in sun or part shade. 6ft (2m)

**Globe Artichoke**
*Cynara scolymus*
A hardy perennial with great decorative and culinary value. Grows best in a sunny spot on retentive soil. The flower buds are edible. 5ft (1.5m)

**Dwarf French Beans**
*Phaseolus vulgaris*
An attractive dwarf bean to grow in the borders. It needs retentive soil and prefers a sunny spot. It looks good in flower and fruit. 1ft (30cm)

**Cucumber** *Cucumis sativus*
A popular vegetable fruit. There are varieties for growing as climbers inside and out and also bush types. All prefer a sunny or semi-shaded spot and must have retentive soil. 1–10ft (30cm–3.5m)

**Endive** *Cichorium endivia*
A salad vegetable, which is generally blanched before use, from late summer through winter. Makes an attractive edging or group in the border. 8in (20cm)

# SEPTEMBER

## 🌺 OUTSIDE 🌺

◆ Continue pruning trained apples.

◆ Begin harvesting onions.

◆ Set up marrows in the sunshine to ripen.

◆ Lift, divide and replant perennials.

◆ Plant evergreen shrubs.

◆ Sow a winter-hardy variety of spinach or, if you have trouble with the crop running to seed, use spinach beet.

◆ Remove and compost summer bedding that has finished flowering and replace with potted flowers or vegetables from standby supply or biennials lifted from nursery bed.

◆ Sow early carrots, lettuce, radish and turnips in the cold frame.

◆ Trap earwigs in chrysanthemums and dahlias.

◆ Begin to lift and store root vegetables.

◆ Lift and replant large evergreens.

◆ Lift gladioli, clean and store the corms.

◆ Plant lettuce for later cloching and spring cabbage.

◆ Remove debris from beans and peas when they've finished producing but leave the roots in the ground to dispense their nitrogen.

◆ Prune peaches and nectarines.

◆ Harvest apples and pears which should be used fairly soon after picking.

◆ Plant spring-flowering bulbs.

◆ Lay turf for a new lawn.

◆ Continue taking cuttings of fuchsias, geraniums, heathers and hydrangeas.

◆ Later in the month, rake out dead thatch from the lawn.

◆ Bring ripened marrows and squashes into the shed for storage.

◆ Dry out onions and garlic bulbs, clean them up and store them.

◆ Put cloches over outdoor tomatoes to assist ripening.

◆ Take hardwood cuttings of gooseberries.

◆ Cut down perennials that are over.

◆ As patches of soil become vacant, dig and manure those that are going to stand fallow.

◆ Clean up the pool and cover it with netting to prevent leaves falling in it.

◆ Prune blackcurrants and gooseberries towards the end of the month.

◆ Weed and clean out the bottoms of hedges.

◆ Prune plums when they have finished.

◆ Sow green manure on vacant ground.

◆ Prune climbing and rambling roses and weeping standards.

◆ Earth up celeriac, celery and leeks to blanch them.

◆ Spray members of the cabbage family with *Bacillus thuringiensis* if you see cabbage white butterfly caterpillars.

◆ Protect the last of the autumn-fruiting strawberries with cloches.

◆ Check the tips of fruit tree branches and bushes for mildew. Cut it off if you see it.

◆ Pot up a few spring-flowering bulbs and plunge in peat; use to fill gaps next spring.

## 🌺 INSIDE 🌺

◆ Check the heating in the greenhouse and repair it if necessary. Remove shading and begin to close the ventilators at night. Reduce watering and damping down.

◆ Sow a winter variety of lettuce and a pot or two of radish.

◆ Take stem cuttings of good varieties of begonias, impatiens and coleus.

◆ Bring inside any plants that have been standing out for the summer.

◆ Pot up bulbs for spring flowering inside, but put them in as cool a spot as you've got.

# OCTOBER

### ❧ OUTSIDE ❧

◆ Divide and replant rhubarb.

◆ Cloche autumn-fruiting strawberries to prolong harvesting. When they've finished, remove the old leaves, weed them and take away the old mulch.

◆ Plant spring cabbages.

◆ Plant new herbaceous plants.

◆ Finish planting biennials and spring bulbs.

◆ Sow winter lettuce to cover with cloches later.

◆ Continue to lift and store root vegetables.

◆ Go through the borders, cutting back herbaceous plants, pulling out any weeds and generally tidying up before the cold weather.

◆ Cut back the old leaves of hellebores when they begin to brown, to make way for new leaves and to expose the flowers later on.

◆ Lift half-hardy perennials you want to save, put them in compost in pots or boxes and bring them into the greenhouse.

◆ Prune blackcurrants towards the end of the month and use the prunings for hardwood cuttings.

◆ Plant autumn onion sets and garlic.

◆ Clip over loose growing conifers like *Chamaecyparis pisifera* 'Boulevard'.

◆ Cut the lawn for the last time and put the mower in for servicing and sharpening.

◆ If you can find the bulbs in the garden centre, plant lilies. Pot them up for later planting if there is no room available.

◆ When leaves of roses have fallen, pick them up and burn them to avoid over-wintering blackspot disease.

◆ Pot up a few roots of mint to grow inside for the winter and sow a pot of parsley.

◆ Take hardwood cuttings of red and white currants and several shrubs like dogwoods, flowering currants, mock orange and willows.

◆ Continue laying turf lawns provided the ground is not frosted.

◆ Sow sweet peas in the cold frame.

◆ Lift a few roots of forcing chicory and store them in sand in a cold spot. Start forcing when supplies of salads are needed.

◆ Cut down the tops of Jerusalem artichokes.

◆ Cut down asparagus and mulch around the plants with compost.

◆ Put grease-bands round apple and cherry trees.

◆ Pick and store late apples.

◆ Plant containers with bulbs and biennials for a spring display.

◆ Remove yellowing leaves from Brussels sprouts.

### ❧ INSIDE ❧

◆ Give as much ventilation as possible during the day now, but close the vents at night. Some heat may be needed.

◆ Clear out old cucumber and tomato haulms as soon as harvesting is over. Clean the greenhouse thoroughly.

◆ Start a regular autumn and winter inspection of plants and immediately remove leaves showing signs of fungus attack.

◆ Pot up a few roses for an early display of flowers next year.

◆ Bring in pot-grown chrysanthemums and feed them regularly.

◆ Bring in citrus fruits and figs that have been grown in pots and stood outside for the summer.

◆ Lift a few herbaceous plants like *Dicentra spectabilis* and lily of the valley and pot them up. Stand them in the frame until December when they can be brought in for forcing into early flower.

# LATE SUMMER PLANTS

**Barberry** *Berberis thunbergii* 'Aurea Nana'
A hardy shrub forming a small mound of
golden foliage. 2ft (60cm)

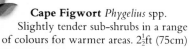

**Cape Figwort** *Phygelius* spp.
Slightly tender sub-shrubs in a range
of colours for warmer areas. 2½ft (75cm)

**Sage** *Salvia* spp.
Evergreen herb. There are many
very decorative forms which are
also useful in the kitchen.
2ft (60cm)

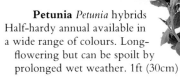

**Petunia** *Petunia* hybrids
Half-hardy annual available in
a wide range of colours. Long-
flowering but can be spoilt by
prolonged wet weather. 1ft (30cm)

**Blackberry** *Rubus fruticosus*
A fruiting climber which can
be useful in this type of garden
but care must be taken to tie
it in regularly or it will
become out of hand.
10–12ft (3.5–4m)

**Melon** *Cucumis melo*
A trailing fruit for growing in
the cold greenhouse or frame in
summer when it will be
fairly prolific. 6ft (2m)

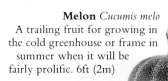

**French Marigold** *Tagetes patula*
Crimson, orange or yellow half-hardy
annual, flowering all summer. Grows
best in sun. 12in (30cm)

**Floss Flower** *Ageratum houstonianum*
A half-hardy annual for the front of
the border. Available in several shades
of blue, purple and white. 6in (15cm)

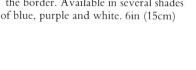

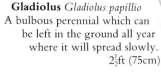

**Gladiolus** *Gladiolus papillio*
A bulbous perennial which can
be left in the ground all year
where it will spread slowly.
2½ft (75cm)

**Feather Grass** *Stipa gigantea*
A fine grass which produces tall,
feathery stems of oat-like grass
from a slowly increasing
hummock. Not invasive. 6ft (2m)

**Raspberry** *Rubus idaeus*
Easy to grow in temperate climates. Summer or autumn fruiting. Does best in well drained
soil in sheltered position.
6–8ft (2–2.5m)

**Honeysuckle** *Lonicera* spp.
There are several honeysuckles that make useful climbers for the pergola, arbour or fence. They will need regular pruning to keep them in check. 20ft (6m)

**Ivy** *Hedera* spp.
The ivies make good ground-cover or climbers over fences or walls. They're excellent attractors of birds, butterflies and other insects.

**Runner Beans** *Phaseolus coccineus*
Prolific vegetable with attractive flowers and foliage. Needs careful soil preparation and retentive soil. 6–8ft (2–2.5m)

**Clematis**
*Clematis tangutica*
A vigorous, small-flowered species which will produce masses of flowers followed by attractive seed-heads. Needs keeping in check. 20ft (6m)

**Oregano** *Oreganum vulgare*
A slightly sprawling herb with peppery leaves and attractive white or pink flowers. Not as widely used in cooking as marjoram. 2ft (60cm)

**Butterfly Bush** *Buddleia davidii*
Fine tall shrub which can be kept small by pruning. Good butterfly attractor. 10ft (3m)

**Senecio** *Senecio tanguticus*
A very attractive, tall perennial with the disadvantage of being very invasive. Best grown in grass. 6ft (2m)

**Garlic Chives** *Allium tuberosum*
A very attractive herb worth growing for its flowers alone but with the bonus of a pronounced garlic flavour. 1ft (30cm)

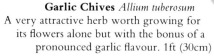

**Sweet Pepper**
*Capsicum annuum*
An excellent vegetable/fruit for the cold greenhouse or frame in summer. Some dwarf varieties can even be grown in pots on the windowsill.
1–3ft (30–90cm)

**Chives**
*Allium schoenoprasum*
A fine herb for the front of the border, producing a succession of bright flowers. There are a few quite dramatic, larger varieties. 1ft (30cm)

# NOVEMBER

## 🌾 OUTSIDE 🌾

◆ Sow a few patches of winter-hardy broad beans and early peas. In colder areas it's wise to cover them with cloches later on.

◆ Sweep up fallen leaves and put them in a wire netting container to make leaf-mould.

◆ Cover those alpines that dislike winter wet, using a piece of glass or clear plastic.

◆ Protect all members of the cabbage family with netting against birds.

◆ Order seed catalogues.

◆ Clear up all debris and make regular slug and snail hunting sorties.

◆ Winter-prune deciduous shrubs, removing dead, diseased or overcrowded wood and a proportion of the old shoots.

◆ When frost blackens dahlia foliage, lift the tubers and store them in the greenhouse or a frost-free shed.

◆ Plant bare-rooted trees and shrubs, including fruit trees and bushes.

◆ Lift leeks and parsnips, put them in peat in case the soil freezes too hard to lift them.

◆ Protect plants in the cold frame with a covering of old carpet or sacking on cold nights.

◆ Winter-prune bush apples and pears.

◆ Sow seeds of the berried shrubs like berberis and cotoneasters and put pots outside.

◆ Remove the top netting of the fruit cage in case it snows.

◆ Check stakes and ties on trees and replace if necessary.

◆ Sow alpines in a coarse compost, cover with grit and put the pots outside or in the cold frame.

◆ Keep strawberries in pots outside but make sure they don't get waterlogged by turning them on their sides.

◆ Protect the curds of cauliflowers from severe frost by snapping a couple of leaves over them.

◆ Brush snow off trees and shrubs if they are in danger of breaking but otherwise leave covered plants because the snow acts as a protection against severe cold.

◆ Remove all weeds from the garden and put them on the compost heap. Lightly fork manure or compost into vacant areas which will be sown or planted next year.

## 🌾 INSIDE 🌾

◆ In the greenhouse, ventilate as much as possible during the day but keep the house closed or with just a tiny chink of ventilation at night. Some heating will be necessary to maintain frost-free conditions.

◆ To reduce heating costs, insulate with bubble polythene sheeting.

◆ Examine stored fruit and vegetables regularly and remove any showing signs of rotting.

◆ As soon as your seed order arrives, check it and then store the seeds in a cool, dry place.

◆ Check all your tools and repair them if necessary, oil them and put them away.

◆ If you have border space available in the greenhouse, sow broad beans, early peas and a winter variety of lettuce.

◆ Check dahlia tubers in store and cut away signs of rotting.

◆ Sow cyclamen if you can maintain a temperature in the propagator of 64°F (18°C).

◆ Feed flowering pot plants.

◆ Clean pots and boxes in very hot water with a little household bleach, ready for the new season.

# DECEMBER

## 🌿 OUTSIDE 🌿

◆ In December the soil will still be warm from the summer though it may not seem so. There is, therefore, still time to plant bare-rooted trees and shrubs, including fruit, and it's much better to do it now than in the new year.

◆ There should be plenty of Brussels sprouts, cabbages and cauliflowers to harvest this month. After you have removed all the sprouts from a plant, or have cut a cabbage or cauli-flower, make sure you pull up the old stump. Good hygiene is a great help in controlling pests and diseases.

◆ If possible, invest in an electric shredder which will take all your prunings and all the old cabbage stumps and turn them into compost material or a mulch for the borders.

◆ Continue to rake up all the leaves you can find and put them into a wire netting enclos-ure to rot down. It's not a bad idea to contact the local council to ask if they will allow you to collect leaves from their depot. If you are prepared to supply the bags and to collect, they may well be pleased to let you have them. There are few better soil conditioners than leaf mould which also makes a superb alter-native to peat in potting and sowing com-posts.

◆ If you feel you have made a mistake with the placing of a tree or shrub, now's the time to shift it. If it's a big plant, take as much soil on the root as possible and wrap it in sacking. After planting you may need to stake the plant against wind.

◆ If you have planted young evergreens, especially conifers, in a windy position, erect a temporary windbreak with the special plastic material available in garden centres or with hessian.

◆ Finish the winter pruning of trees, shrubs and fruit trees this month if you can. It's not a good idea to prune in frosty weather.

◆ Protect tender shrubs and herbaceous plants by covering with cloches or, if they die down completely, with a layer of straw covered with a little soil to hold it down. Some plants, like *Gunnera manicata*, resem-bling giant rhubarb, can be protected by cover-ing the crown of the plant with its own leaves.

◆ Tender plants in pots, like bay, should be moved inside early in the month. Tender per-ennials, like salvias and argyranthemums, should be lifted, either potted or boxed up and put in the cold greenhouse to overwinter.

## 🌿 INSIDE 🌿

◆ If you sowed seeds of winter lettuce in cold frames, they should be ready for trans-planting to their final spacings early in the month.

◆ Take advantage of sunny days to do any necessary repairs to the greenhouse and frame. Cracked glass should be replaced or repaired with special tape; it should never be left as it can drip and damage tender foliage.

◆ If you intend to grow figs, vines, peaches or nectarines in the border soil of the green-house, now's the time to plant them.

# AUTUMN PLANTS

**Virginia Creeper**
*Parthenocissus quinquefolia*
A self-clinging climber for
tall walls or fences. The
foliage is attractive all spring
and summer and turns a fiery
red in autumn. 50ft (15m)

**Crab Apple** *Nalus* spp.
Excellent small trees with flowers,
attractive edible fruits and sometimes
good foliage colour too. 20ft (6m)

**Passion Fruit**
*Passiflora edulis*
The most popular and
prolific passion fruit variety. It needs
the protection of a frost-free greenhouse
in winter. 15ft (4.5m)

**Climbing Nasturtium**
*Tropaeolum tuberosum* 'Ken Aslet'
A semi-hardy climber. Keep it going by
storing a few tubers over winter.
6–10ft (2–3.5m)

**Beauty Berry** *Calli-
carpa bodinieri* 'Giraldii'
A hardy shrub with
insignificant flowers but
grown for its brightly
coloured berries in late
summer. 8ft (2.5m)

**Climbing Monkshood**
*Aconitum volubile*
A perennial climber with typical
blue monkshood flowers. Dies down in
winter. 10ft (3.5m)

**Calabrese** *Brassica oleracea italica*
A form of sprouting broccoli
which matures in the summer.
The spears make an attractive
plant. 3ft (90cm)

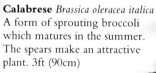

**Pears and** *Cotoneaster frigidus*
Cotoneasters are hardy shrubs or
small trees, bearing white
flowers in spring and red berries.
20ft (6m). Pears are easy in
warmer areas. 10–20ft (3.5–6m)

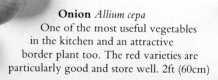

**Onion** *Allium cepa*
One of the most useful vegetables
in the kitchen and an attractive
border plant too. The red varieties are
particularly good and store well. 2ft (60cm)

**Ice Plant** *Sedum spectabile*
A herbaceous perennial for the
front of the border. Its evergreen
leaves and flat heads of flowers
are especially attractive to
butterflies. 1½ft (45cm)

**Orange Peel Clematis**
*Clematis tangutica*
A small-flowered type, rather rampant in growth. The flowers are thick and fleshy. 15ft (4.5m)

**Apple** *Malus sylvestris*
One of the most useful and popular fruits, especially for cooler areas where it is very prolific. 8–20ft (2.5–6m)

**Mountain Ash** *Sorbus* spp.
Excellent small tree with white flowers and berries in a range of colours. Good bird attractor. 20ft (6m)

**Shrubby Veronica** *Hebe* 'Autumn Glory'
A small shrub and one of the hardiest of the hebes. 3ft (90cm)

**Sweet Cicely** *Myrrhis odorata*
An attractive herb, all parts of which are useful in the kitchen and as a medicine. 3ft (90cm)

**Japanese Maple**
*Acer palmatum*
A superb hardy shrub with green foliage, turning red in autumn. 15ft (4.5m)

**Chinese Plumbago**
*Ceratostigma willmottianum*
A moderately hardy shrub for a warm wall or south-facing fence; autumn foliage colour too. 4ft (1.25m)

**Chrysanthemum and**
***Dahlia*** spp.
These two half-hardy perennials are often used for cut flowers for the house and also make attractive border plants. They're available in a wide range of colours. 1–5ft (30–150cm)

**Squashes** *Cucurbita maxima*
Very decorative fruiting vegetables which can be grown in the borders or, in the case of the trailing types, up the pergola or against the arbour. They store until December.

**Celery** *Apium graveolens*
Self-blanching types of celery are ideal for this kind of garden and make attractive border plants too. 2½ft (75cm)

# Chapter 5

# DECORATIVE PLANTS

The title of this chapter is actually a bit misleading! The fact is that *all* the plants in the ornamental kitchen garden are decorative. They wouldn't be there if they weren't. Many of the 'humble' vegetables have superb foliage – carrots, beetroot, fennel, even lettuce look marvellous in a mixed border – while some, like the globe artichoke, have both striking leaves and attractive flowers. Even some roots look good, like those of turnip 'Milan Purple Top' which are like polished rubies in the border on a wet spring morning. And as for the fruit, well you would have to search hard to find a more inspiring sight than an apple tree in full bloom in spring or, for that matter, in the autumn when it's laden with bright fruits.

I could perhaps try to justify my chapter title by claiming that the plants I intend to describe here are *only* decorative, but in some cases that's not quite true. Trees like the crab apples (*Malus* varieties) for example, are highly attractive and their fruit can be used to make jams, jellies and wine. Sunflowers produce a fine crop of seeds that have a hundred and one uses in the kitchen. Even the flowers of some plants, like the English marigolds, can be eaten in salads. Others, like the Poached Egg Plant (*Limnanthes douglasii*), make a wonderful show and also attract hover-flies whose larvae prey on aphids and thus help to keep these pests at bay.

In this chapter you'll find plants that have been selected more for their decorative value than for their productivity. This, in other words, is the aesthetics department!

There's no book in the world, of course, that can accommodate *all* the plants you could grow, so I would suggest that you take my recommendations merely as a starting point. In any case, I continue to discover plants which suit this method of growing, and I'm sure I'll still be coming across them long after this book's out of print! So I make no claims to be comprehensive. I hope my ideas will illustrate the principles of planting this kind of garden and inspire you to try others too.

Quite a lot of the planting is done with 'temporary' plants – hardy annuals, half-hardy annuals and tender perennials. This is because these types of flowering plant not only make an instant, long-lasting and very effective display but can also be used as part of the vegetable rotation. A patch of soil may be used for, say, spring cabbage until June and then replanted with salvias for the summer, while the patch next to it grows pansies all winter and early spring, to be replaced with courgettes in late May. That way you spread the crop rotation system and so lessen the risk of disease, make the best use of the nutrients in the soil and ring the changes so that the garden is a completely different place each season. I can tell you that you never get bored!

## 🦎 TREES 🦎

Choose and plant the trees first. Bear in mind that they will influence all your other planting because of the shade they'll spread and the competition they'll create, but for heaven's sake don't let those factors put you off planting trees altogether. You can always plant them where the shade doesn't matter, and in any case there are plenty of good flowering and foliage plants and lots of vegetables and fruits that will grow quite happily in shade. Obviously you should avoid shading the whole garden, so don't get carried away! Most gardens will want no more than two or three trees and even those should be chosen carefully to avoid giants that will swamp everything else.

When it comes to choice of trees, the criteria for the ornamental kitchen garden are slightly different from those of a traditional garden. If you choose well, your trees can be expected to perform two or three different functions. The best example, I suppose, is the crab apple *Malus* 'Golden Hornet'. It looks superb in flower in spring, and you get another show of colour in the autumn when the bright yellow fruits look exceptionally good. What's more, you can use the fruits to make wine or crab-apple jelly. That keeps you happy, but the tree also pleases the birds which will feed on the fruits when they've exhausted redder berries elsewhere and, if that still isn't enough, in spring it will pollinate most varieties of apple, too. You can't ask for much more than that.

So, the trees should be chosen primarily for their impact on the eye, in terms of colour of foliage, flower, bark and fruit. The next consideration is their usefulness in attracting wildlife by providing perching and nesting sites and food for birds. Then there is their ability to pollinate other trees and perhaps to provide edible fruit as well.

## Recommended trees for small gardens

*Malus*. The crab apples are among the most decorative and useful trees for small gardens. Generally their fruit can be used for wine and jelly, though some are much better flavoured than others. They all provide food for birds, with the yellow-fruited varieties normally being left to last, so choose one of those if you want to enjoy the colour as long as possible. All will grow to approximately 15–25 feet (4.5–7.5 m).

M. 'Aldenhamensis' has purplish leaves that become bronze in autumn. The deep red flowers are followed by reddish purple fruits. A good pollinator for apples.

M. *floribunda*, the Japanese Crab, has crimson flower buds opening to white or pale pink. The fruits are small, red and yellow.

M. 'Golden Hornet' is described above.

M. 'John Downie' has the best fruit for wine and jelly. The spring flowers are white and the large fruits are bright orange and red.

M. 'Profusion' is a very popular variety with a profusion of red flowers and small, blood-red fruits. The leaves are coppery crimson when young.

*Crataegus*. The ornamental thorns are excellent in small gardens. Their rounded heads of twiggy branches are much favoured by birds for nesting sites. The leaves seem to attract numerous ladybirds, the flowers are a good source of nectar for insects, and the fruits are attractive to birds. All species are extremely hardy and put up with industrial pollution and coastal winds. They grow to about 15–20 feet (4.5–6 m).

C. *laevigata* (C. *oxyacantha*) 'Paul's Scarlet' is by far the most popular, producing double flowers of bright scarlet, as the name suggests, followed by masses of bright red berries. 'Aurea' has white flowers and yellow berries while 'Plena' has double white flowers and red berries.

**Cotoneaster.** The cotoneasters are generally seen as shrubs but it is possible to grow them on a longer stem to make an attractive small tree. They have white, often pink-tinged, flowers and generally red berries in autumn which will provide food for birds. Many are evergreen or semi-evergreen, losing their leaves only in severe winters. Height 15–20 feet (4.5–6 m).

*C. frigidus* makes a small, spreading tree which carries huge clusters of crimson fruits in winter.

*C. watereri* is a somewhat variable semi-evergreen with red fruits borne in abundance.

*Malus* 'Golden Hornet' (*see p. 121*).

*Cotoneaster watereri.*

**Ilex.** The hollies are well known and provide food and fine nesting sites for birds, as well as homes for millions of insects. They're tolerant of industrial pollution and salt spray, and are entirely hardy. Usually male and female flowers are borne on separate trees. If you want berries, plant a male and a female plant together. They will grow quite tall and wide but can easily be reduced by pruning or can be clipped to shape.

*I. aquifolium* 'J.C. van Tol' is an excellent self pollinating variety with dark, shining leaves and a regular crop of red berries. The two other popular varieties, 'Silver Queen' and 'Golden King', have silver and gold margined leaves respectively. But remember that the 'King' is a female and the 'Queen' male.

**Sorbus.** This family of trees includes our native Rowan or Mountain Ash (*S. aucuparia*). This and closely related species provide food for birds and will attract insects. Most have white flowers in spring followed by clusters of berries. Some provide distinctive autumn foliage colour too. They grow to about 15–35 feet (4.5–10 m).

*S. aucuparia* 'Sheerwater Seedling' makes a small but vigorous tree with large clusters of orange-red fruits. 'Xanthocarpa' has amber-yellow fruits.

*S. cashmiriana* is a superb species with soft pink flowers in May, followed by drooping clusters of pure white berries.

*S. commixta* has masses of red or orange berries in autumn, set off by richly coloured autumn foliage.

*S. domestica* is our native Service Tree which carries apple or sometimes pear-shaped fruit which is edible, though the flavour is very much an acquired taste!

*S.* 'Joseph Rock' is quite spectacular in autumn, with bright yellow fruits set off by red, copper and purple foliage.

*S. vilmorinii* has marvellous autumn foliage colour, with fruits starting red and gradually turning through pink to white.

**Amelanchier lamarckii** is said to prefer an acid soil though I have seen it growing well in lime. It really is good value in that the young leaves start out coppery red, and serve as a fine background for clouds of delicate white flowers which are a good source of nectar for insects. In autumn the leaves colour richly to red if it's in the sun and yellow if shaded. It grows 15–20 feet (4.5–6 m).

**Betula.** The birches give a woodland effect to the garden and make a very graceful sight with thin, pendulous branches and delicate leaves. They are often grown for their bark colour which varies from silvery white to cinnamon. Height about 25–40 feet (7.5–12 m). They are good insect attractors, providing homes for 200 insect species including many moths. Birds like the cover they provide, and some, such as tits and siskins, feed on their catkins.

*B. utilis* has bark that varies from cinnamon brown to glistening white. Young trees with brownish bark will often become white as they get older.

*B. jaquemontii* is considered by some authorities to be a form of *B. utilis*. What is certain is that it has the whitest bark of them all and is a very striking tree, especially in winter.

**Salix.** Many of the willows are too large for most gardens, but some will not grow enormous and others can be pruned back hard to produce striking bark colours for winter. They support 260 insect species, which in turn attract birds. They have superb catkins to delight you in spring.

*S. caprea* 'Pendula', the Kilmarnock Willow, makes an attractive small weeping tree with white spring catkins opening to bright yellow.

*Sorbus* 'Joseph Rock' *with Rosa rugosa.*

*S. alba* 'Britzensis' (sometimes sold as 'Chermesina'), the Scarlet Willow, produces brilliant scarlet shoots in winter, especially if pruned hard every second year. 'Vitellina', the Golden Willow, sports bright yellow shoots and again needs hard pruning.

*S. daphnoides*, the Violet Wlllow, has violet shoots overlaid with a white bloom. This also needs hard pruning in late March each year or alternate years.

You will have noticed that I have left out fruit trees. Of course there will be plenty of these in the garden, but most will be grown either on the walls, as path edgings or in very specialized shapes, so I have left them for Chapter 8.

### Planting trees

Plant bare-rooted trees during the dormant season from November to March, but preferably before Christmas while the soil is still warm and relatively dry. Container-grown trees can go in at any time.

Prepare the soil really well beforehand, digging the whole border and working in organic matter. Never plant in a hole dug in otherwise uncultivated soil or you'll simply make a sump for the surrounding water and the tree's roots will rot.

Make a hole big enough to take the full spread of the roots or just a bit bigger than the container. With bare-rooted trees the stake can be driven in upright before planting. With container-grown trees put the stake in at an angle to avoid damaging the roots.

## PLANTING TREES

**1** *Always start by watering container-grown trees really well. This will minimize root damage and give them a good start.*

**2** *Dig a hole about twice the size of the pot and cover the excavated soil with garden compost and a handful of blood, fish and bone meal.*

**3** *Plants must always be planted at the level they grew in the pot. Check the depth of the hole with your spade against the plant.*

**4** *Refill the hole with the soil mixture, making sure that it is replaced evenly without spaces round the root-ball.*

**5** *The soil should be firmed in as refilling progresses. It needs to be firm but not solid, so go easy, especially if it's wet.*

**6** *Support the stem with a short stake no longer than a third of the height of the stem. Fix with a proper plastic tree tie.*

Whichever way you drive the stake in, it must be no more than a third of the height of the tree. This then enables the top of the tree to move in the wind, a process which encourages the stem to thicken and the roots to grow stronger. The tree will then be self-supporting when the stake is removed.

Add a little blood, fish and bone meal to the soil around the tree and refill the hole. Make sure, with bare-rooted trees, that you leave no air pockets around the roots. Firm the soil gently with your boot as you refill.

Finally tie the tree to the stake with a proper plastic tree tie which should be fixed to the post with a small nail to prevent it slipping. If your tree is container grown, you *must* make sure you water it afterwards, especially if you plant in spring or summer. Come back at least once a week to check that it's not dry.

After planting, mulch around the tree with well-rotted manure or compost.

### Aftercare

All trees need feeding, but in the ornamental kitchen garden there should be enough nutrients for them left over by the constantly replanted flowers and vegetables. If they're planted in the lawn though, you should feed annually in February with bonemeal.

Some initial pruning may be necessary, cutting the main branches back to a bud to remove about a third and thinning out overcrowded or weak branches. After that, no pruning should be necessary apart from removing dead, diseased or overcrowded wood each year when the tree is dormant.

Water is no doubt the most important factor in aftercare, especially in the first year. Always check new trees on a weekly basis. If they're dry, really flood the soil around them.

## ✿ OUT-OF-REACH PLANTS ✿

Out-of-reach plants are not the ones you can't afford, though I suppose there are bound to be a few of those too! As I've already suggested, the most productive way to manage the borders in the ornamental kitchen garden is to avoid treading on them. If all the borders are straight and only 4 feet (120 cm) or so wide, that's easy because you'll be able to reach to the middle from the side paths. If the garden has been designed informally, however, there are bound to be areas you can't reach. It's there that the taller, permanent shrubs and hardy perennials should go because they'll need attention only once or twice a year. You'll need to feed and mulch them each spring and you may have to prune them from time to time, but that should be all.

When you're choosing permanent plants for this particular style of garden, there is one important limitation that must be borne in mind. If you want to grow vegetables and flowers together – which is, after all, the point of the garden – you'll have to avoid acid-lovers, even if your soil is acid. This is because the vegetables, in the main, prefer a limy soil and will not do well in acid conditions. I shall, in fact, be recommending regular liming in order to maintain fertility. That would not do the acid lovers any good at all.

If you want to grow rhododendrons, pieris, summer-flowering heathers and that kind of plant, you'll either have to confine them to pots or, if you have an acid soil, grow them separately in another part of the garden away from the vegetables.

Once again, there are thousands of suitable plants for this position so I shall have to restrict my list to those I have found especially good in my own garden. Unless you have plenty of space, it's a good idea to choose upright growers which will not spread too far towards the front of the border.

## Shrubs for sunny positions

**Berberis.** There are several suitable barberries for this situation. The main thing to remember is to avoid the really vigorous ones that would take over.

*Berberis thunbergii* 'Aurea'.

*B. thunbergii* 'Atropurpurea' grows to about 6 feet (180 cm) and has shining red foliage that turns brilliant orange in autumn. A smaller version is *B.t.* 'Atropurpurea Nana', which grows to only about 2 feet (60 cm) like the yellow-leaved *B.t.* 'Aurea'. I'm especially fond of the variety 'Red Chief' which is upright in growth with arching branches covered with red foliage. All of these varieties have yellow flowers in spring, followed by red fruits.

*B. linearifolia* 'Orange King' is another good barberry because of its upright growth. It has glossy evergreen foliage, brilliant orange flowers in April and grows to about 6 feet (180 cm).

**Caryopteris clandonensis,** the 'Blue Spiraea', grows to about 3 feet (90 cm), forming a mound of grey foliage. It carries blue flowers in September and October.

**Choisya ternata,** the Mexican Orange Blossom, spreads too far for this garden, but the new introduction 'Sundance' is ideal. It forms a bush no more than 3 feet (90 cm) high and wide, and its foliage is brilliant gold.

**Cornus.** There are several dogwoods that will suit the position, but bear in mind that some of them spread and could cover too wide an area. After a while they'll need to be dug up and shifted, but it's very easy to create new plants from hardwood cuttings (see p. 151).

*C. alba* 'Westonbirt' is the best for red stems, but 'Spaethii' has the bonus of golden variegated leaves in summer.

*C. stolonifera* 'Flaviramea' produces bright yellow stems, so it looks good in winter planted with the above varieties.

All grow to about 6 feet (180 cm).

**Cytisus.** The brooms are many and varied and generally excellent for sun. They are relatively short-lived, but trimming them back lightly after flowering will prolong their lives.

*C. praecox*, the Warminster Broom, is the best of the smaller kinds. Look for 'Allgold', 'Alba' and 'Gold Spear', which will all grow to about 4 feet (120 cm).

**Deutzia** varieties are useful, though you should stick to the smaller growing ones like *D.* 'Mont Rose', which carries large, deep pink flowers in June. It grows to about 6 feet (180 cm). *D. elegantissima* 'Rosealind' is also an erect grower of about the same size with arching branches covered in pink blossom in May and June.

*Potentilla fruticosa (see p. 128).*

**Helichrysum lanatum** makes a rounded bush about 2 feet (60 cm) high, with pretty, silver-grey foliage, a bit like lavender. It has the bonus of yellow flowers in July.

**Hibiscus syriacus** is known as the Tree Hollyhock and makes a compact bush about 6 feet (180 cm) tall with flowers like a hollyhock in late summer. There are several colours to choose from, including blue, pink and white.

**Hypericum.** Nearly all are good for this situation. Avoid like the plague the dreaded *H. calycinum*, the Rose of Sharon, which sounds wonderful but will fill your garden with an inexhaustible supply of rampageous suckers.

*H. indorum* 'Elstead' is one of the best. It makes a 3 foot (90 cm) tall shrub with yellow flowers for a long period in summer, followed by bright red fruits. It is sometimes a little prone to rust disease.

*H.* 'Hidcote' is one of the most popular, and for good reason. It reaches about 4 feet (120 cm) and is covered with large, saucer-shaped yellow flowers all summer. It seems to be immune to rust.

**Ilex.** The hollies are superb for all-year-round colour and will grow almost anywhere. Choose one of the smaller varieties like *I. meserveae* 'Blue Angel' or *I. m.* 'Blue Princess', both of which have bluish stems and foliage and brilliant red berries. They'll grow to about 5 feet (150 cm). These two are both female, so if you want two bushes it might be sensible to choose *I. m.* 'Blue Prince' which is male, and could act as a pollinator for either of the other two.

**Ligustrum ovalifolium** 'Aureum' is better known as Golden Privet and is much looked down on. Nevertheless, it makes a superb small shrub which can be clipped to any size. It is evergreen except in the hardest winters.

**Lonicera nitida 'Baggesen's Gold'** is often used for hedging but is superb as a yellow foliage shrub. It can be clipped to size.

**Olearia haastii** is the most popular of the genus, making a rounded bush about 4 feet (120 cm) high with white, fragrant flowers in July and August. But, if you have a sheltered spot, much better is *O. scilloniensis* which is about the same size but with attractive grey foliage that literally disappears under a mass of white blossom over a long period in early summer.

**Paeonia suffruticosa,** the Tree Peony, is worth growing for its superb foliage alone, giving a touch of the exotic to the garden. New American and Japanese varieties have introduced some really wonderful flower colours, and most have exotic blotches and markings on the petals. You can choose from a wide range, including white with a yellow centre, bright scarlet and lustrous pink. They grow to about 6 feet (180 cm).

*Rosa* 'Graham Thomas' (*see p. 128*).

**Philadelphus.** The Mock Oranges grow, in the main, too large for our purposes. There are two exceptions. The variety 'Manteau d'Hermine' is well worthwhile, making a small shrub up to about 3 feet (90 cm), covered with sweetly scented white flowers in June/July. The foliage variety *P. coronarius* 'Aureus' has brilliant yellow leaves that will brighten up any garden. It grows to about 6 feet (120 cm) but can happily be pruned back to size.

**Phlomis fruticosa,** the Jerusalem Sage, grows to about $2\frac{1}{2}$ feet (75 cm) and has grey-green leaves resembling sage. In June and July it produces clusters of bright yellow flowers.

**Potentilla fruticosa,** its varieties and several hybrids from it are invaluable for their long flowering period. There are several to choose from, ranging from the brick-red 'Red Ace' to the primrose-yellow 'Katherine Dykes' and the white 'Abbotswood'. They'll grow to about 2 feet (60 cm).

**Roses** are excellent subjects for the centre of the borders and I have made good use of bush varieties. Many of the species or 'shrub' roses are too tall and spreading, but the 'English' roses are ideal. They are the result of back-crossing old-fashioned varieties with modern ones to produce flowers that have the old cottage garden appearance coupled with a repeat-flowering habit. They are available in a whole range of colours and flower shapes. My favourites are 'Graham Thomas', a superb deep yellow, and the blush-pink 'Sharifa Asma'. Both have a strong fragrance.

**Spiraea** is another large group with some invaluable plants for our purposes.

S. arguta, the spring-flowering Bridal Wreath Plant, grows to about 6 feet (180 cm) and is covered with foams of white flowers in April and May.

S. bumalda is summer-flowering. The variety 'Anthony Waterer' is valuable for its large, flat clusters of carmine flowers from July to September. 'Goldflame' has bright golden foliage splashed red in spring and crimson flowers in July. Both these varieties will grow to about $2\frac{1}{2}$ feet (75 cm) and can be pruned hard to restrict height.

**Syringa.** The lilacs are deservedly popular but generally too large for this position. There's one exception, though, that merits a place. *S. velutina*, the Korean Lilac, makes a bush only about 5 feet (150 cm) tall, and it can be pruned back to keep it to size. It bears numerous scented, lilac-pink flowers in June and July.

**Viburnum** species are very numerous and varied. The variety *V. bodnantense* 'Dawn' is well worth growing if you have the space because it produces its round clusters of powerfully scented pink flowers over a long period in winter and early spring. It grows to about 7 feet (210 cm). Of the spring-flowering varieties small enough for the centre of the border, my favourite is *V. juddii*. It has very sweetly scented pink flowers in April and May and grows to only about 5 feet (150 cm).

## Shrubs for shade

**Arundinaria** or bamboo species are generally too big and spreading for this position, but there are a few exceptions. I would certainly look at *A. viridistriata* (syn. *Pleioblastus viridistriata*) which forms small clumps of purplish canes up to 6 feet (180 cm) high with foliage of dark green, broadly striped rich yellow.

**Aucuba japonica 'Crotonifolia'** is the best of the Spotted Laurels. It's a well-known evergreen shrub growing to about 5 feet (150 cm) with leaves boldly splashed with gold.

**Berberis thunbergii** varieties will also do well in shade and these are described on p. 126.

**Cornus** varieties, described on p. 126, will also do well in shade.

**Cotoneaster.** Good shade plants, but generally either ground coverers or too big and spreading for this position. There is one exception,

*Mahonia media* 'Winter Sun'.

*C. hybridus* 'Pendulus', which is usually grown as a small weeping standard tree. In autumn it is covered with bright red berries which are eventually taken by birds, generally in January or February. In most winters it will retain its shiny green leaves.

*Elaeagnus pungens* '**Maculata**' forms a rounded bush about 5 feet (150 cm) high. Its bright green and gold evergreen leaves will light up the darkest corner, even in winter.

*Fatsia japonica* is usually grown as a house plant, when it's called the Castor Oil Plant, but it is in fact quite hardy if grown out of the wind. The glossy green, palmlike, evergreen leaves add a touch of the exotic to the garden. It grows to about 5 feet (150 cm).

*Hydrangea* species are superb in light shade and you should not restrict yourself to the well-known mop-head Hortensias, *H. macrophylla*. These are excellent shrubs, of course, growing to about 5 feet (150 cm) and producing large heads of pink, red or white flowers (not blue, which requires acid soil), from July to September. The Lacecaps have flattened flower-heads, with the central disc of flowers surrounded by a ring of florets of different colours. Also suitable for this position are the varieties of *H. serrata*, which grow to about the same height. *H. s.* 'Grayswood' is superb, with a blue or pink centre surrounded by florets of white at first, changing to deep red.

*Hypericum.* All will also grow in shade and are described on p. 127.

*Ilex.* The hollies will grow in shade as well, and they are described on p. 127.

*Mahonia* species have attractive evergreen foliage and sprays of sweetly scented yellow flowers in winter or spring. Among the best are *M.* 'Charity' which flowers in winter and grows to about 6 feet (180 cm) and 'Buckland' which has the same yellow flowers but longer, stiffer leaves.

*Photinia fraseri* '**Red Robin**' is an outstanding introduction from New Zealand. An evergreen, it grows to about 6 feet (180 cm) and its most striking feature is the brilliant red young foliage. To keep it to size, prune it back after the young foliage has turned green. New red growths will then appear.

*Skimmia.* Evergreen, though grown mainly for the flowers. One of the best is *S. japonica* 'Rubella', which carries striking red buds right through winter. They open to form sweetly scented white flowers with yellow anthers. Height 3–5 feet (90–150 cm).

*Viburnum davidii* is a handsome evergreen reaching about $2\frac{1}{2}$ feet (75 cm). Its long, shiny leaves set off white flowers in May. These are followed by bright blue berries if several plants are grown together to ensure cross-pollination.

*Skimmia japonica* 'Kew Green'.

## Hardy perennials for sunny positions

Herbaceous perennials are very accommodating plants and convenient for this kind of garden. Whereas shrubs really do need to get their roots down and remain where they are for life, most hardy perennials actually thrive on being moved every few years. So they can be planted in the borders wherever you think they'll be best and, if you find you've made a mistake, or you require more room for vegetables and fruit than you at first thought, just dig them up and shift them. That thought makes life a lot more relaxing straight away.

Most perennials die down in winter, so there's nothing to see until spring. I don't think that's a great disadvantage, however. In winter your thoughts are generally turned to other things and, since there's much less to do outside, you tend to give the garden less attention. And somehow the thrill of seeing the first fresh green leaves of spring and the

*Campanula persicifolia.*

gradual unfolding of the new year's garden makes the dull winter well worth while. Still, you won't want a completely bare garden in winter, so the mixture with shrubs and trees is certainly the best way.

**Achillea.** The Yarrows are easy-to-grow, attractive plants with feathery foliage and flattened flower heads. Undoubtedly the best is *A.* 'Moonshine' which has silvery leaves and bright yellow heads of flower over a long period in summer. Some of the new German hybrids are also worth hunting out. They grow to about 2 feet (60 cm).

**Agapanthus.** The African Lilies form attractive clumps of grassy foliage topped in late summer by large heads of pendulous blue flowers. They need a sheltered spot and are not all reliably hardy. The best are the deep blue *A.* 'Bressingham Blue' and the clear white *A.* 'Bressingham White'. Height about 2–3 feet (60–90 cm).

**Allium.** The Onions include some superb plants for the middle of the border though some are better suited to a position nearer the front. *A. aflatunense* makes a magnificent plant 3–4 feet (90–120 cm) tall. It flowers in late spring, producing large spherical heads of tiny deep lilac flowers. The leaves die away soon after flowering. *A. giganteum* is much the same but flowers late in the summer. It can grow even taller at 4–5 feet (120–150 cm). *A. bulgaricum* will reach 3 feet (90 cm) and bears heads of much larger, bell-shaped, pendulous flowers of green with a purple tinge. The seed-heads are also very attractive.

**Anchusa azurea.** A well loved old garden plant with flowers of deep blue, held on drooping spikes like giant forget-me-nots. One of the best is 'Loddon Royalist' which is certainly the richest shade of blue. It grows to about 3 feet (90 cm), and flowering is from June to August.

**Asphodeline lutea.** The Asphodel forms clumps of stiff, grassy foliage and bears 3 foot (90 cm) tall spikes of fragrant, bright yellow flowers. The seed-heads are also very attractive.

**Aster.** The Michaelmas Daisies are well-known and valuable late-flowering plants. They have the disadvantage that many are subject to attack by mildew and the worst offenders are best avoided. The varieties of *A. novae-angliae* are more disease resistant than the *A. novi-belgii* types which are what are normally described as Michaelmas Daisies. Height is 2–5 feet (60–150 cm), depending on variety, and they are available in many shades. Look out also for the old hybrid *A. frikartii* 'Monch' which produces lavender-blue daisy flowers from July to October.

**Astrantia major.** The Masterworts bear interestingly shaped flowers of greenish white, pink or plum red. They grow to about 2 feet (60 cm). The variety *A. m.* 'Sunningdale Variegated' has attractive green foliage splashed with yellow. Look out also for *A. maxima* which has light pink flowers with a 'collar' of pure rose pink.

**Campanula.** There are three of the Bellflowers that I certainly wouldn't want to be without. *C. lactiflora* will grow to 4–5 feet (120–150 cm) with its stout stems covered in large heads of lilac flowers. *C. latifolia* will grow to 4 feet (120 cm), the spikes carrying violet or white tubular flowers. It's a prolific seeder, so make sure you remove the seed-heads after flowering. *C. persicifolia* grows to about 3 feet (90 cm) and again carries bell-shaped flowers of lilac or white.

**Centaurea dealbata.** The perennial Cornflowers, are easy to grow and bloom for a long period in summer. The variety 'Steenbergii' carries deep pink flowers on $2\frac{1}{2}$ foot (75 cm) stems above the jagged silvery foliage.

**Chrysanthemum.** There are several hardy types that are worth growing for flowers in the autumn. Named varieties like the double crimson 'Anastasia' and the orange 'Peterkin' are worth looking out for. *C. rubellum* is very free flowering and available in a range of colours, according to variety. They all grow to about 2–3 feet (60–90 cm) and carry daisy-like flowers.

**Coreopsis verticillata** is easily grown and makes an upright bush about 2 feet (60 cm) tall. It has finely divided leaves and is covered in rich yellow daisies for a very long period in summer through to autumn.

**Crocosmia.** There are several new introductions of this striking perennial that are worth a place. The leaves are upright and strap-shaped and the flower stems arch over at the top where they produce eye-catching blooms in various shades of red, yellow and orange.

*Helenium autumnale* 'Moerheim Beauty' (*see* p. 132).

**Delphinium.** A 'must' for the ornamental kitchen garden. Tall spikes of flowers in shades of blue or white rise up on noble spikes 4 feet (120 cm) high. There are also pink varieties which are not so impressive.

**Echinacea purpurea** was once called *Rudbeckia* and resembles that plant. It bears numerous purple daisies with a strong central boss. There is also a good white form, 'White Lustre'.

**Echinops ritro.** The Globe Thistle has grey, jagged foliage and bears 4 foot (120 cm) spikes of steely blue, spherical flower-heads. A useful and easy-to-grow plant.

**Eryngium.** The Sea Hollies are blue-flowered, with jagged foliage. They are excellent for drying. *E. oliverianum* is one of the best of the hybrids, growing to 2 feet (60 cm) tall with spiny flowers.

**Euphorbia.** The Spurges are accommodating plants which will grow in full sun or shade. *E. characias* 'Margery Fish' is a superb ever-green with handsome winter foliage and striking spikes of sulphur-yellow flowers. It grows to about $3\frac{1}{2}$ feet (105 cm).

**Helenium autumnale** has given rise to several excellent hybrids suitable for the middle of the border. 'Butterpat' has pure yellow daisy flowers with a brown centre, while 'Moerheim Beauty' has rich bronze flowers. They are invaluable as they flower from August to October. Height 4–5 feet (120–150 cm).

**Helictotrichon sempervirens** is a fine grass. Non-invasive, it forms clumps of narrow, erect, blue-grey leaves topped by waving flower stems of grey. Height about 3–4 feet (90–120 cm).

**Hemerocallis.** The Day Lilies are extremely easy to grow. The leaves are long and strap-shaped and the sometimes perfumed flowers are lily-shaped. Because they come in such a wide range of colours, the best bet is to consult a catalogue. Height about 2–3 feet (60–90 cm).

**Lilium.** Most hybrid Lilies do well in sun. They produce striking, trumpet-shaped flowers in many colours, depending on variety. *L. regale* has a powerful scent and is easy to grow. Height about 3–5 feet (60–180 cm).

**Lupinus.** The Lupins are too well known to need description, but they are invaluable plants for this kind of garden. Easy to grow, they produce attractive divided foliage which catches and holds drops of rain or dew. The stately spikes of flowers come in different single colours and combinations, depending on variety. Lupins are easily raised from seed but do not come true to type and colour.

**Lychnis.** The Maltese Cross, *L. chalcedonica*, is an ancient garden plant and well worth growing. The flat heads of blossom are a really eye-catching red and borne on stems about 3 feet (90 cm) tall. *L. coronaria*, the Dusty Miller, forms clumps of grey, felted leaves with flowers of red, pink or white. Both bloom from mid to late summer.

**Monarda didyma** is better known as Berga-mot. Hooded flowers, slightly resembling sage, are borne on 3 foot (90 cm) stems. There are several good hybrids in colours ranging from white, through red to deep purple. Flowering time is June to September .

**Paeonia.** The Peonies produce exotic-looking flowers like silky cabbage roses in a range of colours from deep red through pink to white, according to variety. Flowering time is usually late spring or early summer. The foliage is highly attractive and would guarantee the plants a place even without flowers. Height 2–3 feet (60–90 cm). Peonies don't relish being moved.

**Penstemon.** Marvellous plants which seem to go on and on for most of the summer. They produce pendulous, bell-shaped flowers in abundance, ranging in colour from deep purple, through red and pink to white. Height 1–3 feet (30–90 cm).

**Phlox.** Another easily grown old cottage garden flower that is a 'must' for this garden. Most garden centres would offer *P. paniculata*, which is available in many different cultivars of a variety of colours, including pink, orange, red and white, often with an attractive central 'eye'. They can be subject to eelworm, so make sure you buy plants that have been grown from root cuttings from a reputable nursery. Look out too for *P. maculata*, which has slightly smaller flowers in softer colours but is ideal for this type of border. Both types will grow to about 3 feet (90 cm) and be in flower from July to September.

**Phygelius.** This plant somewhat resembles a hardy fuchsia. The flowers are long and tubular, and borne in summer in great abundance. One of the best is *P.* 'African Queen', which carries numerous long narrow trumpets of pink with a yellow throat. It grows to about 2½ feet (75 cm).

**Rheum.** Of course you'll be growing rhubarb in the borders for eating, but there are a few ornamental species which match them for effect. *R.* 'Ace of Hearts' grows to no more than about 2 feet (60 cm) and has narrow, pointed red leaves which are topped at flowering time by 4 foot (120 cm) spikes of pink flowers.

**Rudbeckia.** If, like me, you love daisies, don't miss Black-Eyed Susan (*R. hirta*) and her relatives. *R. fulgida* 'Deamii' produces a long-lasting display of bright yellow petals with a black centre. The variety *R. f.* 'Goldsturm' is especially good. It grows to about 2 feet (60 cm).

**Scabiosa caucasica.** The flower of this well-known cottage garden plant looks like a pincushion surrounded by a ring of petals. There are a few good varieties, including the favourite *S.* 'Clive Greaves' which has lovely lavender-blue flowers, the darker *S.* 'Moerheim Blue' and *S.* 'Loddon White'. They grow to about 2 feet (60 cm).

**Thalictrum aquilegifolium.** The Meadow Rue forms clumps of dainty, light green foliage like a Columbine. The flowers are fluffy, in shades of purple and lilac, and borne on 3 foot (90 cm) stems.

**Verbascum.** Several of the Mulleins are biennial but there are also some good perennials. *V. chaixii* produces spikes of small yellow flowers with a purple eye on stems 3 foot (90 cm) high. There is also a white one, *V. c.* 'Album'. The Purple Mullein, *V. phoeniceum*, has produced many good hybrids in various tints but is not truly perennial (it is worth growing if you propagate it by root cuttings regularly).

## Perennials for shade

**Aconitum.** The Monkshoods are so called because the flowers very much resemble a monk's cowl. They are easy to grow and produce 4–5 foot (120–150 cm) spikes of various shades of blue, pink or white flowers. They do best if lifted and thinned out each spring. *A. napellus* is the most commonly grown and has given rise to many hybrids. Look out also for *A. septentrionale* 'Ivorine', a plant growing to about 3 feet (90 cm) and producing spires of ivory-white flowers.

**Anemone hybrida.** Often sold as *A. japonica*, the Japanese Anemones flower for a very long period in late summer and autumn. They produce lovely single or semi-double flowers in shades of pink or white. One of the best is the old variety 'Honorine Jobert' which has pure white flowers with a gold centre. They grow to about 5 feet (150 cm).

**Aquilegia.** The Columbines are marvellous old cottage garden plants which enhance the border in May and June. The foliage is delicately divided and fresh green, while the flowers are attractively bell-shaped with spurs sweeping back behind. They are available in a wide colour range with some bicolours too. Height 2–3 feet (60–90 cm).

*Attractive grouping of perennials.*

**Astilbe.** These lovely plants form clumps of attractive foliage from which arise feathery plumes of flowers in various colours from deep red, through pink to white. They vary in height from 2–4 feet (60–120 cm). There are also some dwarf varieties which are not, of course, suitable for the middle of the border.

**Brunnera macrophylla.** In April and May, this superb plant is a mass of vivid blue forget-me-not type flowers. When they have faded, the heart-shaped leaves assume a larger and more impressive size. (There is also a variegated variety which is worth seeking out.) Height about 2 feet (60 cm).

**Cimicifuga.** The Bugbanes are graceful plants with attractive fern-like foliage. The bottle-brush white or cream flowers are borne on wiry stems which require no staking though they often grow to 5 feet (150 cm).

**Dicentra.** *D. spectabilis*, Dutchman's Breeches, Bleeding Heart or Lady-in-the-Bath is another marvellous cottage garden plant

that you shouldn't be without. It flowers quite early in the spring, producing intricately shaped flowers of red and white or pure white. There are also some excellent hybrids like 'Bacchanal' which has masses of deep crimson flowers, and 'Luxuriant', a very long-flowering variety with red flowers.

*D. eximia* 'Adrian Bloom' has greyish leaves and masses of red flowers. It will also stand a little more sunshine than most.

**Digitalis.** The common Foxgloves are biennials, but there are a few perennials which are well worth growing. Most grow to about 2 feet (60 cm) and produce spikes of typical foxglove flowers but in a range of colours. *D. grandiflora*, for example, is creamy yellow, while *D. lanata* bears beautifully marked yellow, purple and grey flowers. *D. mertonensis* is a reddish colour, marked with copper. They're not long lived but easily raised from seed.

**Geranium.** I have included the Cranesbills because some are so good in dry shade – the most difficult situation. However, you will certainly have to lift, divide and throw away, most years! Some types spread quite rapidly. One of the best in shade is *G. phaeum*, the so-

*Astilbe × arendsi* 'Koblenz'.

called Mourning Widow. It grows to about 2 feet (60 cm) and the nodding flowers are dark maroon.

**Helleborus corsicus.** Most of the lovely Hellebores are better suited to nearer the front of the border, but this species will reach 2 feet (60 cm). It forms a bushy plant with attractive, divided, spiny, dark green foliage. The green, cup-shaped flowers are produced very early in the year.

**Hosta.** Many of the Hostas are better suited to nearer the front, but there are a few tall-growing varieties. They are grown mainly for their attractive foliage but their tall spikes of mauve or lavender flowers are an added bonus. There are several good American introductions, like 'Big Daddy', which has intense blue leaves, and 'Royal Standard', with green leaves and white flowers. The striking *H. sieboldiana* has magnificent blue–grey leaves of great size.

**Polygonatum.** Solomon's Seal is a well-known cottage garden plant and ideal in this type of border. The most commonly grown is *P. hybridum* which is sometimes sold as *P. multiflorum*. It produces 3 foot (90 cm) tall, arching stems from which hang dangling, bell-like white flowers. Much better in my view is *P. canaliculatum* which, as if just to confuse you, is sometimes sold as *P. giganteum* and sometimes as *P. commutatum*. Whatever they call it, it grows to about 5 feet (150 cm) and makes a superb display in late spring.

**Rheum.** The Giant Rhubarbs will do well in sun or shade and are described on p. 133.

**Rodgersia.** These are handsome plants with bold foliage like enormous hands, some of them bronze tinted, especially when young. The flower-heads are fluffy and rather like *Astilbe*, only cream or pink. One of the best is *R. pinnata* 'Superba' which has shiny bronze leaves and flower-heads of bright pink borne on 3 foot (90 cm) stems.

## 🪲 FRONT-OF-BORDER PLANTS 🪲

The front 2 feet (60 cm) of the borders are kept, in the main, for vegetables, annuals and tender perennials. This is where most of the work is done because that's about as far as you'll be able to reach comfortably. But obviously you won't want to simply leave a uniform 2 foot (60 cm) strip along the paths. That would look awful most of the time.

In order to make an attractive cottage garden border with enough room for your temporary flowers and vegetables, while still maintaining a structure and an interest in the front, you need to plant judiciously. The permanent shrubs and perennials are arranged to leave 'bays' of bare soil between them, and it's here that you plant your temporary plants.

Naturally these front-of-border plants need to be on the short side so that they neither hide the out-of-reach plants at the back nor shade the annuals and vegetables in the front. They also need to be relatively well behaved. Invasive plants like, say, the ornamental Dead-nettle (*Lamium maculatum*) or, worse still, Rose of Sharon (*Hypericum calycinum*) are to be avoided at all costs. They would soon take over the border and your vegetables would disappear under the onslaught.

Again, please bear in mind that my list consists of plants that I have grown in my own garden. There are hundreds more.

*Front-of-border plants need to be short.*

## Shrubs for sunny positions

*Berberis thunbergii.* The variety B. t. 'Atropurpurea Nana' forms a rounded bush slowly reaching 2 feet (60 cm). The bronze foliage becomes vivid red in autumn. A smaller variety, 'Baggatelle', will reach only half that size. Even more striking is the yellow version, 'Aurea', though it's important to site this one out of cold winds.

*Cytisus kewensis* is a superb prostrate broom, growing no more than 1 foot (30 cm) high. It will need clipping back to restrict its growth but that will encourage production of its creamy yellow flowers which appear in May.

*Euonymus fortunei* is a prostrate evergreen that is often grown in groups for ground cover, but it also makes a good, bright shrub when grown singly. It benefits from trimming back annually and so is easily kept in check. The varieties 'Emerald Gaiety' with white and green variegated leaves, 'Emerald 'n Gold' with green, yellow and pink-tinged leaves and 'Sunspot', green with a central splash of gold, are all to be recommended. They grow to about 1 foot (30 cm).

*Fuchsia.* The hardy fuchsias are very prolific flowerers from midsummer to autumn. They are available in a range of colours and combinations, depending on variety. F. 'Tom Thumb' has flowers of violet and carmine, while F. 'Riccartonii' is scarlet and purple and F. *magellanica* 'Aurea' has red flowers and striking yellow leaves. They grow to about 1–2 feet (30–60 cm).

*Genista pilosa.* The dwarf varieties of this shrub form spreading mats no more than 1 foot (30 cm) high, covered in yellow flowers in spring. The best varieties are 'Lemon Spreader' and 'Vancouver Gold'.

*Hebe.* The shrubby veronicas are not all hardy, so choose with care and, as an insurance, take cuttings in summer to house in the green-

house. *H. pinguifolia* 'Pagei' forms 1 foot (30 cm) high hummocks of attractive grey foliage and is covered in white flowers in summer. *H. pimeleoides* 'Quicksilver' is more spreading with silvery leaves and white flowers in summer, while *H.* 'Carl Teschner' forms low, dark green hummocks covered with violet flowers with a blue throat.

*Hypericum.* There are several dwarf hypericums used on rock gardens, but I have found the 9 inch (23 cm) *H. olympicum* with its large yellow flowers and its variety 'Citrinum' with lemon-coloured flowers most effective in this position. They flower for a long period in summer.

*Lavandula.* Lavenders are well-known cottage garden plants and superb in this garden since they provide grey foliage, blue, purple or white flowers, wonderful perfume and a terrific attraction to bees and butterflies. Who could ask for more? Use a low-growing variety of Old English Lavender (*L. spica*), like 'Hidcote', which can grow up to 24 inches (60 cm) but can be clipped to size if necessary. Indeed, all lavenders should be clipped back after flowering to keep them bushy. If your soil is well drained, look out also for French Lavender (*L. stoechas*), which has peculiarly shaped flowers of two shades of purple.

*Roses.* Miniature roses are excellent in the front of the border and are available in a wealth of colours, heights and habits. They are covered in tiny but perfectly formed flowers all summer long and are pruned just like ordinary bush roses.

*Santolina chamaecyparissus,* or Cotton Lavender, makes a fine silver foil of filigree foliage which sets off the leaves of something like beetroot or ruby chard very well indeed. It produces masses of yellow buttons in summer but this tends to spoil the foliage so it's best to prune back hard in spring to promote new growth. It grows to about 2 feet (60 cm).

*Senecio greyi.* A popular grey-leaved shrub which grows to about 2 feet (60 cm) and bears bright yellow flowers in summer.

*Spiraea japonica.* There are dwarf varieties of this Spiraea suitable for the front of the border. 'Alpina' forms a compact mound and bears deep pink flowers in summer. It grows to about 18–24 inches (45–60 cm). 'Little Princess' has deep pink to crimson flowers while 'Shirobana' produces red and white flowers on the same plant. Flowering is from about mid to late summer.

## Shrubs for shade

There are very few shrubs suitable for the front of the borders in shaded conditions (fortunately, there are several herbaceous perennials).

*Berberis.* The varieties listed above will also thrive in shade.

*Euonymus.* Again, those described previously are suitable.

*Sarcococca humilis* is a low-growing evergreen reaching about 18 inches (45 cm), with white, perfumed flowers in early spring. But it spreads to form quite extensive clumps, so you'll have to restrict it regularly.

*Viburnum davidii* is a bushy evergreen that grows slowly to about $2\frac{1}{2}$ feet (75 cm). It's worth having for its large leathery leaves alone, but it also carries clusters of white flowers in June.

## Perennials for sunny positions

*Anaphalis triplinervis.* A fine, grey-leaved plant which forms spreading mats which may have to be restricted from time to time. Just cut round with a spade and dig out roots that spread too far. They reach no more than about 1 foot (30 cm) and are covered in pearly white, everlasting daisies in late summer.

*Anthemis.* There are two forms of chamomile which I wouldn't be without. *A. cupaniana* forms low mounds, about 15 inches (38 cm) high, of finely divided silver-grey foliage which is covered in white daisies in May and June. *A. tinctoria* is available in several varieties, the best of which in my view is 'E.C. Buxton' which forms an 18 inch (45 cm) mound of ferny green foliage topped by creamy yellow daisies all summer. A marvellous plant.

*Armeria.* The thrifts vary in size and colour and several will suit this situation. I would grow *A. maritima* 'Dusseldorf Pride' which forms neat hummocks of grassy foliage about 6 inches (15 cm) high with light red flowers from about May to July. I can also specially recommend a white-flowered variety, *A.m.* 'Alba'.

*Astilbe.* There are a few shorter-growing varieties of this attractive plant which will grow in sun or part shade provided the soil is water-retentive. *A. chinensis* 'Pumila' grows to about 1 foot (30 cm) and forms spreading mats of attractively cut foliage with slender spikes of pinkish-purple flowers. *A. simplicifolia* 'Sprite', of similar height, has pink flowers followed by attractive seed-heads. The flowering period for Astilbes is from about July and lasts many weeks.

*Bergenia.* The Elephants' Ears are well named, having large evergreen leaves many of which will turn vivid red or bronze in winter. Most will grow to about 1 foot (30 cm). Bold flower spikes are produced in spring, usually rosy-red, pink or white. (These plants will also do well in shade though they flower slightly more shyly.)

*Carex.* There are two sedges that are well worth growing in the front of the border. *C. petrei* makes clumps of fine, grassy leaves of pinkish brown while *C. morrowii* 'Evergold' has bright golden leaves with a narrow green margin. Each grows to about 1 foot (30 cm).

*Lavender (see p. 136).*

**Dianthus.** An absolute 'must' for any cottage garden. Most Pinks have greyish leaves and superbly scented flowers of pink, white or red. They grow about 6–12 inches (15–30 cm) tall, depending on variety.

**Diascia cordata 'Ruby Field'.** A delightful front-of-border plant, reaching no more than about 6 inches (15 cm) and covered throughout summer in salmon-pink flowers over spreading mats of fresh green foliage.

**Euphorbia.** There are a few Spurges that are short enough for this position. *E. myrsinites* produces prostrate stems of blue-grey foliage, which radiate from the centre and end in lime-green flowers in early spring. *E. polychroma* makes small mounds about 15 inches (38 cm) high, covered in bright yellow heads over a long period in spring.

**Geum.** These well-known and easily grown perennials form large clumps of foliage about 1 foot (30 cm) high which are covered in flattish, bright flowers of yellow, apricot, orange or red, depending on variety. I particularly like the orange *G. borisii*, *G. rivale* 'Lionel Cox', which is a creamy apricot colour, and *G. chiloense* 'Lady Stratheden', which has double yellow flowers and grows rather taller.

**Heuchera.** Newer hybrids have improved this plant no end. It forms clumps of evergreen, rounded foliage and carries spires of small flowers. Look out for *H.* 'Greenfinch', which is olive green, and *H. villosa*, with cream flowers. Two foliage Heucheras I would strongly recommend are the now popular *H.* 'Palace Purple', with deep red foliage topped by white flowers, and the not so well known *H. americana*, which has green foliage mottled with brown and peculiar green and brown flowers. They all reach about 2 feet (60 cm).

**Iris.** There are some wonderful dwarf varieties of Iris which are well worth growing. *I. graminea*, for example, grows to about 15 inches (38 cm) and has purple flowers with a strong, delicious perfume. The 10 inch (25 cm) high Bearded Iris hybrid 'Green Spot' has ivory-white flowers with green markings. In fact there are short varieties of Bearded Irises, some as little as 4 inches (10 cm) high, in all the colours of the rainbow. The flowering period is April to May.

*Miniature rose 'Red Rascal' (see p. 136).*

**Linum perenne.** The Blue Flax is a wonderful plant, about 15 inches high. It produces clear blue flowers over a very long period in summer. Each lasts only a day but is always replaced by another the following day.

**Lychnis flos-jovis.** The Flower of Jove grows to about $1\frac{1}{2}$ feet (45 cm) and forms tight tufts of foliage with many heads of reddish-purple flowers in early summer. 'Horts Variety' is clear pink.

**Molinia caerulea 'Variegata'** is one of the best grasses for the front of the border. It forms neat tufts of vivid green and cream leaves and carries feathery plumes of flowers of pale buff in autumn. Height about 18 inches (45 cm).

**Oenothera.** The Evening Primroses produce lovely clear yellow flowers from mid to late summer. *O. missouriensis* has prostrate stems covered in 4 inch (10 cm) flowers of the brightest yellow over a long period. *O. glaber* makes small rosettes of shining red-brown leaves from which arise stems tipped with cup-shaped yellow flowers. It grows to about 1 foot (30 cm).

**Phlox.** The prostrate, alpine types are superb for colour and are available in various shades of blue, pink, red, lilac and white. They do, however, tend to become a bit invasive, so you may need to do some judicious weeding out each year. Flowering time is late spring or early summer, depending on species.

**Potentilla.** There are many garden hybrids of this easy-to-grow plant. It has strawberry-like leaves on sprawling stems which in summer carry brilliant flowers for a very long period. They last until well into autumn. They are available in scarlet, yellow, orange and copper colours, depending on variety, and grow to about $1\frac{1}{2}$ feet (45 cm).

**Prunella webbiana.** This Self-Heal can be a bit invasive, so keep it in check with your spade each year. It produces short flower spikes somewhat like dead-nettles in red, pink or white. Height up to about 6 inches (15 cm).

**Saponaria ocymoides,** Bouncing Bette, is a vigorous trailing plant which covers its small dark leaves with bright pink blossoms over a long period in summer. Well worthwhile.

**Silene schafta.** A lovely small plant providing bright rose-pink flowers from late summer into autumn. It grows to about 6 inches (15 cm).

**Viola.** There are numerous species and hybrids of this popular plant, which will do well in the front of the border in sun or part shade. The many varieties of *V. cornuta* are mostly in shades of blue or white and are all suitable, growing to about 6–12 inches (15–30 cm). The named varieties of the garden Pansy (*V. × Wittrockiana*) are specially worth seeking out. 'Irish Molly' is brown overlaid with lime green, 'Maggi Mott' is pale mauve, while 'Jackanapes' is bright yellow and reddish-brown. Then there are black ones, cream ones, yellow ones and white ones, all good and flowering most of the summer.

*Anthemis* 'E. C. Buxton' (*see p. 137*).

## Perennials for shade

*Alchemilla mollis,* Lady's Mantle, forms clumps of fresh green foliage which catches raindrops. In June it produces frothy sprays of yellow stars, rising to $1\frac{1}{2}$ feet (45 cm). There are also smaller species, such as *A. erythropoda,* which grows to about 6 inches (15 cm).

*Aquilegia.* There is one dwarf Columbine well worth growing. *A. flabellata* grows to about 6 inches (15 cm) and has bluish leaves and superb blue and white flowers in early summer, while 'Nana Alba' is white.

*Astilbe.* The Astilbes, mentioned on p. 137, will also do well in partial shade.

*Bergenia.* Bergenias, described on p. 137, will also thrive in shade, though their flowers will be less prolific.

*Chiastophyllum oppositifolium.* A huge mouthful for a small and exquisite plant. It makes rosettes of succulent green leaves which in June are covered in small yellow flowers on red stems. Height about 6 inches (15 cm). (It is often found in catalogues under its former name of *Cotyledon simplicifolia.*)

*Dicentra formosa.* With more divided foliage than the Bleeding Heart (*D. spectabilis*), this species makes ferny hummocks about $1\frac{1}{2}$ feet (45 cm) tall. There are small purple-pink, pendulous flowers in spring and early summer.

*Epimedium.* The Barrenworts are really a bit invasive and therefore on the borderline for this garden. They'll certainly have to be controlled. However, they're very good for the most difficult dry, shady places. Most have wonderful new leaves of light brown or green, veined reddish brown, and delicate sprays of tiny flowers of shades of red, green or cream. They grow to about 9 inches (23 cm).

*Helleborus.* The lower-growing hellebores like the white *H. niger* and some of the varieties of *H. orientalis* will do well in this position. The cup-shaped, pendulous flowers are generally mauve, pink or white, often with intricate markings inside.

*Heucherella* 'Bridget Bloom'. An interesting and delightful plant like a delicate Heuchera with marbled foliage and spikes of pale pink flowers over a long period in late spring and summer. It grows to about $1\frac{1}{2}$ feet (45 cm).

*Hosta.* There are many Plantain Lilies which look marvellous in the front of these borders, especially when contrasted with the foliage of some of the vegetables. There is a range of leaf colour from white-edged green to metallic blue. Most have lilac or white flowers.

*Liriope Muscari.* This tough plant, 9 inches (23 cm) high, forms clumps of evergreen foliage from which spring spikes of lilac-blue flowers rather like a Grape Hyacinth.

*Primula.* There are many Primulas which will do well in this position and provide flower over a long period. *P. denticulata,* the Drumstick Primula, is quite familiar. Growing to about 1 foot (30 cm), it produces large round heads of lilac. *P. vialii* has unusual flower spires, on long tapering stems, with red buds opening to lilac, while *P. auricula* has greyish leaves and usually yellow or purple flowers. *P. vulgaris* is our own native yellow Primrose, but certainly not to be despised.

*Pulmonaria.* Don't be without the Lungworts. They provide good foliage colour throughout the year, and many have leaves spotted white or silver. The flowers, which appear in spring, come in a variety of blues, reds and white. *P. saccharata* 'Margery Fish' has silver-spotted foliage and superb pink and blue flowers, while 'Sissinghurst White' is the clearest, purest white possible. 'Highdown' is blue and *P. rubra* 'Redstart' bears rosy red flowers for a very long time. All grow to about 1 foot (30 cm).

*Tiarella collina* produces clumps of green leaves with spikes of pink buds opening to white in summer. It reaches 1 foot (30 cm).

## 🦋 BULBS 🦋

You could say that bulbs and corms take up no room in the garden at all. They're the bottom layer of planting, underneath the shrubs and herbaceous perennials, and many of them can be planted so that they grow through them. Indeed, this is certainly the best way to grow spring-flowering bulbs. You plant them in among herbaceous perennials that die down completely in winter. The big-leaved types, like hostas, are best. When the bulbs have finished flowering, the herbaceous plants grow up to cover their untidy foliage. It's a perfect arrangement.

But I must say that after the initial planting of the garden I rarely plant dry bulbs. What I do is to pot them up in the autumn, putting several bulbs in a pot. I then leave them outside, plunged in bark or even sunk into the border somewhere, and plant them out in the spring when I can see clearly where they're needed. After flowering, you can leave them in if you wish. Alternatively, you can lift them and heel them into a trench, closely spaced with just their foliage showing to help them build the bulb for next year. Then you repot them again in the autumn. This is really a way of using bulbs as 'bedding' and is an excellent method for things like narcissi, tulips and hyacinths.

If you do decide to do it this way, you must plant the bulbs at the correct depth in the pots. With larger bulbs, like narcissi, this is sometimes impossible because the pots aren't deep enough. In this instance you must plunge the bulbs in peat so that they are at the right depth below the surface. When you plant, set them quite deep so that only the green part of their stems is showing, with the white parts that have been below the peat buried again.

You'll want to leave many of the bulbs in the ground to multiply, of course. Things like lilies and allium should stay where they are and be treated just like herbaceous perennials, but the tender types, like gladioli, must be lifted each autumn and stored in a dry, frost-free place for replanting the following spring.

Once again, there are dozens of species and varieties to choose from so I've restricted myself to those I have grown myself and found successful. (I am using the term 'bulb' for all the plants in the following lists, though some are corms or tubers.)

### Out-of-reach bulbs

There are a few bulbs that are tall enough to go in the middle of the borders.

*Acidanthera.* These produce 2–3 foot (60–90 cm) stems of large, white, scented flowers with maroon blotches at their centres. They flower from July to October and are superb for cutting. Plant mid-May, 3 inches (7.5 cm) deep and 6 inches (15 cm) apart in full sun.

*Allium.* The Onions produce rounded flowers, quite striking when they rear up through lower-growing herbaceous plants. *A. aflatunense* and *A. albopilosum* will grow to 2–3 feet (60–90 cm) and both have spherical lilac coloured flowers about June. Plant them in the autumn 2–3 times their own depth and 9 inches (23 cm) apart.

*Gladiolus.* The large-flowered Gladioli are difficult plants, in my view, to place in the border. But they make such good cut flowers that I like to grow a few. They hardly need describing since their spikes of flowers are widely known. They are available in a wide range of colours and grow to about 3–4 feet (90–120 cm). They are, of course, tender so must be lifted each autumn after flowering and replanted in April. The Butterfly and Primulinus types are perhaps better suited as border plants since they're shorter and more delicate.

*Lilium.* The Lilies are superb for this kind of garden. Some thrive in a sunny spot while others like partial shade. But all prefer shaded roots and a fertile soil. Therefore, even the sun-lovers are ideal for growing through her-baceous plants, which will shade the roots while allowing their heads to be in the sunshine. Most should be planted about 6 inches (15 cm) deep with the exception of the Madonna Lily (*L. candidum*) which should only just be covered. They vary in height from 1 to 5 feet (30 to 150 cm).

*Lilium hybridum.*

**Narcissus.** The Daffodils certainly need no description. The larger varieties grow to about $1\frac{1}{2}$ feet (45 cm) in height and belong to the area just between the front and the middle of the border. There are, of course, dozens of varieties, from the pure yellow and most popular 'King Alfred' to 'Sempre Avanti' which is white with an orange cup. Plant them at least twice to three times their depth in August. Shallow planting can lead to blind-ness after the first year. After they have fini-shed flowering, don't cut off the leaves or tie them into neat bunches until at least six weeks afterwards, to enable them to manufacture food to build flowers for next year.

**Tulipa.** Like the larger daffodils, the taller Tulips are difficult to place in this type of garden, but I have included the odd few to add a splash of spring colour in an otherwise green area. They vary from about $1–2\frac{1}{2}$ feet (30–75 cm) and are available in a range of colours. They start with the Single Earlies which can flower in late March, followed by Double Earlies, Mendel, Triumph and Darwin tulips in April, and Lily-flowered and the frilly Parrots from May onwards. All are best planted 4–6 inches (10–15 cm) deep in September.

### Front-of-border bulbs

**Allium.** There are several members of the onion family short enough to grace the front part of the borders. *A. flavum* produces clumps of blueish foliage and heads of yellow bell-like flowers on 1 foot (30 cm) stems from mid to late summer. *A. pulchellum* grows to no more than 6 inches (15 cm) and has pendulous bells of lilac (there is a white form too). Equal in beauty is *A. tuberosum*, known as garlic chives and grown as a herb (see p. 174).

**Anemone.** The first to flower is *A. blanda*, in February. Delightful massed in groups at the front of a border, the large daisies are produced in shades of blue, pink and white. They need full sun when in flower but a little shade on their corms later, so this type of garden should be ideal. Plant in September about 1 inch (5 cm) deep.

There are two popular strains of the Poppy Anemone, *A. coronaria*. St Brigid has semi-double flowers and De Caen single flowers, both in a variety of colours including red, blue, white and violet. Plant these 1 inch (2.5 cm) deep in autumn for spring flowering and in spring for flowers in the summer.

**Chionodoxa,** Glory of the Snow, has charm-ing, pendulous, bell-shaped flowers of blue or lilac, generally with a white eye. They grow to about 6 inches (15 cm) and are easy to grow in sun or partial shade. Plant in the autumn about 2 inches (5 cm) deep.

**Colchicum.** These attractive autumn flowerers are called Autumn Crocus despite the fact that they're not crocuses at all. They do, with some stretching of the imagination, look a bit like large crocuses and come in shades of purple and white. Plant them in July or August, in a shady spot, covering them with about 3 inches (7.5 cm) of soil. They're best when growing through low-growing plants to provide the floppy stems with support. Height 6–9 inches (15–23 cm).

**Crocus.** Excellent plants for this garden since they flower early in spring when there's little else. They can be used as bedding plants, and a good way to do this is to pot them up during autumn in the net pots often used for water plants, then plant them out in spring. After flowering, simply lift the whole pot out and heel it in somewhere out of the way. They are available in a very wide range of colours. Height about 6–9 inches (15–23 cm).

**Erythronium dens-canis.** The Dog's-Tooth Violets do best in part shade and are most successful bought as plants rather than as dry bulbs. The leaves are attractively blotched brown and the flowers are rosy mauve with reflexed petals. There are white and cream forms too. All grow to about 6–9½ inches (15–23 cm).

**Galanthus nivalis.** Snowdrops are a 'must'. They come very early in late January or February, bringing the first splash of spring cheer. They grow to about 6 inches (15 cm), and of course have lovely white flowers with green markings. They are best planted in late spring, having been either pot-grown or recently lifted – the dry bulbs are rarely very successful.

**Muscari.** The Grape Hyacinths are easy to grow in a sunny spot. They reach about 6 inches (15 cm) and carry heads of tiny, almost spherical blue flowers in mid-spring. Again, I grow them as bedding, putting them into net pots and lifting them after flowering.

**Narcissus.** There are several species of narcissi suitable for the front of the border. Varieties of *N. triandrus* grow to about 6–12 inches (15–30 cm), the petals are attractively swept backwards and they come in lemon yellow or white forms. *N. cyclamineus* hybrids reach about the same height. Look out for 'February Gold', which has deep golden yellow flowers with swept-back petals, and 'Tête-à-Tête', which carries one or two deep yellow flowers on a 6 inch (15 cm) stem. Plant them in August at two or three times their own depth.

**Scilla.** The Squills are quite breathtaking when grown in large drifts, but in this garden they can still look good planted in clumps. Again, I use them as bedding, planted in large net pots to form good clumps. *S. bifolia* is an easy-to-grow type with loose heads of small starry flowers of deep blue, pink or white in February and March. They grow to about 4–6 inches (10–15 cm). *S. siberica* grows from 4–6 inches (10–15 cm) and has bell-shaped flowers of deep blue. Plant Scillas in the autumn about 3 inches (7.5 cm) deep.

*Scilla siberica.*

## ❧ RAISING FROM SEED ❧

The cheapest way to grow plants, without a doubt, is from seed. It's also one of the most exciting ways, and even more so if you collect the seed yourself from your own plants. All but a few of the permanent vegetables are raised from seed, and so are all the annuals and biennials, and even some of the perennials too. Of course, trees and shrubs can be raised in this way as well, but that's a much more specialized business and not for this book.

### Direct sowing

Many flowers and vegetables can be raised by direct sowing outside, but the technique in the ornamental kitchen garden is just a bit different.

First of all, don't bother sowing anything until the soil is warm enough. It needs to be about 45°F before seeds will germinate, though unless you go to the lengths of checking the temperature with a soil thermometer you won't know it precisely. So wait until March at the earliest for sowing anything in the open ground. In colder areas you may even have to delay until April. If you have

cloches you can get a start about a month earlier, but make sure you put them where you're going to sow at least three weeks beforehand in order to warm the soil.

One of the great advantages of this garden is that everything is done in small areas, so it's not a lot of trouble to cover a few bits of soil with clear polythene in early winter. This will keep it dry and warm it up so that you'll be able to make a start at least a fortnight before everyone else.

My sowing technique has become quite a ritual. Each step is practised religiously every time I sow, whether it's at the beginning of the season or after lifting another crop.

Bear in mind that all the plants should be grown in patches rather than in long rows. So you'll have a smallish, irregular-shaped plot, in most cases roughly circular or oval. The first job is to prepare the soil by putting a bucketful of well-rotted compost on the top and lightly forking it in. You will find, incidentally, that you do some damage to the roots of neighbouring plants. Not only do I think this does not matter a lot – provided, of course, that you're as careful as you can be – but I actually believe it to be necessary, as a form of pruning to avoid undue competition.

### DIRECT SOWING

**1** *Prepare a patch with compost and fertilizer, rake it to a fine tilth and mark a series of drills using a cane.*

**2** *Always sow seeds thinly. I find the best way is to tip them into the palm of one hand and to take the seed in small 'pinches'.*

**3** *For the earliest sowings, make sure the patch is exactly the size of the cloche by gently pressing it into the soil first. Cover after sowing.*

With the kind of highly fertile soil we're going to create in this garden, I have never found it to restrict growth very much. But there's no need to fork deeper than about 6 inches (15 cm).

Then scatter a handful of blood, fish and bone fertilizer over the top. Some gardeners, in particular vegetarians and Jehovah's Witnesses, don't like the idea of using blood, fish and bone, in which case an alternative must be used. If you can get hold of a good quantity of farmyard manure, that will supply all you need. Or you can buy concentrated fertilizers based on animal wastes like chicken or duck manure.

After forking over, level the ground with a rake or the back of the fork, and firm it down either by treading lightly or with the back of the rake. Then scratch the seed drills in the soil with a pointed stick. I have tried all kinds of implements for this job, from the corner of the rake to an onion hoe, but I always come back to my primitive stick! It certainly enables you to scratch a *shallow* drill, which is essential.

The distance apart of the drills depends on what you're sowing, but you should bear in mind that you can nearly always space them a little closer than is generally recommended.

This is because you need no access paths between and because of the high fertility of the soil. For example, I would sow most hardy annual flowers at about 6 inches (15 cm) apart. They only need a little thinning in the rows and will grow into a fine clump.

Sow thinly. There's never a need to crowd seeds together and this will only make thinning more necessary and more difficult. After sowing, cover the seeds either by raking a little soil over them or just brush it over with your hand, and pat it down.

If the soil is dry, you should water first. Don't water after sowing because this tends to 'cap' the soil, forming a hard crust on the top which seedlings find hard to push through. So pour a little water down the drills *before* sowing and cover with dry soil.

Vegetables are sown in exactly the same way though distances here do vary somewhat. I have listed suggested sowing distances under each particular vegetable in Chapter 7.

### Sowing in the greenhouse

The greenhouse is useful for starting off tender ornamental plants, and quite a few vegetables too, both tender and hardy.

---

SOWING IN THE GREENHOUSE

**1** *Water the compost well and then tap the seeds from the palm of your hand so that they trickle down the channel.*

**2** *Small seeds often need no covering, but larger ones can be covered with sieved compost.*

**3** *An electric propagator is ideal for germinating seeds that need temperatures up to about 65°F (18°C).*

There are two things to check first of all, before you sow anything at all inside. First is whether or not the seeds require light to germinate. Some things, like impatiens and celery, will do much better if they're not covered, though most prefer darkness. Secondly, it's essential to check the preferred germination temperature. This usually can't be controlled exactly in the amateur gardener's greenhouse, but you should try to get as near to it as possible.

For germination, only small containers are needed, so I generally sow them in pots or pans or, at the most, half-trays. That gives more than enough seedlings for most gardens.

Use a soilless compost which should not be over-firmed. Fill the tray, and firm by pushing your fingers into the compost a couple of times. Then scrape the compost level with the top of the container and finally firm with a presser board or a flat piece of wood.

Then it's most essential to water *before* sowing. Watering afterwards is likely to wash the seeds into patches or even out of the container altogether!

Sow the seeds by putting them into your left hand, which should then be half closed to make a channel, and tapped on the uppermost side with a finger of the other hand. You'll find that the seed can be accurately dribbled down the groove in your palm and distributed very thinly.

After sowing, cover the seeds with a little compost, unless they are very tiny, using a fine sieve. But don't overdo it! More seeds fail because they're sown too deeply than for any other reason, so don't let it happen to you.

If the seed is very fine, don't cover it with compost. Just press it in a little with the board and leave it at that. If it's one of those that needs light to germinate, the best bet is to cover it with fine vermiculite. Make sure it's the horticultural grade, which you can buy from the garden centre. This will ensure that the seed is stabilized in the compost but will let the light in too.

Seeds that prefer to be in the dark should be covered with opaque polythene and those that like it light with clear sheeting or a piece of glass. Put the container in a propagator if necessary, but remember that it's often worse to exceed the recommended temperature than to get below it.

As soon as the first seedlings germinate, remove the cover and take the container out of the propagator into a slightly lower temperature. The seedlings will now need maximum light to ensure short, bushy plants, but don't allow the hot sun to scorch the delicate foliage. If it shines on the seedlings directly, cover them with a sheet of newspaper.

As soon as the young plants are big enough to be easily handled by the leaves (never handle them by the stem, which will damage them), they can be transferred to wider spacings to grow on to planting size (known as 'pricking out') or they can be potted to make larger plants.

## Sowing in modules

A method that's becoming increasingly popular is to sow in plastic or polystyrene modules. These are like seed trays only divided into numerous square cells. I find them invaluable for sowing annuals in particular (see p. 155), and I do some vegetables in them too.

They're filled in exactly the same way with soilless compost. The seed is then sown, a tiny pinch to each cell. If the seeds are big enough, you can of course sow them individually, but with small annual seed I sow a few seeds and I don't bother thinning them later. They simply form a single bushy plant which can be transplanted to its final position later without root disturbance. You can save a week or two this way and always end up with better plants. And of course, it saves a tremendous amount of fiddly, tedious and time-consuming transplants.

## Hardening off

*Harden off gradually in the cold frame.*

Hardening off requires a cold frame – an essential piece of equipment in the ornamental kitchen garden – and it's just a case of gradually acclimatizing plants to the lower temperatures outside. Put greenhouse-raised seedlings into the cold frame about three weeks before you want to plant them in the garden. On the first day, keep the frame closed all the time. Then open it a crack on the second day but close it at night. Continue this gradual opening until the frame lid is fully open, but always close it up at night. Then start opening at night, too, in just the same gradual way. The plants then get gradually used to a harder regime and they won't stop growing as they would if they went straight out.

## Sowing perennials

There are three ways to raise your own herbaceous perennials from seed. If you have room in the greenhouse, sow them in very gentle heat in March in pots or trays, prick them out later and finally transfer to 3 inch (7.5 cm) pots before planting in their final positions.

Alternatively, sow them in modules and grow them on to planting size without a shift. That way you should get them into the soil earlier but they'll be slightly smaller plants. Either way, they should be hardened off for a week or two before planting out and they should flower the same year.

If you haven't got greenhouse space, they can be sown in a seedbed outside in May and transplanted to their final positions in the autumn of the same year or the spring of the next. You'll produce some superb plants this way, very cheaply, but they won't flower until the year after sowing. If you have no room in the borders for a seedbed, then simply sow in the same way in modules.

## SOWING IN MODULES

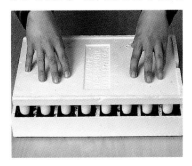

**1** *Fill the modules with sowing compost and gently press it down with the special board provided with the kit.*

**2** *Put the seed on to a piece of folded card and push the required number into each cell using the tip of a knife.*

**3** *To stabilize the seeds in the compost, it's best to cover them with a little silver sand. This stops them pushing out as they root.*

## Sowing hardy annuals

These can be sown directly in the soil in March or April, as soon as the soil is warm and dry enough. Alternatively, sow them in February or March in modules in the cold frame. They need no heat and the frame will be empty at that time, so it's a good way. Then plant them out as soon as they've made enough root, or pot them up as standby plants to go in as soon as a space appears in the borders.

## Sowing half-hardy annuals

Unlike their hardy cousins, these will not stand even a touch of frost. Start sowing them in a heated greenhouse at the end of January and go on until April (see p. 145). They can be sown in pots and pricked out into trays, or sown directly into modules (see p. 146). Potting them into 3 inch (7.5 cm) pots will produce better plants but naturally more expensively. Some should be potted, though, to serve as standby plants awaiting a space.

Make sure they're hardened off, as described on p. 147, before planting out in late May or the first week in June when all danger of frost has passed.

## Sowing biennials

Biennials are generally sown in a seedbed outside in exactly the way described for perennials. Start in May and transplant them to spacings 6 inches (15 cm) apart when they're large enough to handle comfortably. Then plant them in their final quarters in the autumn when the summer bedding comes out. An alternative is to sow them directly in their flowering positions in July or August. The snag with that is that the space will be filled by annuals, which will be looking at their best. So if you don't have room for a seedbed or to space the plants in rows to grow on, sow in modules as described for hardy annuals, but in late June, either in the well-ventilated frame or outside. Then transplant to their final positions.

## Collecting seed

It's quite easy to collect your own seed from certain plants. Most of the perennials and a few of the annuals will be eligible. But avoid $F_1$ and indeed most garden hybrids unless you wish to gamble on the outcome, because the resulting plants won't be the same as their parents.

All you need is a paper bag and a sharp eye. It's essential to collect when the seed is ripe, but you must catch it before it falls. This means daily excursions to the plant after you've noticed the seed-pods go brown. As soon as the first pod opens, cut the whole head and put it into a paper bag or lay it on a sheet of newspaper in the greenhouse. Hang it upside down in a cool shed where it'll be out of the sun but very, very dry. The seed will eventually fall and can then be cleaned and either sown straight away or stored.

Unfortunately, it's very difficult to know which should be sown straight away and which saved until spring and sown in heat, so it's best to hedge your bets at first. Split the seeds into two and sow one lot straight away into a pot of seed compost. Cover with coarse grit and leave the pot in the well-ventilated cold frame. Leave the rest until spring and sow in gentle heat. If you keep a notebook, you'll soon discover the most successful way.

*Collecting seed from your own plants is easy.*

## 🦎 PROPAGATION BY CUTTINGS 🦎

If you find it hard to believe that a lump cut off a plant and stuck into a pot is going to make a brand new one, join the club! Even after 30-odd years of gardening I still don't really believe it when I take a cutting, and I still marvel when it eventually produces roots. It's a fascinating business this gardening lark!

But root it certainly will if you do things the right way, and this makes a cheap means of increasing the plants in your garden. If friends or neighbours have plants you envy, ask them if you can take a cutting or two. If they're gardeners they'll be only too pleased.

In the ornamental kitchen garden, tender perennials are an important part of the planting scheme, and with these a mastery of the cuttings technique is essential. Otherwise you'll have to buy new plants each spring and that's inconvenient, expensive and not half as exciting. What's more, despite the twinges of pessimism about your success, which we all get, plant propagation by cuttings is really not at all difficult to achieve.

### Cuttings of tender perennials

These include geraniums (*Pelargonium*), half-hardy fuchsias, chrysanthemums, salvias, dahlias, cosmos, etc. (see p. 161). They are all plants which are planted out in late May or early June and brought into the greenhouse in November after the first frost. They are kept there until spring when they can be started into growth once more to produce shoots for cuttings.

Cuttings of dahlias, cosmos and some salvias are best taken from the overwintered mother-plants in spring, but fuchsias, geraniums and chrysanthemums are taken in late summer or early autumn and kept in the greenhouse. Then another batch can be taken in spring either from the overwintered mother-plants or even from the tops of the cuttings you took in the late summer. The technique is the same for all, with just a couple of minor exceptions.

Look for healthy side-shoots and remove them just above a leaf joint, making them about 3 inches (7.5 cm) long. With a really sharp knife, cut just below the bottom leaf joint and remove the bottom leaves. Geraniums have small, leafy stipules under each leaf stem and these should be removed as well.

It's a bit difficult to advise on how many leaves should be allowed to remain. This is something which comes with a bit of experience but, as a general rule of thumb, say about four if they're small like a fuchsia, and three or even two if they're as large as a geranium.

TAKING CUTTINGS OF TENDER PERENNIALS

**1** *Take short shoots from the mother plant and trim them just below a leaf joint. Remove the lower leaves.*

**2** *Dip the tip of the cutting into hormone rooting powder and dibble it into a cuttings compost.*

**3** *Water well and, to maintain humidity, cover the pot with a polythene bag and put it into a shady spot, preferably with a little heat.*

Most plants will benefit from a bit of hormone rooting powder on the base of the cutting, but you should never overdo it. Surprisingly, too much powder will actually inhibit rooting. After dipping the cutting into the powder tap off the excess. Then dibble it into a compost which consists of equal parts of peat (or preferably one of its alternatives) and horticultural vermiculite (I stress 'horti-cultural' because the grade used by builders for insulation is too fine and dusty and could impede drainage; buy it from the garden centre). After setting the cuttings about 2 inches (5 cm) apart in the pot, put it inside a propagator which will provide gentle bottom heat – about 68°F (20°C) is ideal. They should root in a week or two.

There are just two exceptions, both relating to geraniums. Here there's no need to use hormone rooting powder. In fact they have plenty of rooting hormone already at each leaf joint and too much will prove counter-productive. They also don't like too humid an atmosphere, so put those on the open bench. But if you can provide a little gentle heat it'll help rooting no end.

Once rooting takes place and the cuttings visibly perk up, they can be potted into 3 inch pots using a soilless potting compost.

## Cuttings of shrubs

One of the easiest ways with many shrubs is to take softwood cuttings in June. I have had success with a very wide range of plants so I

## BOX CUTTINGS

**1** *In summer remove the cuttings from the mother plant, taking shoots that have grown in the current year. My 'nursery' is the result of five years' cuttings.*

**2** *Put the cuttings into a polythene bag and keep them in the shade until you can deal with them. The first job is to trim off the bottom leaves.*

**3** *The best area for rooting on most cuttings is just below a node (leaf joint), so trim the cutting there with a very sharp knife.*

**4** *Box cuttings generally root quite readily, but hormone rooting powder will normally speed them up. Make sure the powder is fresh.*

**5** *Dibble the cuttings into a compost consisting of fifty-fifty peat (or preferably coconut-fibre peat) and vermiculite. Then give them a good watering in.*

**6** *Cover the cuttings with thin polythene so that it rests on the leaves. Put them in a shady spot and they should root in about six to eight weeks.*

would suggest that you try this method first with everything.

When you take the cuttings, look for strong young shoots that have grown this year. Cut them just above a leaf joint to leave them about 3–4 inches (7.5–10 cm) long. If you're raiding a friend's shrub, take them from round the back where they can't be seen but take at least half a dozen for each plant you want. Put them into a polythene bag and keep them out of the sun until you can deal with them.

When you get home, trim them in the same way I described for tender perennials, cutting below a joint and removing the lower leaves. Dip them in hormone rooting powder, tap off the excess and put them into a pot or tray of equal parts peat alternative and vermiculite.

Then take a piece of very thin clear polythene. The sort of stuff your suit comes back from the cleaners in is ideal. Gently wrap this over the top of the cuttings so that it actually touches them and tuck it underneath to form a hermetic seal.

The containers then go into the cold frame, and the fun begins. You need to strike a balance, allowing the cuttings sufficient light to manufacture some food from sunlight by photosynthesis but not enough to cause them to wilt. It's not easy but worth taking trouble over, because it really is the key to success.

Shade the frame with plastic greenhouse shading net. You can buy this at the garden centre. Check the weather forecast each morning and, if it's going to be a bright day, cover the frame with two thicknesses of net. If it promises to be about normal, use one thickness. But, if it threatens to be dull, use none at all. If you can't be bothered with all that messing about, cover with one piece of net and keep your fingers crossed. Don't expect the results to be quite as good, however.

The cuttings should root in about six to eight weeks when they can be split up and potted individually for growing on.

Conifer cuttings are taken in the same way except that it pays to wound the bottom of the shoot. Do this by simply pulling off the leaves rather than carefully cutting them off.

## Hardwood cuttings

Some shrubs root so easily from hardwood cuttings that it's not worth bothering with more sophisticated methods. The job's done in the autumn simply by cutting off a length of shoot from the current season's wood. Make it about 9 inches (23 cm) long. Trim the top above a leaf joint and the bottom below one and put the cuttings into a trench in a corner of the garden, with about 3 inches (7.5 cm) of the top of the shoot showing. If your soil is

## HARDWOOD CUTTINGS

**1** *Hardwood cuttings are taken in the dormant season. Shoots about 9 inches (23 cm) long are trimmed below a leaf joint at the bottom and above one at the top.*

**2** *Make a narrow slit trench in a corner of the garden and, to aid rooting, line the bottom with a little sharp sand.*

**3** *Put the cuttings in so that only about 3 inches (7.5 cm) show above the soil and firm them in. They'll be ready for moving the following autumn.*

heavy, line the bottom of the trench with a little sharp sand. Firm the cuttings in with your boot and the job's done. They should have rooted and be ready for transplanting at the end of the following year. The kind of shrubs suitable for this method are the willows, flowering currant, forsythia, buddleia, cornus, philadelphus, etc.

*Divide herbaceous plants in autumn or spring.*

## Another way with shrubs and herbaceous plants

An alternative and very successful way to propagate herbaceous plants and some shrubs copies the technique used by commercial nurserymen. Cuttings from the tips of shoots are taken at any time of the year you're able to find them. This generally means from about April to October.

They are taken in exactly the way described for tender perennial cuttings and put in the propagator at the same temperature. It's advisable to maintain a slightly higher humidity by lining the bottom of the propagator with capillary matting, which you can buy at the garden centre, or with a good thickness of kitchen paper, which should be kept wet. Cuttings should root this way in three weeks plus, depending on the subject and the time of year.

## Division

Many herbaceous plants can easily be increased by dividing the roots. This is obviously restricted to those plants that form a clump with a diverse root system and is not suitable for plants with a single stem and a taproot.

The best time to do the job is in the autumn or spring. Simply dig up the plant and split it into pieces to make several new plants. Many herbaceous plants spread outwards from the centre and it's the pieces on the outsides of the clumps that are youngest and most vigorous. So retain these for replanting and throw the old centres away.

If the clump is difficult to split, borrow another garden fork and prize the clump apart by driving the forks into the middle back to back and levering them apart.

Some plants with fleshy roots, like hostas, are best left until spring. Just as they start to grow, you'll be able to see where the buds are. You can then split between them either with a sharp spade or a large knife.

Before replanting, always revitalize the soil with a bucket or so of compost and a dusting of fertilizer. And remember that the new plants may need water, especially in spring.

## 🦎 PLANTS FOR THE SCREE PATH 🦎

The scree path looks wonderful when the planting matures to cover the hard edges of the paving slabs. But it does become somewhat difficult to negotiate and it's no place for a gardener in a hurry! That, in my view, is a great advantage because it *forces* you to slow down and enjoy your surroundings. It does, however, present a planting problem.

However careful you may be, you will inevitably have to tread on some of the plants in the scree path, so a careful choice must be made. While it's perfectly possible to plant the more delicate subjects right at the side of the slabs, anything which is going to spread to the middle must be tough. That cuts the list down considerably, but leaves quite enough to make a really attractive job. In the following lists I have indicated where the plants should be planted. Again, this is only a small selection and a trip to an alpine nursery is strongly recommended.

*Acaena.* Most of the New Zealand Burrs are ideal since they'll take some wear. They form wide mats of blue-grey or bronze foliage covered with flowers which have bristles that are generally red.

*Antennaria dioica.* A good carpeter, the grey leaves forming a spreading mat. In early summer, heads of white flowers are carried on short stems. The variety 'Rosea' has rich pink flowers. It can be used in the middle of the path where a little bruising from feet will do some much needed pruning.

*Arabis ferdinandi-coburgii* **'Variegata'.** I'd grow this plant just for the name, but it's also excellent for the edge of the paving. It will be damaged if walked on but is vigorous enough to regenerate quite well. It forms tight rosettes of creamy white splashed green and carries small white flowers in spring.

*Arenaria balearica.* A delightful, delicate plant forming a film of tiny green leaves and thousands of small white flowers. Best in shade.

*Armeria.* The Thrifts are hummock-forming plants which prefer full sun. They need to be planted at the side of the path where they won't get damaged. *A. alpina* forms tidy mounds with pink flowers on 4–6 inch (10–15 cm) stems. *A. juniperifolia* also has fine heads of pink flowers which are almost stemless.

*Campanula.* There are one or two Bellflowers that are suitable. *C. cochlearifolia* is a delightful spreader, forming wide mats of tiny, shining green leaves above which dangle hundreds of 'fairy bells' on 1 inch (2.5 cm) stems. They range in colour from white through lavender to deep blue, depending on variety. They are really best grown at the side of the path since you won't want to risk treading on them. *C. carpatica* 'Turbinata' makes compact clumps for the path edge and has masses of rich blue, saucer-shaped flowers in summer. There is also a white form.

*Frankenia.* Prostrate evergreens with pink, white or red flowers in summer. The best species for the scree path are *F. hirsuta*, with red flowers in summer, *F. laevis*, which has tiny green leaves and pink flowers in profusion, and *F. thymifolia*, which has greyish leaves and carries numerous stemless rose-pink flowers. Plant this at the edge and allow it to grow into the middle.

*Geranium.* A few of the dwarf Geraniums are suitable for the edges and will grow into the middle. *G. cinereum* 'Ballerina' makes neat mounds of grey-green leaves above which are carried large, cup-shaped flowers of lilac pink veined purple. 'Apple Blossom' is very similar but with clear pink flowers. *G. sessiflorum* 'Nigricans' makes dense mats of brownish foliage with white flowers.

*Helichrysum bellidioides* forms prostrate mats of tiny grey-green leaves with white flowers on the end of each branch. It's an easy plant to grow though said by some to be a risk in wetter areas. It will stand some wear and tear.

*Mentha requienii.* If you have a cool, shady spot on the path, grow this Mint. It makes a film of tiny, peppermint scented leaves topped with minute lavender flowers in spring and summer. Walking on it will cause damage but it seems to regenerate quickly.

*Nierembergia repens.* An absolutely prostrate member of the potato family, which spreads by creeping stems underground. It carries large, white, bell-shaped flowers in summer and can be grown near the middle of the path.

*Raoulia australis.* A superb plant if you can grow it. It forms dense mats of tiny silver leaves, studded with minute yellow flowers. It may suffer in wet weather but, provided you haven't skimped on the grit and the drainage is good, it's well worth a try. Plant it at the side of the path.

*Saxifraga.* The Saxifrage family is enormous and very variable. The members of it that are suitable for growing near the edge of the path form encrusted mounds of foliage topped by flowers of various colours, including white, pink, red and yellow. The hybrid 'Irvingii' makes tight mounds of grey rosettes and almost stemless pink flowers. 'Iris Pritchard' also makes lovely, lime-encrusted mounds with buff-apricot flowers, while 'Lady Beatrix Stanley' is similar but with red flowers.

*Scree path softened by mature plants.*

*A dwarf Geranium (see p. 153), like* 'Laurence Flatman', *makes a good edging plant.*

**Sempervivum.** The Houseleeks are definitely not to be trodden on but are excellent when planted at the edge of the path. Rather like hardy cacti in appearance, their succulent leaves form attractive rosettes in various colours from grey-green through to mahogany. There are dozens of suitable varieties.

**Thymus.** The creeping Thymes are all excellent and have the bonus of aromatic foliage which carries well into the air when the plants are stepped on. It's therefore a good idea to grow it where the leaves will be bruised from time to time. There are several excellent species and varieties. *T. longicaulis* forms spreading mats of scented green leaves covered in early summer with rosy-mauve flowers. *T. minimus* is a very prostrate grower with woolly leaves and tiny pale pink flowers. There are several varieties of *T. serpyllum* which are excellent. 'Albus' has white flowers, 'Coccineus' is crimson, while 'Lanuginosus' makes mats of grey-green, woolly leaves and pretty pink flowers.

**Veronica prostrata 'Trehane'** makes low carpets of yellow foliage which acts as a superb background for its short spikes of sky blue flowers in early summer – another one to start at the edge of the path.

## ANNUALS

'Bedding out' is an important feature of the ornamental kitchen garden. While the shrubs and herbaceous perennials form the backbone of the borders, the temporary annuals, biennials and tender perennials not only add colour to the scheme but also take part in the rotation of crops.

As I've explained, the permanent plants are arranged to form 'bays' of bare soil any one of which might be filled with, say, lettuces in February, followed by radish in May, and then bedding dahlias in June. Or you may have an area devoted to wallflowers from October until June, when they're pulled out and replaced with courgettes. There again, Brussels sprouts could be underplanted with spring bulbs so that the sprouts, predominant during wintertime, are removed in spring to show off the bulbs to best effect. The bulbs are replaced, after flowering, with pansies and later with autumn-flowering bulbs. This way the garden will always be taking on a fresh new look and the rotation of different crops will be as wide as possible. Not only will you make the best of your resources, in terms of the use by the plants of nutrients, but you'll have the pests and diseases so confused they'll need psychiatric care!

The bedding plants in this garden are definitely *not* laid out as you might see them in the municipal park. Attractive though a formal scheme may be, with perhaps masses of pink geraniums, fronted by rows of bright red salvias in regimented lines like soldiers, it just wouldn't do for our purposes. Here, all the planting must be on 'cottage garden' lines with the plants set out in informal drifts. There should be considerable variation in height too, with patches of lower-growing plants drifting towards the back of the border here and taller ones creeping towards the front there.

If you haven't done it before, it may sound like a planning nightmare. But the beauty of this garden is that it's not necessary to sit down with a plan of the garden and a set of coloured pencils to try to work out the scheme before planting. The process is a continuous one, with small areas becoming vacant from time to time, so that all you have to do is to apply your mind to that particular spot.

It's for this reason that I like to keep a reserve of bedding plants in pots on the patio. Then, whenever a space becomes available, I have the choice of filling it with a vegetable to maintain the succession of harvesting or, if the border is beginning to lose colour, I can liven it up with a flowering plant. It's a fascinating and very rewarding way of gardening.

### Hardy annuals

These are the easiest and cheapest flowering plants of all. They'll stand a few degrees of frost, so they can be sown directly outside without any fuss or bother and without the need for expensive heating.

The ideal time for sowing outside is March. Just scratch a few drills in the soil with a stick, making them about $\frac{1}{2}$ inch (13 mm) deep and 6 inches (15 cm) apart. Sprinkle the seeds down the rows as thinly as you can and cover with a little soil. Firm the soil with the back of a rake or with your hand and the job's done. It is possible just to sprinkle the seeds all over the area you wish to sow, raking in afterwards or sieving a little soil over the top, but this has one big disadvantage. When the seedlings appear, so will the weeds and you'll be hard put to know which is which. If you've sown in rows, it's the ones in straight lines that you want to keep. When the seedlings are big enough to handle, thin them to 6–9 inches (15–23 cm) apart.

Another way to do it is to sow into plastic modules, with just a tiny pinch of seed to each cell (see p. 146). There's no need for heat as the seedlings will germinate readily in the cold frame. Several seedlings will come up in each cell but there's no need to thin them out. Just push each little clump of plants out of the cell

and plant the lot. It's important to water well before planting since soilless composts are difficult to wet once the plants are in the soil.

The plants can be held in the modules for several weeks if there's no space available, but once they start to look yellow it's best to pot them into 3 inch (7.5 cm) pots.

Good hardy annuals for the ornamental kitchen garden include:

**Agrostemma.** Height 3–4 feet (90–120 cm). Soft pink, trumpet-shaped flowers.

**Anchusa.** Height 9 inches (23 cm). Star-like blooms in shades of blue, lavender and white. A good bee plant.

**Bartonia.** Height 2 feet (60 cm). Large, brilliant gold flowers all summer.

**Calendula.** Height 1–2 feet (30–60 cm), depending on variety. The marigolds are well-known cottage garden plants with yellow or orange, many-petalled flowers.

**Calliopsis.** Height 2 feet (60 cm). Large daisies with golden yellow petals and brown centres.

**Clarkia.** Height $2\frac{1}{2}$ feet (75 cm). An old favourite with superb double flowers in rich shades or red, pink and white.

**Convolvulus minor.** Height 1 foot (30 cm). Ideal for a sunny spot. Lots of trumpet-shaped flowers in shades of blue, pink and white. Good hoverfly plant.

**Eschscholzia.** Height 1 foot (30 cm). The Californian Poppies produce in abundance large flowers in shades of red, pink, orange, yellow and white.

**Larkspur (Delphinium solida).** Height $1\frac{1}{2}$–3 feet (45–90 cm), depending on variety. Tall spikes of flowers in pink, lavender, violet and white.

**Lavatera.** Height 2 feet (60 cm). Bushy plants which are covered in large trumpets of pink or white all summer.

*Limnanthes.* Height 6 inches (15 cm). The Poached Egg Flower produces masses of bright yellow-and-white flowers over a long period. A good hoverfly attractor.

*Nasturtium.* Height 1 foot (30 cm). Well-known and very easily grown plants producing attractive foliage and masses of large trumpets in shades of red, orange and yellow. The seeds are used as a substitute for capers. There are also climbing varieties.

*Phacelia.* Height 9 inches (23 cm). A delightful plant with flowers of the deepest gentian blue.

*Sunflower.* Height 4–8 feet (120–240 cm), depending on variety. Enormous heads of yellow flowers are produced, the central brown disc later carrying edible seeds. An excellent bird plant.

*Sweet Pea.* Well-known climbers, ideal for growing through trees or shrubs or to trail through fruit trees or on wires on the fence. The sweetly scented flowers are available in a wide range of soft pastel colours.

## Half-hardy annuals

These are more showy plants generally, but certainly more difficult and expensive to grow. They have to be raised in the greenhouse and hardened off in a cold frame before planting out when all danger of frost has passed.

Sowing starts in late January and a small propagator is really essential. Though the seed packets will tell you to germinate different varieties at a whole range of different temperatures, this is quite unrealistic for the amateur gardener. Those requiring a really high temperature, above 70°F (21°C), are probably best germinated in the airing cupboard, though considerable care must be taken. Don't put the containers immediately above the hot water tank which is normally too hot. One shelf above is generally about right. And check them daily for germination.

The container should be brought out and taken into the greenhouse as soon as the first seedling shows through.

For most seeds, however, an electric propagator will suffice, even though most are set to operate at about 65°F (18°C). There is a certain leeway with most seeds, though it has to be said that some can be a little temperamental.

Sow into soilless compost in small containers. For most modern gardens the amount of seedlings you can raise in a 4 inch (10 cm) pot will be plenty. Full details of how to sow can be found on p. 145.

When the seedlings are large enough to handle, they can be transplanted to wider spacings in seed trays while some can be potted up into 3 inch (7.5 cm) pots. These make bigger and better plants and, because of the increased volume of compost, can be held over while awaiting a planting space.

About a month before the plants are to be planted out, they should be hardened off in the cold frame to get them used to lower temperatures outside (see p. 147).

Suitable varieties for the ornamental kitchen garden include:

*Ageratum.* Height 9 inches (23 cm). Good plants for the front of the border, with masses of fluffy blue flowers all summer.

*Antirrhinum.* Height 6 inches–3 feet (15–90 cm), depending on variety. The Snapdragons are well-known and easily grown plants. They produce spikes of flowers of unusual shape in a range of colours including white, red, bronze, crimson, yellow and pink.

*Aster.* Height 9 inches–3 feet (23–90 cm), depending on variety. The annual Asters are useful in that they flower in late summer. The flowers range from single blooms, like many-petalled daisies with a yellow centre, to the Ostrich Plume types which form large heads of numerous quill-shaped petals. They are available in shades of red, blue, pink, yellow and white.

*Ageratum* 'Blue Champion' (*see p. 157*).

**Begonia.** Height 6–12 inches (15–30 cm). The fibrous-rooted Begonias are exceptional value in the front of the border. They flower in a range of reds, pinks and white all summer and their glossy succulent foliage, which is either bright green or red, makes a wonderful foil.

**Cineraria maritima.** Height 12 inches (30 cm). This has silvery-grey foliage which is a fine contrast for brighter bedding.

**Cosmos.** Height 3 feet (90 cm). One of the best for the back of the border. The fernlike foliage acts as the perfect foil for masses of delicate, dahlia-type flowers of red, pink and white. Not to be missed.

**Dahlia.** Height 2 feet (60 cm). The dwarf bedding Dahlias resemble their bigger brothers but are raised from seed each year. They are available in a wide range of colours.

*Brilliant silken-petalled poppies (see p. 160) look best in groups of five or more.*

*Begonia* 'Pink Avalanche'.

**Dianthus.** Height 6–12 inches (15–30 cm). The annual Pinks closely resemble their perennial relatives. They come in shades of red, pink and also in white and are very sweetly scented.

**Gazania.** Height 12 inches (30 cm). Large exotic daisy flowers in shades of red, pink, orange, bronze and yellow with circular markings towards the centre of the flowers. They must have a sunny spot.

**Impatiens.** Height 6–12 inches (15–30 cm). The Busy Lizzies are among the best annuals for a shady spot. In sun or shade they'll be covered in flowers all season, in a range of reds, pinks and white.

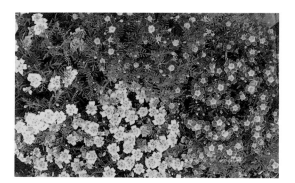

*Tagetes* 'Starfire' (*see p. 160*).

*Lobelia* 'Mrs Clibran' (*see p. 160*).

*Verbena hybrida* 'Tropic' (*see p. 160*).

**Ipomoea.** The Morning Glory is a showy climber bearing large trumpets of white or blue.

**Lobelia.** Height 6 inches (15 cm). You may have noticed that I excluded Alyssum from my list. This is because it often finishes well before other annuals, so I grow white Lobelia instead. This superb edging plant is completely covered in flowers all season. They are light or dark blue, white, or blue with a white 'eye'. I am not impressed with the red and pink shades but, of course, you may be.

*Lobelia* 'White Lady'.

**French Marigold.** Height 6–12 inches (15–30 cm). Grown *en masse*, these showy plants can be too glaring for this type of garden. However, in small doses, they can be used underneath taller-growing plants, vegetables, for example, to good effect. They are yellow, orange or bronze.

**Mimulus.** Height 6–12 inches (15–30 cm). Another useful plant for shaded places, the annual Musk produces marked and spotted flowers in shades of yellow, orange, red and pink.

**Nemesia.** Height 9–12 inches (23–30 cm). Upright, bushy plants covered in flowers in the widest colour range possible. Mixtures look extremely good – like a Persian carpet.

**Nicotiana.** Height 12 inches (30 cm). One of the best of all annuals. Look out for *N. affinis* (*N. alata*) which grows to 3 feet (90 cm) and carries numerous sweetly scented white trumpets all summer. There are also many varieties of this, in shades of cool green, white, yellow and red. Some are low-growing and compact.

**Petunia.** Height 12–18 inches (30–45 cm). Perhaps the showiest of all summer bedding plants, but some varieties can be damaged in wet weather. I have found them ideal for containers and baskets. They produce large trumpets in the widest possible range of colours. For this garden, it pays to avoid the over-gaudy!

**Poppy.** Height 12–24 inches (30–60 cm). The Poppies produce lovely flowers in pastel shades that look for all the world like silk. They must be grown in groups of five upwards for best effect. Look out for the variety 'Summer Breeze' which is especially good.

**Rudbeckia.** Height 2 feet (60 cm). Very similar to some of the hardy herbaceous Rudbeckias, the annuals produce wonderful daisies of warm yellow and rusty-red shades. Superb for the middle of the border.

**Tagetes.** Height 9–15 inches (23–38 cm). The flowers are somewhat like French Marigolds, but the plants are much more delicate and less brassy. They look marvellous under sweet corn.

**Verbena.** Height 6–12 inches (15–30 cm). Very floriferous plants producing large heads of flowers in shades of red, pink, blue and white. Each flower has a white 'eye' in most varieties.

## ❧ TENDER PERENNIALS ❧

The aristocrats of the garden, I suppose, are those perennial plants from warmer climes, which flower their hearts out all summer but succumb to the first frost. Most are refined, subtle plants with none of the gaudy brashness of the French or African marigolds or the brilliant red salvias. They need a little extra care, but most will root quite easily from cuttings taken in the autumn and over-wintered in a greenhouse which is kept just frost-free. The alternative is to lift the plants in the autumn, box or pot them up and take cuttings in the spring. Either way, it's a little extra expense admittedly, but it's worth it.

I also put a few into pots and grow them on to bigger plants especially for decorating the patio. They have to be brought into the greenhouse for winter where, I must admit, they take up a lot of space. If your space is limited, put them in the most sheltered spot you have in the garden and either plunge the pot in the soil or wrap it with sacking. This way it might come through the winter unscathed, but you should always take a few cuttings just in case.

*Argyranthemum.* Height 2–3 feet (60–90 cm). These used to be called *Chrysanthemum* until the botanists had one of their regular brain-storms and decided to change it. They include plants like *A. frutescens*, the Marguerite, which has white flowers with a yellow centre. The variety I grow, which in my view is best of all, is 'Jamaica Primrose' which produces simple but wonderful cool yellow daisies all summer. I wouldn't be without it. The variety 'Vancouver' has semi-double flowers of rich pink. *A. foeniculaceum* has smaller white flowers but in greater profusion and again all summer. Treat them like the ordinary chrys-anthemums, lifting the plants in autumn, storing them in pots or boxes over winter in a frost-free greenhouse and take cuttings in the spring.

*Chrysanthemum.* The ordinary florist's Chrysanthemum is not ideal for this type of garden, but I like to grow a few as cut flowers. There are hundreds of varieties to choose from in a wide range of colours and flower shapes. After flowering, cut the plants down, lift them and store them in boxes in a frost-free place. Take cuttings in spring.

*Cosmos atrosanguineum.* Height 2 feet (60 cm). A lovely relative of the Dahlia with the deepest maroon flowers which smell strongly of chocolate. It needs a sunny spot and might overwinter in warmer areas, especially if mulched over the top when it dies down. However, it can be lifted and its tuberous roots treated just like a Dahlia, storing it in a frost-free place and taking cut-tings in spring. It is perhaps a little shy of rooting but will normally take with a little bottom heat from the propagator.

*Dahlia.* Most are too overpowering for this garden but there are a few that are suitable, like the superb *D. merckii* which gives a con-tinuous display of small single lilac flowers with a dark maroon centre. Its height is 3 feet (90 cm). Treat it like any other Dahlia, lifting and boxing the tubers in the autumn, storing them frost-free and taking cuttings in spring.

*Euryops pectinatus.* Height 2–3 feet (60–90 cm). This has attractively divided grey foliage and brilliant yellow daisies all summer. Sometimes it will stand the winter and some-times it won't, so leave the plants in if you like to take the risk but take cuttings in the autumn. *E. acraeus* is a smaller version ideal for a sunny spot at the front of the border or at the edge of the scree path. It's actually hardy but short-lived, so treat it as if it were tender and take cuttings at least every other year.

*Fuchsia.* Height 1–2 feet (30–60 cm). Several varieties of half-hardy Fuchsia are worth growing and I also run up a standard or two on a 3 foot (90 cm) stem which makes a good

*Fuchsia (see p. 161).*

*Osteospermum* 'Lady Leitrim'.

focal point plant. Again, either lift the plants and store them frost-free, taking cuttings in spring, or take them in the autumn and risk leaving the plants in.

***Nepeta govaniana.*** Height 3 feet (90 cm). A delicate, airy plant for a shady spot. It carries tall, open spikes of tubular yellow flowers all summer. This is best raised from seed which is easy to collect from the plants each year.

***Nicotiana langsdorfii.*** Height 3 feet (90 cm). Another tender perennial to raise from your own collected seed. It carries sprays of small greenish-yellow bells on tall stems all summer.

***Nicotiana sylvestris.*** Height 4–5 feet (120–150 cm). A stately plant producing a succession of long, tubular trumpets of pure white that are heavily scented. Collect seed each year.

***Osteospermum.*** Height 6–24 inches (15–60 cm), depending on variety. These are sun-loving South African plants which are available in quite a wide variety. Look out for

'Buttermilk', a soft yellow with a brown eye, 'Whirligig', which has white petals with a blue reverse and curiously crimped petals, and 'Tresco Purple', which is a shorter plant bearing deep purple flowers with a black eye. They can all be easily propagated from cuttings in the autumn. Alternatively, the plants can be lifted and potted for cuttings in spring.

***Pelargonium.*** Height 12–18 inches (30–45 cm). The Geraniums are indispensable plants for a bright display over a long period. They're especially useful for containers and hanging baskets, and available in every possible shade of red, orange, pink, purple and white. They can be easily grown from seed, sown in January or February, though it's quite an expensive way and not guaranteed to be successful. Cuttings taken in autumn are easy and, in my view, the best way of bringing Geraniums though the winter. You can then take more cuttings from the cuttings once they start to grow in the spring.

***Salvia patens.*** Height 2 feet (60 cm). A beautiful tender perennial with gentian-blue, hooded flowers all summer. This produces tubers and so can be lifted and treated like a dahlia, or you can take cuttings in the autumn with the help of a little bottom heat in the propagator.

## CLIMBERS

Climbing plants are generally fast-growing, so they will add more or less instant height to the garden. They can be used to cover the walls or fences where they'll mix with the trained fruit. Care must be taken, of course, to control rampant growth so that the climbers never overpower the fruit. A good covering of climber will restrict growth and reduce yields too, so it's best to use only the less vigorous types here.

On the pergola and arbour, climbers grow up each post and eventually scramble over the top, providing shade as well as colour and perfume. Here ornamental plants can be allowed to mix freely with climbing fruits and vegetables. These can quite happily hold their own, so with a little trimming and tying here and there as necessary they can, on the whole, be left to fight it out.

*Clematis* 'Niobe' (*see p. 164*).

*Vitis coignetiae* (*see p. 165*).

Finally, a few of the less vigorous climbers can be useful to add out-of-season colour by allowing them to scramble over shrubs and through trees. Again, you must be careful with your choice of varieties and always be prepared to use your secateurs to admonish anything that gets over-exuberant.

*Aconitum volubile.* A herbaceous perennial with blue flowers just like the border Monks-hoods. They die down completely in winter but reappear in spring and will reach a good 8–10 feet (240–300 cm) in the season. They are particularly good when allowed to scramble through a small tree or a tall shrub and they can be grown on the fence or pergola.

*Actinidia chinensis.* The Chinese Gooseberry is a vigorous climbing shrub with attractive young shoots that are red and large heart-shaped leaves. If you buy a specially selected fruiting type and are prepared to grow two (a male and a female plant), you can produce edible fruit in warmer areas. The flowers are creamy white and fragrant and produced in late summer.

*Actinidia kolomikta.* An unusual climber with white, scented flowers, but it is chiefly grown for its foliage which is striped green, creamy white and pink. Plant in full sun to get the best variegation.

*Celastrus orbiculatus.* The plant is a strongly twining shrub which produces brown fruit capsules in autumn, which split open to reveal glistening red seeds. At the same time the foliage turns a clear golden yellow. As you can imagine, it's quite a sight.

*Clematis.* Undoubtedly the most popular of all climbers and deservedly so. There is a wide range of flower shapes and colours to choose from and great variation in flowering time too. If you decide to grow your Clematis through a tree, or scrambling over a shrub, or on the pergola, make sure you choose one of the less vigorous varieties. A rampant species like *C. montana* or *C. tangutica* would swamp all but the largest tree. Much better choose something like *C. viticella* or one of its varieties or, if you prefer an early flowerer, a slender variety like *C. alpina*. The large-flowered garden hybrids are nearly all suitable too. If you're concerned about pruning, a good rule of thumb is to prune right down to the ground in February all varieties which bloom after June. If they flower before, either leave them alone or, if the plant is getting out of hand, just trim back some of the side-shoots.

*Eccremocarpus scaber.* This is an evergreen in some warmer areas, but in cold winters it dies down to the ground, only to grow to its full 12 feet (360 cm) in the season. It carries masses of scarlet to orange-yellow tubular flowers over a long period in summer. It can be used to good effect on the fence or pergola but is too rampant and dense to grow through shrubs. It freely produces seed and some should be collected in case the parent plant suffers during a hard winter.

*Hedera.* The Ivies are useful, self-clinging climbers for walls or fences and provide homes for many insects and nesting sites for birds. There are several variegated varieties that will make a bright splash of yellow or silver.

*Humulus lupulus 'Aureus'.* The Golden Hop is a vigorous climber with soft yellow leaves. Ornamental kitchen gardeners who are also beer enthusiasts may be tempted to grow the green hop, but it's really much too vigorous for gardens.

*Jasminum nudiflorum.* Really a wall shrub and very popular as such. Its bright yellow flowers adorn the naked branches from November to March.

*Jasminum officinale.* The common white Jasmine is a strong twining plant ideal for the pergola or rose arbour. It is covered with small white, very fragrant flowers from June to September.

***Passiflora caerulea.*** The Passion Flower needs a warm, south-facing wall or fence, when it will produce a mass of vigorous shoots and numerous blue, white and pink flowers. It will die down completely during the winter in all but the warmest areas.

***Rhodochiton atrosanguineum.*** This slender climber is ideal for growing intermingled with other plants on the pergola or rose arbour, or scrambling over shrubs in the borders. It never becomes a nuisance and produces all summer dozens of superb tubular flowers of purplish red with a black calyx. They are tender and so will be cut down by the first frost. However, they can be easily raised from home-collected seed each year.

***Roses.*** What better plants for the rose arbour, of course, than roses? Use either climbers or ramblers, the difference being that climbers are generally less vigorous but flower repeatedly throughout the season, while ramblers climb higher and spread further but often flower just once or sometimes twice a season. There are, of course, numerous colours and flower shapes to choose from but in this garden there is one important factor to bear in mind. Roses are very subject to attack by the fungus diseases black spot and mildew, so avoid varieties that are particularly prone. If you find one growing in the garden which is attacked each year, it's best to root it out and replace it with something more resistant.

***Solanum crispum.*** A relative of the potato, this vigorous climber carries numerous potato-like flowers of deep purple with a bright yellow eye. The variety 'Glasnevin' will flower over a longer period, from about June to September.

***Sweet Pea.*** Well-known annual climbers easily raised from seed and useful to grow up trees, through large shrubs and on the pergola and arbour. They are, of course, available in a wide range of colours, though it's well worth sticking to perfumed varieties.

***Tropaeolum tuberosum.*** Related to the nasturtiums, this is a superb bright climber with attractive foliage and masses of orange-scarlet flowers. Look out for the cultivar 'Ken Aslet' which is very free flowering over a long period in summer. It's not hardy, so the tubers must be dug up in autumn and kept in the way you would store a dahlia. They can simply be replanted in spring.

***Vitis.*** The vines make superb vigorous climbers with very attractive foliage which turns rich shades of red and purple in the autumn. There are purely decorative varieties grown for their foliage, like *V. coignetiae* which has large, heart-shaped leaves that turn crimson and scarlet in autumn. Or grow fruiting vines which are decorative and can be used for wine-making or dessert (see p. 236).

##  POOL AND BOG PLANTS

The pool, whether it be a half-acre or half a beer barrel, is a small, self-contained ecosystem and, like everywhere else in the garden, needs a balance of life to make it work well.

Small pools in particular are very often garden disasters because, only days after they're filled, the water turns a ghastly green and within a very short while begins to smell putrid – not what is needed in your beautiful garden and certainly not attractive to a wide range of wildlife. The only living organisms that are going to love it are the microscopic algae and blanket weed that make it green. Establishing the right sort of plants is essential, after which insects and other animals will follow. Some can be introduced but most will simply arrive.

### Necessary plants

A well-planted pool is a very beautiful feature. But many of the plants are there not just to look pretty; they have a job of work to do.

First, there must be some whose main purpose is to oxygenate the water. This is vital for the well-being of the animals and plants that live there. The second function of aquatic plants is to help prevent the build-up of those organisms that turn plant matter to slime and the colour of the water to pea soup.

## Oxygenating plants

*Elodea crispa.* A green, trailing weed, very much like Canadian Pond Weed, to which it is related, but less vigorous. It is therefore ideal for smaller pools, where the rampant *E. canadensis* would need to be drastically thinned at least once or twice a year. Ideally, plant it in the soil at the bottom of the pool.

*Ceratophyllum demersum.* Hornwort has attractive, feathery underwater foliage and is easily controlled. It doesn't need planting – just throw it in.

*Nymphaea* 'James Brydon'.

## Aquatic plants

The algae that make pond water green thrive on sunlight, which they need for photosynthesis, and the mineral salts present in the water. If you can restrict these, you'll go a long way towards eliminating the algae. The oxygenating plants and other water plants will help use up the minerals. The sunlight can be restricted by plants whose leaves spread out on the surface of the water. The obvious choice for this purpose, and for their aesthetic value, are the Water-lilies (*Nymphaea*). All ponds should have them. But when you make your choice, you must be very careful to choose varieties that will suit the depth of water you can provide. There are Water-lilies for the shallowest and the deepest pools.

When you plant them, ideally put the roots into the soil at the bottom of the pool. If you can't do that, pot them into netted pots and make sure the top of the pot is at the correct depth.

For water up to 6 inches (15 cm) deep:

*Nymphaea pygmaea.* A tiny Water-lily with white flowers with a yellow centre. The variety 'Helvola' has soft yellow flowers and a stronger constitution, so is recommended.

For water 9–24 inches (23–60 cm) deep:

**N. 'Froebelii'.** An old favourite with crimson flowers. A very reliable flowerer.

**N. laydekeri.** There are a few hybrids of this variety which are among the best for small pools. 'Lilacea' varies from soft mauve-pink to deep rose. 'Fulgens' has crimson flowers while 'Purpurata' is wine red to crimson-purple.

For water 1–3 feet (30–90 cm) deep:

**N. 'James Brydon'** is considered one of the best of all. The foliage is purple, turning green later, and the flowers are deep pink or red and perfectly shaped.

*N. marliacea* has several hybrids that are ideal for this depth. 'Chromatella' has soft yellow flowers, 'Carnea' is very pale pink, 'Rose Arey' is deep pink and 'William Falconer' is rich crimson.

Apart from the Water-lilies, there are many other plants with floating leaves that can be planted at the bottom of the pool that are well worth growing. The best bet is to get hold of an aquatic plant catalogue.

*Aponogeton distachyus.* The Water Hawthorn does the same shading job as a Waterlily, with large floating leaves. It produces striking white flowers with black centres throughout spring and summer.

*Azolla caroliniana.* Fairy Moss is a floating fern with tiny reddish-brown leaves which will multiply to cover quite a good surface of water.

## Marginal and bog plants

Planting around the edges of the pool is important both to make a gentle transition between the water and the surrounding garden and to provide cover for wildlife. You'll find that hundreds of birds and millions of insects and even the odd hedgehog will use the pool as a source of drinking water, so it's a really effective way to attract them into your garden. They'll feel a lot happier if they have some kind of plant cover from which they can emerge to drink and dash back into if they feel threatened. Also, of course, a good wide margin of boggy soil around the pool will give you room to grow a whole range of plants that would otherwise be denied you.

Once again, I must stress that there are dozens of plants you could use and the following list is just a suggestion of the delights in store.

*Acorus.* Height 3 feet (90 cm). The Sweet Flag, *A. calumnus* 'Variegatus', has tall, swordlike leaves striped green and cream, while *A. gramineus* 'Variegatus' is much the same but

much smaller. Grow both in about 2 inches (5 cm) of water.

*Arum italicum* **'Pictum'.** Height 15 inches (38 cm). This lovely winter foliage plant has superb large spear-shaped leaves that are glossy green and mottled with white. In September this plant bears spikes of red berries.

*Astilbe.* Excellent in boggy soil and described on p. 134.

*Caltha palustris.* Height 1 foot (30 cm). The Marsh Marigold flowers in early spring. Varieties particularly worth growing are 'Plena', which has double yellow flowers, and 'Alba', a good single white form. *C. polypetala* has larger flowers.

*Caltha polypetala.*

*Euphorbia palustris.* Height 4 feet (120 cm). A handsome plant with great heads of green and gold flowers all summer.

*Gunnera manicata.* Only for the largest bog gardens, this giant foliage plant grows to about 8 feet (240 cm), producing huge, parasol leaves. The resting buds should be protected in winter.

*Iris.* Height 18–24 inches (45–60 cm). There are several good Irises which thrive in boggy soil. *I. kaempferi* bears lovely flowers of rich red-purple, lavender or white. *I. laevigata* has lavender-blue flowers and there are also varieties in deep blue or white. The variety 'Variegata' has blue flowers and variegated foliage. *I. pseudacorus* is slightly taller and has creamy yellow flowers while *I. versicolor* 'Kermesina' is rich claret in colour.

**Lobelia cardinalis.** Height $2\frac{1}{2}$ feet (150 cm). This striking plant forms tall shoots of deep red foliage topped in late summer with blood-red flowers. It's not entirely hardy so it's best to cover the crowns in winter and to take some cuttings as a safeguard.

**Lysichiton.** Height 3–4 feet (90–120 cm). The marvellous Bog Arums must have deep mud to grow in and are only for the large bog. If you can grow them you won't be disappointed by their huge yellow or white spathes of flower in spring followed by large leaves.

**Mimulus.** Height 1 foot (30 cm). The Monkey Musk (*M. luteus*) has small yellow flowers marked and spotted red, while *N. ringens*, the Lavender Musk, has blue flowers.

**Myosotis scorpioides 'Mermaid'.** Height 3 inches (7.5 cm). An improved Water Forget-me-not that is compact. It has typical blue flowers over a very long period in summer.

**Primula.** There are several Primulas which thrive in moist soil. *P. bulleyana*, 18 inches (45 cm), grows in sun or shade and produces whorls of orange flowers in May and June. *P. florindae*, 3–4 feet (90–120 cm), the Himalayan Cowslip, carries drooping, bell-shaped flowers of sulphur yellow from July to September. *P. japonica* is of the Candelabra type, with large spikes of pink, white or magenta flowers in April and May, and following it comes *P. pulverulenta*, height 2 feet (60 cm), which has red flowers.

**Trollius.** Height $2\frac{1}{2}$ feet (75 cm). The Globe Flowers carry large balls of lemon or deep yellow flowers over a long period in summer.

## ATTRACTING WILDLIFE

When you come to think about it, the very thought of 'controlling' pests and diseases is pretty arrogant. People who make a living from the land very soon understand that they simply can't control nature. On the contrary, nature controls us and the sooner we realize it the better.

Any farmer or grower will tell you that, though some temporary respite from attack from pests can be achieved with chemicals, it's not long before resistant races evolve and newer, stronger poisons have to be used. We are only now beginning to realize the cost.

In fact, nature has the control of pests and diseases very much in hand and all we have to do is to follow the rules and provide the right conditions. Indeed, we're in a position to provide even better conditions than those that occur naturally. For in nature you'll rarely find the wide diversity of plant species that can be provided in a garden. The more diverse the planting, the greater the variety of wildlife you'll attract, and, as I've pointed out, though that will certainly include some villains, there will always be enough predators to police your patch.

So the first rule in planting the ornamental kitchen garden is to provide as wide a diversity of plants as possible.

Trees, of course, are important because they attract birds by providing perching and nesting sites and, if you choose your varieties carefully, food from berries and fruits. While it isn't necessary to grow only native species, it's a good idea to include some near relatives. There are, for example, cultivars of our native thorns, mountain ash and crab which will keep quite a few indigenous insects happy as well as providing for the birds.

There are some ornamental plants that serve especially well as attractors of predators and as homes for wildlife. Ivy, for example, makes one of the best nesting sites and food for birds, provides winter hibernation quarters for some species of greenfly-eating hoverfly larvae and many other insects, provides nectar for butterflies and other insects and is a food plant for the larvae of the Holly Blue butterfly.

Flowers with an open structure, like the Poached Egg Plant, marigolds and the dwarf convolvulus, allow the female hoverfly, which has a short feeding tube, to have a meal before laying her eggs, while others, like *Sedum spectabile*, *Buddleia davidii* and many more, will attract butterflies in their hundreds.

But, all things considered, I'm not an advocate of restricting planting to just those plants that will serve a useful purpose in this way. I'm quite sure that the best way is simply to plant as large a mixture of different plants as you can and let nature do the rest. I'm equally sure that you'll never really know which plants are the best attractors of some insects until you try them. I have found, for example, bushes of *Skimmia japonica* simply covered with hundreds of ladybirds in spring. Ladybirds, of course, are voracious devourers of aphids, but why they took to my skimmias I have no idea.

### Plants to attract birds

There are hundreds of shrubs, trees and herbaceous plants which will attract birds so this list is by no means exhaustive: antirrhinum, aucuba, berberis, blackberry, cherries, cosmos, cotoneaster, elaeagnus, elder, euonymus, hawthorn, hollies, honeysuckle, Michaelmas daisy, pyracantha, roses, scabious, sorbus, sunflower, symphoricarpos, yew.

### Food plants for bees

*Annuals:* alyssum, borage, candytuft, clarkia, coreopsis, cornflower, french marigold, godetia, larkspur, lobelia, nasturtium.
*Perennials:* amelanchier, berberis, celandine,

chaenomeles, chives, cornus, cotoneaster, delphinium, echinops, lavender, lupin, Michaelmas daisy, monkshood, pulmonaria, scabious, sedum, thyme, veronica.

### Plants to attract butterflies

Alyssum, armeria, aubrieta, buddleia, cornflower, dianthus, forget-me-not, hawthorn, honeysuckle, hyssop, lavender, lilac, michaelmas daisy, nepeta, petunia, polyanthus, primula, scabious, sedum, solidago, thyme, viola.

### Plants to attract moths

Honeysuckle, jasmine, lychnis, nicotiana, petunia, saponaria, silene, verbena.

*A Comma butterfly enjoying ivy flowers.*

## CONTAINERS

Tubs, troughs and baskets have an important function in the ornamental kitchen garden and, properly planted, they illustrate the basic philosophy in microcosm.

It's possible to make containers colourful all year round. They brighten the paved areas and bare spaces that show up in winter. The patio, for example, will be partly covered in summer with small plants in pots waiting to go into the borders, but from midsummer to late spring there will necessarily be bare spaces. They can be decorated to good effect with plants in containers. The pergola will look marvellous in spring and summer but perhaps a little bare early in the year, and certainly fairly dull in winter. That can be brightened up with hanging baskets.

## Tubs and troughs

All containers will need a well-drained compost. I find the best general purpose mix to be 2 parts of good garden soil to equal parts of a peat alternative and coarse grit. To every 2 gallon (9 litre) bucketful of compost mix in about 1 oz (28 gm) of blood, fish and bone meal fertilizer.

The most colourful regime for tubs is to use annuals and biennials which are replanted twice a year. Start in late spring, after all danger of frost has passed, by planting half-hardy annuals and perennials.

Tall perennials, like geraniums, argyranthemums, osteospermums or fuchsias, are ideal in the centre to give height. Around those and nearer the front use shorter plants, like petunias, salvias or marigolds, and right

*A colourful tub of petunias and lobelia interspersed with cherry tomatoes.*

on the edge use edging plants, like lobelia, alyssum or ageratum. Also at the edges use trailing plants, like trailing lobelia, trailing geraniums and nepeta.

Don't neglect the vegetables in containers. I have used tomatoes especially to very good effect. There are now varieties available that are eminently suitable. In warmer areas you could even use peppers, which look very exotic indeed. Even small lettuces and beet-root look handsome in tubs.

When the frosts come, these tender plants will die, of course, so the containers are then replanted with spring-flowering subjects. Bulbs are ideal, but try short varieties, especially if you're using tulips (which have weaker stems than daffodils and narcissi). You can make an attractive show by planting bulbs on top of each other in layers. In the bottom of the container, plant daffodils on a 4 inch (10 cm) layer of compost. Cover with the same amount, and plant another layer. Finally, top off with a layer of crocus to provide a real potful over an extended period.

You could also use wallflowers, bellis, pansies and forget-me-nots to make a very bright-looking container.

Winter containers are less successful, but they can work when filled with hardy subjects. For example, winter-flowering heathers mixed with ivies and perhaps the odd foliage shrub like a variegated pieris would look good all winter.

## Hanging baskets

Hanging baskets can be planted in much the same way as tubs and troughs. The art of a good basket is to finish up with a complete ball of colour, and that's not difficult to achieve. Start with the right basket. The shallow plastic types are really quite useless. Get the old-fashioned wire basket, or you can buy a similar pattern in plastic.

Line it with sphagnum moss which you can buy from the florist if you can't find your own. Put a saucer or a small square of poly-thene in the bottom to help retain water and three-quarters fill with compost. Then set in the same plants recommended for tubs and troughs, and in much the same way. Top up with compost and finally push some trailing lobelia through the moss and into the compost. This is done all round the bottom of the basket so that it eventually makes a complete globe of flower.

And there's no need to exclude the veg-etables even here. I've grown some very good tomatoes and several herbs in baskets, which look marvellous and taste wonderful too.

## PLANTING UP CONTAINERS

**1** *To make a hanging basket, start by lining a large wire basket with sphagnum moss. A piece of poly-thene in the bottom will help retain moisture.*

**2** *The plants can be really crammed in with taller ones in the centre, shorter ones to the outside and trailers on the edges.*

**3** *Further trailing plants can be pushed through the moss from the outside once the basket is hanging up. The result will be a complete ball of colour.*

# Chapter 6

## HERBS

Herbs have been used for centuries in medicines, as dyes, for perfumes, love potions and magic spells, and, first and foremost, to flavour our food. And it's for this latter purpose that the ornamental kitchen gardener will normally grow them.

They're tailor-made for the borders in this type of garden, of course, because most are very attractive and easy to grow, and many are a magnet for bees and butterflies. The taller ones make an eye-catching display mixed with cottage garden plants. Indeed, you feel when seeing them in this setting that this is the way they were *meant* to be grown. Lower-growing herbs like the thymes can be established between the paving slabs on the scree path, while others would be quite happy and would look fine in pots on the patio, though they all will grow well in the borders.

Alternatively, if you have enough room, herbs can be grown separately in a formal setting like a parterre (see p. 46). If you do that, though, check on the height and spread of the herbs first and grow only those easy to restrain that will not take over the plot.

The perennials will need little attention – just the odd clipping over perhaps, though regular harvesting generally does that job for you. The annuals are a little more trouble, but well worth it. They can be raised quite readily from seed sown in a slightly heated greenhouse in February or March or in a cold frame in March or even sown direct outside.

It's a good idea to propagate the perennial herbs to provide a few replacements now and then. If you're not vigilant with the pinching back, you may find that some, like rosemary and the sages, will become straggly. Once that happens, the only real solution is to dig up the plant and replace it. Most are very easy to propagate from softwood cuttings taken in June (see p. 150).

When you're choosing herbs, remember that some of the more ornamental varieties are just as good in the kitchen as their less colourful counterparts. Variegated sage, for example, looks good in the borders and has a very similar flavour to the green variety, while some of the golden thymes can be used for much the same purposes as the all-green ones.

**Balm (*Melissa officinalis*),** perennial, height 1 foot (30 cm)
Use in stuffings for poultry and in fish dishes. The leaves must be used young or they tend to become stringy and lose their flavour.

It prefers semi-shade and a moist root run, though too much shade will result in pallid leaves. Balm does well in tubs or containers.

Sow in a cool greenhouse or frame in March, or outside in April. Established plants can also be increased by division.

Cut the plants back quite hard in the autumn to encourage new young shoots to keep them bushy.

**Sweet Basil (*Ocimum basilicum*),** annual, height 1 foot (30 cm)
Use in egg, chicken and pasta dishes.

This is a plant that loves warmth and so it must be grown as an annual in cooler areas. It grows taller than bush basil. There's a good purple variety, *O. b.* 'Purpurascens', which has a slightly milder flavour.

Sow in modules or small pots in a slightly heated greenhouse in March, harden off in the cold frame and plant out in a sunny spot in late May or early June when all danger of frost has passed.

Keep well watered and pinch off flower buds if they appear or growth will slow down. In the autumn, a few plants can be cut down and potted and brought into the heated greenhouse or put on the windowsill, where they'll produce another crop of leaves for at least a few months.

**Bush Basil (*Ocimum minimum*),** annual, height 8 inches (20 cm)
Grow and use in the same way as sweet basil. This one is lower growing and slightly easier to grow, though the flavour is a little milder.

**Bay (*Laurus nobilis*),** perennial
Use in casseroles, stews and sauces. It can also be cooked with roast meat. Excellent both dried and fresh.

In cooler areas this shrub is best grown in a tub which can be moved inside in hard winters, since it is not reliably hardy. In warmer areas it can be left outside. It will grow into quite a large tree but can be clipped back regularly to keep it small. It's often grown as a formally clipped bush, so its height can be varied at will.

Trained specimens are very expensive, but bay plants can be propagated (though not easily) from softwood cuttings taken in June (see p. 150). Take more than you need to be sure of success.

During the growing season, make sure the pot doesn't dry out and feed weekly with a manure solution. The leaves can be picked and dried in the sun to preserve them.

**Borage (*Borago officinalis*),** annual, height 2 feet (60 cm)
Use in summer drinks and salads for its cucumber flavour. It can also be cooked like spinach.

One of the most attractive of herbs, this is more or less obligatory in the ornamental kitchen garden for its succession of fine blue flowers. It seeds itself readily so there will be no need to sow it more than once. It won't come up in the same place twice, of course, but in this garden that shouldn't matter. It's quite easy to lift the seedlings and transplant them when they're young. Sow in small pots inside in March or directly outside in April. It prefers a sunny spot.

Borage (*Borago officinalis*).

**Chervil (*Anthriscus cerefolium*),** annual, height 1 foot (30 cm)
Use in salads and fish, chicken and egg dishes for its parsley flavour. It makes a delicious soup and can be added to vinegar.

Chervil is a wonderfully cool-looking plant with heads of white like a dainty cow parsley. Unfortunately it has a tendency to run to seed if it becomes dry or suffers a check to growth. So grow it in semi-shade and water if necessary. Sow directly outside from March onwards at monthly intervals. Pick off flowers as soon as they're seen. Towards the end of the season, collect seed for next year or allow the plants to seed themselves.

**Chives (*Allium schoenoprasum*),** perennial, height 9 inches (30 cm)
Use as a garnish for salads and soups, and to add a mild onion flavour to cheese.

A good plant for the front of the border where it will provide plenty of fresh leaves and a flush of attractive round, pink flowers (keep a few clumps free from flowers by

*Chives (Allium schoenoprasum).*

picking them off: this will improve the flavour).

It's very easy to grow, preferring a sunny spot but not at all fussy. Propagate it by lifting the plants in spring and dividing into individual bulbs before replanting. They can also be started from seed sown in gentle heat in March or outside in April.

There are several other species of *Allium* that are worth growing, especially for their dramatic ornamental effect. The Welsh onion (*A. fistulosum*), for example, will grow much taller and stronger and look quite striking planted among the flowers. Garlic chives (*A. tuberosum*) has white, starry flowers in summer and the leaves have a marked garlic flavour excellent in salads and with cheese dishes.

**Dill (*Anethum graveolens*),** annual, height 3 feet (90 cm)
Dill has a wide range of uses since the whole plant can be utilized. The seeds flavour soups, fish dishes and even sweet dishes, while the flowers can be used in pickles. The leaves can be used in salads, and in meat and fish dishes, and also as a garnish.

Dill also produces wonderful yellow flower-heads, which have a strong aromatic perfume, and the foliage is feathery and attractive. All in all, it's one not to miss.

It likes a dry, sunny situation out of the wind and is best sown where it is to grow in April and then in succession every month or

so. Collect seeds at the end of the season for next year or allow to self-seed. Do not grow it near fennel or cross-pollination will occur.

**Fennel (*Foeniculum vulgare*),** perennial, height 6 feet (180 cm)
Its pleasant aniseed flavour adds a freshness to many dishes. The seeds have the strongest flavour and are crushed and used in sweet and savoury dishes while the leaves are used with salads, fish, poultry and meat.

Sow outside in April or in modules or small pots in gentle heat in March. Fennel likes full sun and a fertile soil because it has a useful life of up to five years. It will self-seed each year and the seedlings can be transplanted.

**Garlic (*Allium sativum*),** annual, height 1 foot (30 cm)
Use in all kinds of savoury dishes, with salads and to flavour bread.

Garlic demands, and should get, the sunniest spot in the garden. It is grown as an annual, by splitting bulbs into individual cloves and planting them every year. Put them in a patch about 6 inches (15 cm) apart so that they are just buried. The best time to plant them is the autumn – October or November – but if you miss the boat you'll get a good but slightly reduced crop from an early spring planting. In August or September, lift and dry them and hang them inside, making sure you save some cloves for replanting the following year.

**Lovage (*Levisticum officinale*),** perennial, height 9 feet (270 cm)
The leaves have a spicy, peppery taste and can be used in a variety of soups, stews and casseroles. The young stems are used in vegetable and poultry dishes and the seeds give a spicy flavour to cakes, biscuits and bread.

Lovage can be grown from seed sown in March in modules or pots but it's best to buy a plant initially. You certainly won't need more than one! Indeed, you will probably want to lift the plant and divide it after a few years because it does form very large clumps.

*Mint is one of the most useful herbs in the kitchen (see p. 176).*

*Bay (Laurus nobilis) (see p. 173).*

**Pot Marjoram (*Origanum onites*),** perennial, height 2 feet (60 cm)

This herb is used in all kinds of dishes that otherwise have a bland flavour – meat, fish, and egg dishes, stuffings, vegetables and salads.

It is the easiest marjoram to grow but has

*A well-stocked herb garden: both beautiful and useful.*

the least flavour. The small, pale pink or white flowers make it an attractive plant for the border and, like all marjorams, it attracts bees.

All the marjorams like a sunny spot and rich soil. They can be raised from seed sown inside in March or outside in April but germination is slow. Alternatively, take root or stem cuttings or divide the clumps. At the end of the season, pot up a clump or two and bring them inside where they'll continue to produce. They do well in pots outside if they're in full sun.

### Sweet Marjoram (*Origanum majorana*),
half-hardy perennial, height 18 inches (45 cm)
The most aromatic and flavoursome of the marjorams. It can be used in the same kind of dishes as pot marjoram.

Grow as for pot marjoram.

### Oregano (*Origanum vulgare*), perennial,
height 2 feet (60 cm)
This is the peasant of the three, with a stronger, penetrating flavour. It has good white or pink flowers but a slightly sprawling habit. Grow and use as pot marjoram.

### Mint (*Mentha rotundifolia*), perennial,
height 1 foot (30 cm)
This is probably the best known herb of all. Traditionally used to flavour lamb, peas and potatoes, it is also delicious in other vegetables, and for flavouring cold drinks and cold soups.

Mint is best bought as a plant, but grow it in a pot because the roots are very invasive indeed and must be contained. Even in a pot, you must make regular inspections to ensure that it hasn't hopped over the top and escaped! It's very easy to cultivate in sun or shade, demanding only a moist soil for the best supplies of leaves.

A winter supply can be grown by placing lengths of root in a box of potting compost in November and forcing the plants on the kitchen windowsill. If you wish to propagate more (though that's very doubtful!), do so in the same way, by root cuttings.

### Parsley (*Petroselinum crispum*), annual,
height 9 inches (23 cm)
Another popular herb, used as a garnish for just about anything and everything and to flavour fish and vegetables, soups and sauces.

Raise it from seed sown in modules in March or sow directly outside. It's slow to germinate so make sure it has adequate water. If the soil is dry at sowing time, water the drills well before sowing. Then all you need is patience and perhaps more water in dry weather.

It does well in pots and makes a fine edging plant for paths or as separations in the parterre or formal garden. It can also be grown in the greenhouse or on the windowsill.

### Rosemary (*Rosmarinus officinalis*),
perennial, height 3–4 feet (90–120 cm)
This hardy shrub looks handsome in the border, with blue flowers and grey-green aromatic foliage. It would be worth growing as a decorative plant even if it had no culinary usefulness. It's used in many meat dishes, notably lamb, and with vegetables, fish and in soups. It has a fairly strong flavour so should be used with caution.

Rosemary hates bad drainage, so if you have a heavy soil it's a good idea to lighten it with coarse grit. It can be raised from seed but takes a long time to reach any size. It's better to buy a plant from which you can take cuttings in June (see p. 150). Since it's evergreen, it will provide leaves all the year round and is certainly best kept well clipped in order to prevent it becoming straggly.

### Sage (*Salvia officinalis*), perennial,
height 2 feet (60 cm)
A well-known and very decorative herb which thrives in full sun. There are several coloured-leaved varieties which make excellent plants for the borders. The leaves are used widely in stuffings, in meat and cheese dishes and is sometimes mixed into pastry.

Plants can be raised from seed, but it's best to start with a plant from which cuttings can be taken. They root easily in June (see p. 150). An even easier way is to peg a shoot down to the ground, when it will root along its length to make several new plants. Give all sages a sunny spot and clip them regularly to prevent them becoming straggly. They should be replaced every few years.

*Gold-variegated sage (Salvia officinalis 'Icterina').*

## Summer Savory (*Satureia hortensis*),
annual, height 2 feet (60 cm)

A rather floppy annual with a peppery flavour, used notably with broad beans, in sausages, soups and stews, and in meat dishes.

It prefers a sunny spot and a well-drained soil. Raise it from seed sown inside in March or outside in April. Thin the seedlings to 6 inches (15 cm) apart. The yield is not high, so grow plenty. This plant has the advantage of being a superb bee attractor.

## Winter Savory (*Satureia montana*),
perennial, height 15 inches (38 cm)

Used for the same purposes as summer savory, but of course, being a perennial evergreen, it provides leaves all year round. It can be raised from seed sown outside in August. When sowing, don't cover the seeds because they need light to germinate. The plant can also be propagated from cuttings in June or by division. It's necessary to keep propagating since it's a short-lived plant and will need replacing every few years.

Like summer savory, it's an excellent bee plant.

## Tarragon (*Artemisia dracunculus*),
perennial, height 2 feet (60 cm)

Described as the 'king of the herbs', French tarragon is used in fish and chicken dishes, in stuffings, salads, vinegar, mayonnaise and with many meat dishes. It is an essential ingredient of Bearnaise and other sauces. In other words, it's indispensable.

Tarragon can't be successfully propagated from seed, so buy a plant to start with and propagate from cuttings taken in June (see p. 150). Give the plants a sunny spot and a well-drained soil and divide them every four years to prevent deterioration.

## Thyme (*Thymus vulgaris*),
perennial, height 3–12 inches (8–30 cm)

There are several types of thyme, from the creeping ones used on the scree path to the more upright common thyme which has the best flavour for cooking. It's worth growing a few varieties, which all look good and attract a million bees, and trying them out in the kitchen. Common thyme is best for stuffings, sauces and soups, poultry, shellfish and game, and especially for fatty foods. Lemon thyme is preferred by some cooks for its fruitier, less pungent flavour.

Thymes prefer sun and like a limy soil, so add lime at planting time if necessary. Common thyme is easy to raise from seed sown inside in March or outside in a warm spot in April or May. Others are best bought as plants and propagated from cuttings taken in June (see p. 150). To prevent thyme getting leggy, it's important to keep cutting it for the kitchen or, if you can't use enough, trimming it back hard in June. If it begins to spread farther than you want it to, simply chop it back with a spade. It does well in containers.

# Chapter 7

# VEGETABLES

The basic plan for the ornamental kitchen garden is to provide a self-sufficiency of vegetables and fruit right through the season, while at the same time enhancing the visual attraction of the garden. It's a tall order.

Of course, it would be silly to suggest that you could be self-sufficient regardless of the size of the plot. No one can produce a continuity of produce all year round from a postage stamp. But I'm quite certain that the methods described in this book will give you the highest yields possible from each square yard (sq. m).

The first thing you have to decide is the ratio of vegetables to ornamentals that you wish to sustain. This will vary depending on your fresh food requirement and the importance you place on filling the garden with flowers. A chap with a large family will probably want to increase the vegetable content, while a single person won't need nearly as much.

However much room you think you may need for produce, don't cut down on the ornamentals too much. Remember that they form a vital link in the natural chain, attracting the predators that will work for you as pest controllers. And however much of a philistine you may be, a few cheery flowers will certainly lift your spirits.

 ## PLANNING A CONTINUITY OF PRODUCE

There are two ways to maximize the yields from your garden. The first is to maintain such a high state of fertility that the plants can be grown at the greatest possible density. I believe the soil management principles I have suggested will achieve that. There's a constant need to maintain the input of organic matter and natural plant foods, but you'll be amply rewarded by heavier yields.

The second way is to spread the season over as long a period as possible. The longer you can increase the harvesting period at both ends of the season, the more your annual yields will increase. To achieve this, you'll certainly need a greenhouse, a cold frame and a few cloches, plus a supply of polythene sheeting.

Start the season by sowing in the greenhouse in pots, seed trays and modules. Sowing normally starts in the last week of January or early February. There's not a lot of point in starting earlier because plants respond to day length as well as temperature. So, however warm it may be in your greenhouse in December, day-length sensitive plants will not respond until the days get longer.

The first crops will come from those grown to maturity in the greenhouse, either in pots, growing bags or in the border soil. Salads like lettuce and radish will mature quite happily in pots, or they can be sown directly in the borders. The problem with relying on this method is one of space. I know I never have enough room at that time of year for much extra.

So the cold frame and cloches come into their own. Use the cold frame to take the overflow from the greenhouse when it's necessary. The lower temperatures will slow growth a little, but you'll still get much earlier yields. Put the cloches out at least two weeks before sowing or planting to warm up the soil and you'll be harvesting much better quality vegetables from a week to a full month before those grown in the open ground. Elsewhere, you should certainly cover pieces of ground with polythene sheeting in early winter to keep it dry and to warm it up for the earliest start.

If you have room outside but none in the greenhouse, it's a good idea to make use of a hotbed for raising early vegetables. For urban gardeners who have no access to farmyard manure, the system produces a double benefit.

In most areas, even right in the centre of large industrial cities, fresh horse manure is available. If you have difficulty finding it, check the trade telephone directory under 'Riding Stables'. I guarantee you'll always find at least one or two.

You should never put fresh manure on the garden, of course. It'll need to be stacked for at least six months and preferably a year before use. Pile it into a heap at least 3 feet (90 cm) square and the same height – bigger if possible. Cover the top with about 6 inches (15 cm) of good soil or compost and leave it for a week or so to warm up. You can test the temperature by pushing a stick into the heap and feeling it when you pull it out.

Once it has warmed up, put your cold frame over the top and sow or plant your early crops in the topsoil. Naturally the heap will begin to cool after a while but by that time the weather will have warmed up and your plants will be away. At the end of the season you're left with a heap of well-rotted manure for the borders.

At the other end of the season, you can use your cloches to cover later sown or planted crops which would otherwise not mature before the first frosts. Things like bush tomatoes often benefit from cloche cover in autumn as it helps to ripen the last of the fruit.

In the frames and the greenhouse, various crops can be sown which will overwinter to mature very early the following year.

Planning a succession of sowing outside can be a bit of a headache. It's very easy to advise that lettuce, for example, should be sown at intervals to give a continuity of cropping, but I know from bitter experience how difficult that is in practice. It's the easiest thing in the world to forget that vital sowing and to be left with nothing for a few weeks. If that happens in my garden, I always make myself go without for a time rather than buying in. That soon disciplines the mind, because I'm quite keen on my fresh vegetables!

Fortunately, it's a lot easier with this system of gardening, because everything is grown in small patches. You get quite used to assessing what's needed when you walk round from time to time.

Try also to perfect the art of having a few plants waiting in the wings to go on. My patio is always full of plants in pots and boxes, waiting for a space. You may have to throw the odd one or two on the compost heap, but it doesn't seem to happen often.

*Making a hotbed.*

## SELECTING WHAT TO GROW

If your garden is enormous, grow every possible vegetable you can. There's no greater enjoyment to be had from the land and certainly no healthier way to eat. Alas, most of us have to make do with less than enough space, so we have to make a few hard choices.

The first rule, I suppose, is to avoid those crops that the farmer or grower does as well or better than you at much the same price or, I have to say it, cheaper. Maincrop potatoes are a perfect example. You'll never grow them as cheaply as the farmer can and, since you have to store them as well, the quality and freshness are no better. Having said that, you *do* have the opportunity to grow them organically, of course, so there are some advantages. Maincrop peas are another case in point. The freezer companies can afford to pick them all on the one day the crop's at its best, and to freeze them more or less immediately. There's not a lot of difference in flavour in my view. So, if you're short of space, perhaps those two should go. Mind you, I would certainly grow early potatoes because the flavour is so much better when they're dug fresh, and I wouldn't be without mangetout peas.

Next I would suggest you grow those vegetables that taste a lot better fresh than when they've hung around the wholesale market and then in the shop for up to a week. Crops like spinach and lettuce are much better picked fresh and used before they begin to wilt. Sweet corn is much, much sweeter when it's picked fresh, because the moment a cob is taken from the plant the sugar in the seeds begins to turn to starch. Old gardeners reckoned you should put the saucepan on to boil, take a stroll down to the vegetable plot, cut the cob and run back!

Some crops are better home grown because the gardener has the choice of varieties with a superior flavour. While the commercial grower looks to a variety to produce high yields, disease resistance, uniformity and a good appearance and worries little about flavour, the gardener has the luxury of being able to choose his varieties for what they taste like. Try growing 'Ailsa Craig' tomatoes or 'Concorde' early potatoes, for example, and you're bound to agree.

Finally, go for those vegetables that are expensive or unobtainable. I'm quite sure the growers of globe artichokes are all millionaires, because the prices are just ludicrous. I can grow them in my garden to taste five times better than shop-bought ones, and at only a fifth of the cost. That's when you can find a shop that stocks them!

## CHOOSING VARIETIES

When you've decided what to grow, get hold of a seed catalogue and choose your varieties. You'll find yourself faced with an agonizing choice because every one of them is described in glowing terms. In this garden there are a few points to bear in mind.

First, look for varieties which have some form of pest or disease resistance (see p. 245). This is one of the great advantages in modern plant breeding and is of enormous help to the organic gardener. I'm certain that the breeding of resistant varieties will be the way pest control will go in the future. There are already many varieties worth growing for that reason.

Selection for flavour is, of course, something you must learn over the years. So it's a jolly good idea to grow a few new varieties every season or you may never know what you've missed.

Look for those varieties that are attractive in the borders too. There are quite a few that taste just as good as their plainer cousins but look much better. Ruby chard, for example, tastes every bit as good as ordinary Swiss chard and the red Brussels sprout 'Rubine' has a wonderful flavour.

Finally, there is the vexed question of $F_1$ hybrid varieties. You'll sometimes see the symbol F$_1$ on seed packets or in the catalogue alongside some newer varieties. These have to go through the complicated process of hand rearing every time new seed is needed, so they're quite a bit more expensive than those that are pollinated by insects in the field. Though they do certainly have the great advantage of what the breeders call 'hybrid vigour', you must bear in mind that they have all been bred with the commercial grower in mind and that his requirements could be quite different to ours. He wants, for example, to harvest all his Brussels sprouts in one go, while that's the last thing we want. He wants all his crop to be of uniform size and shape, but the home gardener may well want a big cabbage on the day Auntie Maud and her family visit and a small one when he's on his own. Remember, too, that flavour is often the last thing in the commercial grower's list of priorities, so treat F$_1$ hybrid varieties with caution. I suppose a season's trial is really the only way of knowing.

## ✺ FEEDING ✺

Vegetables in the borders will thrive on a diet of well-rotted manure or compost plus the applications of blood, fish and bone meal I have suggested before planting or sowing each crop (see p. 76). However, plants grown in pots will have to be fed with a liquid fertilizer.

Seaweed is a good tonic, but not very high in nutrients. It's best, if you can, to make your own. If you have access to animal manure, a good liquid fertilizer can be made by filling a sack with manure and hanging it in a tank of water. The resulting liquid is used neat. If you are unable to obtain the manure, there are several proprietary organic brands of fertilizer available at the garden centre.

## ✺ SOWING ✺

I have already explained the technique of sowing flowers and vegetables in patches rather than in straight lines (p. 80), but there are a couple of points worth adding.

Sometimes it's easier to sow in 'stations' than in rows. This simply means that for those crops with big seeds, like beetroot, peas or beans, instead of sowing in a row and then removing most of the plants later, you sow two or three seeds at the distances you'll eventually want them. When they germinate you then thin to leave the strongest seedling.

Sowing will go on right through the summer. This can mean putting seeds into dry soil, which is never a good idea. To avoid it, draw the drills and then run a little water into them. Allow the water to drain away, sow the seeds and then cover with dry soil. Don't water again until the seeds germinate. This avoids the formation of the hard crust that forms on the surface when you water after sowing.

*Feeding with a liquid seaweed fertilizer.*

## 🐿 THE VEGETABLES 🐿

### Asparagus

Asparagus needs a well-drained soil. On heavy land, improve drainage by raising the area and working in coarse grit and organic matter. Its fern-like foliage makes it an attractive plant for the border.

*Varieties.* Choose an all-male variety which expends no energy producing seeds. 'Lucullus' is an excellent, proven one while the newer 'Franklim' produces thicker spears and a heavier crop.

*Raising.* Asparagus can be raised from seed sown in gentle heat in February. Transfer the seedlings into small pots and plant out after hardening off, in June. Generally it's quicker to buy crowns. Make sure they're one-year-olds as these will establish better.

*Planting.* If you buy crowns, soak them in water for an hour as soon as they arrive. Plant them immediately, setting them in threes or fives, with 1 foot (30 cm) between the crowns.

*Cultivation.* Make sure the plants don't go short of water and give them a feed of blood, fish and bone meal in the spring. Cut down the yellowing foliage in autumn and mulch the crowns with good compost.

*Harvesting.* Cutting can start in the second year with these new varieties, but don't cut more than one spear per crown until the third year. Allow the spears to grow about 4 inches (10 cm) above ground and cut below the soil as far as you can. Always leave some shoots to make leaf to build up the plant for next year.

### Globe Artichokes

A real gourmet treat and a superb border plant too. Its striking, thistle-like grey foliage makes a dramatic effect, especially if underplanted with low-growing flowers in blues or reds.

*Varieties.* 'Green Globe' is an old favourite and difficult to beat.

*Globe artichoke.*

*Sowing.* Artichokes are easy to raise from seed germinated at a temperature of 65°F (18°C) in late January or February. Sow two seeds per 3 inch (7.5 cm) pot and thin to leave the strongest seedling.

*Planting.* Plant out in April, putting single plants towards the middle of a sunny border. If you grow more than one in a group, space them 18 inches (45 cm) apart.

*Cultivation.* There's not much to do except watering and weeding. They can be retained to grow on the following year but will need more room, so thin out to 3 feet (90 cm) apart.

*Harvesting.* Cut the flower-heads while they're still closed for the tenderest flesh.

### Jerusalem Artichokes

A tall perennial not suitable for the borders. Grow it in a row at the end of the garden for a superb summer windbreak. The tubers are indispensable in winter. They contain no starch and are therefore ideal for slimmers.

*Varieties.* 'Fuseau' is the smoothest, and therefore easiest to peel.

*Planting.* Plant the tubers 1 foot (30 cm) apart in early spring.

*Cultivation.* Cut down the stems in early winter.

*Harvesting.* Dig during the winter as required.

*Jerusalem artichoke 'Fuseau'.*

## Aubergines

In cooler areas the aubergine must be regarded as a greenhouse vegetable. It's easy to grow in pots and could be stood outside in a sunny, sheltered spot if greenhouse room is scarce. Grown well, most plants should produce about six fruits.

*Varieties.* Several varieties are offered by seedsmen but I can find little difference between them. 'Moneymaker' and 'Black Prince' both produce good crops of well flavoured fruit.
*Raising.* Sow at a temperature of 65–70°F (18–21°C) in February or March. Transfer the seedlings to 3 inch (7.5 cm) pots when the seed-leaves are large enough to handle and reduce the temperature to 60°F (15°C).
*Planting.* When the roots form a good cover on the outside of the root-ball, transfer the plants into 9 inch (23 cm) pots of soilless potting compost.
*Cultivation.* Support the plants with canes and feed them at every watering with a liquid tomato feed. Pinch out the tops of the plants when they're about 1 foot (30 cm) tall. Also, pinch out the side-shoots when you can see that the plants have formed small fruits. Allow only about six fruits per plant.

If plants succumb to attack by whitefly when they're in the greenhouse, put the pots outside (provided all danger of frost has passed), and spray them with a strong jet of water (though, of course, not strong enough to damage the plants!). It won't be long before the whitefly disappear. Alternatively, hoover them off.
*Harvesting.* Pick the fruit while it's still shiny. Once the shine goes off the skin, the fruits will be tough.

## Broad Beans

A useful vegetable for this garden because it provides plenty of nourishing, protein-packed food, lots of green waste for the compost heap and nitrogen compounds made by bacteria in the roots, which are released to the next crop when the tops are cut off.

*Varieties.* Under cloches, use 'The Sutton', a short variety which fits under them for longer. For the main crop use 'Jubilee Hysor', or 'Relon' if you prefer green beans.
*Sowing.* In February, start sowing in the greenhouse in small pots or modules for planting out under cloches in March. Alternatively, sow directly under cloches in February, setting the beans about 6 inches (15 cm) apart. Sow the main crop in March or April outside, setting the seeds two to a station in a rough circle with about 6 inches (15 cm) between each station.
*Cultivation.* Remove the cloches as soon as the plants grow to touch the tops. To support maincrop beans, put a 4 foot (120 cm) cane in the middle of the circle and hold the beans with loops of string.
*Harvesting.* Pick the beans in succession as they mature. Leave one or two pods on the plants to dry. These can be re-sown in August or early September in the same way, but this time it's the tender tops of the plants that are picked in October or November – they're delicious stir-fried or lightly boiled. After harvesting all the beans, cut the tops off at ground level, putting the haulm on the compost heap and digging the roots back in to release the nitrogen compounds formed in them.

## French Beans

French beans are generally grown as small bushes though there are also climbing varieties which are grown in the same way as runners. Like broad beans, they make nitrogen compounds in their roots.

*Varieties.* 'Daisy' produces long round pods which are held above the plants making them easy to pick. 'Kinghorn Wax' has bright yellow pods which look most attractive in the borders, while 'Purple Queen' has deep purple pods. All three produce beans of fine flavour. If you prefer climbing beans, go for 'Purple Podded', which looks very attractive and tastes delicious, or 'Blue Lake', which can be allowed to develop large beans for use as haricots.

*Sowing.* French beans like warm conditions, so don't sow too early. I like to produce some plants in pots in the greenhouse, sowing two seeds to a 3 inch (7.5 cm) pot in March and April. When they germinate, thin to leave the strongest seedling. Start sowing outside under cloches in early April and without protection in early May. They look best in threes though they can, of course, be grown singly.

*Planting.* Plant out in late May or early June.

*Cultivation.* There's little to do except to keep the plants watered and weeded. In hot, dry weather it'll pay to mulch round the plants with coarse bark, partly to help conserve moisture and partly to deter slugs.

*Harvesting.* Pick the pods for immediate eating, when they are still young. When they get old, they tend to become stringy so it may be necessary to harvest every couple of days or so. For haricot beans and storing in airtight jars, leave the pods on the plants until they become dry and brown.

## Runner Beans

Pretty certainly the most prolific of all vegetable crops. You simply can't do without runners. If you choose the right varieties they can also make very attractive flowering plants. Climbing beans are grown in the same way.

*Varieties.* The most attractive of all is the old variety 'Painted Lady', with contrasting red and white flowers. However, if you prefer more modern varieties, you can achieve the same effect by growing a red-flowered variety like 'Polestar' next to the white-flowered 'Mergoles'.

*Sowing.* The method I prefer is to sow in the greenhouse in April as it generally avoids slug damage. Sow two seeds in a 3 inch (7.5 cm) pot and thin to leave the strongest seedling. Alternatively, sow against the canes in early May, sowing two seeds per cane and again thinning.

*Planting.* Ideally, set the canes 1 foot (30 cm) apart along the pergola or on the rose arbour. Runners look extremely attractive as ornamental climbers, especially among roses. Alternatively, make a wigwam of canes, again

*Runner bean 'Mergoles'.*

1 foot (30 cm) apart in a border, or grow them up the fence on canes fixed to wires. Plant out after all danger of frost has passed, generally in early June.

*Cultivation.* You may have to help the plants up the right canes to start with but they soon take hold. Protect the young plants from slugs with plastic bottles (having cut off the bottoms) or by mulching with coarse bark.

*Harvesting.* Pick the beans when they're still very young. Letting them get too big produces stringy beans and also discourages the production of more pods. If you have to go on holiday, get a neighbour to keep picking.

## Beetroot

The snag with beetroot is that its red leaves and its delicious roots make it such an attractive and useful border plant that you're likely to grow too much! Try to keep a succession of young roots ready for harvest plus a main pulling for winter storage.

*Varieties.* There are plenty of seeds in a packet, so don't waste money by buying more than one variety. 'Boltardy' will produce good baby beet and will store well too.

*Sowing.* The first sowing can be made in February, in the greenhouse in modules. Beetroot seed consists of several seeds in a single cluster. Sow two clusters of seeds per cell and don't thin the seedlings when they appear. Make the first outdoor sowing in March under cloches or in early April without cover. From then on sow at three-weekly intervals until July. Sow in stations with two seeds per station, setting them about 2 inches (5 cm) apart. Because of their decorative value, they are best sown near the front of the border in a patch of about six stations. When the seedlings appear, there's generally no need to thin. The plants will simply push each other out of the way to grow into excellent baby beet. The main crop for storage is sown, again in patches, in July but

these are thinned to leave a single plant every 9 inches (23 cm).

*Planting.* Young beet plants raised in modules can be planted out under cloches in early April and outside without cover later in the month. Plant them in patches with about 9 inches (23 cm) between each cluster.

*Cultivation.* Simply keep them well watered and weed-free.

*Harvesting.* Pull when the roots are still young and tender. Harvest the main crop in autumn and store in boxes of sand in a frost-free place.

## Broccoli

Under this heading I have included calabrese, which is harvested in summer, and sprouting broccoli, which is ready to eat in winter.

*Varieties.* For the earliest crop of calabrese use 'Mercedes', which is ready in July. Follow this with 'Corvet', for harvesting in September, and then the very decorative 'Romanesco', which has most attractive yellow heads like a cluster of coral and is ready in late autumn. For sprouting broccoli which will mature in late winter and early spring, use 'White Sprouting' or 'Purple Sprouting' but remember that they are very large plants and take up room for a long time. Only for the bigger garden really.

*Sowing.* Sow calabrese and sprouting broccoli in short rows in April or May.

*Planting.* Water the rows well and lift the seedlings when they're 3–4 inches (7.5–10 cm) high and transplant them to the borders. You won't need many plants of sprouting broccoli because they produce well, so three or four plants towards the middle of the border will do. Plant 'Romanesco' nearer the front of the border where its attractive head can be seen. If you plant groups of plants, space calabrese 1 foot (30 cm) apart and sprouting broccoli 2 feet (60 cm) apart.

*Cultivation.* Remove yellowing leaves from the bottom of the plants.

*Harvesting.* Cut the central head of calabrese first and side-shoots will grow later. Pick sprouting broccoli regularly to encourage further production. Remove the stumps immediately after the plants have finished and crush or shred them for the compost heap.

## Brussels Sprouts

It has to be said that this is not an attractive plant in the winter, so place it where it will be unobtrusive. It's certainly a very useful winter vegetable and not to be missed.

*Varieties.* There is just one attractive variety which you should certainly be growing in full view. 'Rubine' will not achieve the weight of crop of some of the hybrids, but it's blessed with attractive red leaves and sprouts and a very fine flavour indeed. Follow that with 'Montgomery', which does not have a pretty face but crops from December until March.
*Sowing.* Sow in short rows in March or April.
*Planting.* When the seedlings are 4 inches (10 cm) tall, plant them out either singly or in groups with 2 feet (60 cm) between plants. Fill in around them with low-growing annuals like marigolds for best effect.
*Cultivation.* Remove yellowing leaves and support over-tall plants with a cane if necessary.
*Harvesting.* Pick the sprouts from the bottom as they mature, removing the leaves up to where you've picked.

## Cabbage

You can grow cabbages all the year round and they form an important part of the diet. I never grow them during the height of the summer, however, because I don't want them when there are beans, peas, courgettes, etc. For the rest of the year they're indispensable. If you think they won't look attractive, try growing them singly or in threes, surrounded by wallflowers or, later on, tagetes. Certainly

you continually need to remove yellowing leaves to keep them looking good, but you should always do that anyway. If your soil is plagued with club root you will have to take special precautions (see p. 248).

*Cabbage 'Ruby Ball'.*

## Spring Cabbage

The first to be harvested during the year and very welcome in the 'hungry gap' of April and May.

*Varieties.* 'Myatts Offenham Compacta' can be used for spring greens or left to heart up later. 'Pixie' can be planted closer and makes a small heart with few outer leaves.
*Sowing.* Sow thinly in short rows in early August.
*Planting.* Plant when the cabbages are about 4 inches (10 cm) tall, preferably in threes or fives, allowing 6 inches (15 cm) between plants.
*Cultivation.* Don't let them go short of water in the early stages. In late January it pays to give them another dressing of blood, fish and bone meal to get them going again after the winter.
*Harvesting.* In April there will be spring greens to harvest. Pull up every other plant to allow

1 foot (30 cm) between the remaining plants. They can be left to heart up later or can also be pulled for greens if required.

## Summer Cabbage

*Varieties.* 'Hispi' is still the best variety, producing very early, pointed hearts of the finest quality.

*Sowing.* The first sowing is made in the cool greenhouse in late January. Sow in a seed tray or small pot at a temperature of about 60°F (15°C). When the seedlings are large enough to handle, transplant to wider spacings in seed trays. Later, in March, sowings can be made outside in short rows. In my view, later sowings than this are not required but it is possible to sow outside until May.

*Planting.* Plant the greenhouse-raised plants under cloches in March, setting them 9 inches (23 cm) apart. Transplant the outdoor-raised plants singly, or in groups of three or five, at the same spacings.

*Cultivation.* Just keep the plants weed-free and watered.

*Harvesting.* Cut the hearts when they are hard and dig up the stalk.

## Late Summer and Autumn and Winter Cabbage

*Varieties.* 'Castello' is an excellent autumn variety which stands for three months before bursting. For winter, 'Tundra' is one of the hardiest, standing in good condition from November to late April. If you want red cabbages, go for 'Ruby Ball', which stands from August until January, looking attractive all the time. The crinkled, blueish leaves of Savoys always enhance the border. 'Taler' is ready in October and 'Wivoy' from January to April.

*Sowing.* Sow thinly in short rows in April.

*Planting.* Transplant 2 feet (60 cm) apart when the plants are 4 inches (10 cm) tall.

*Harvesting.* Leave the plants in the ground over winter and cut them as required.

Cauliflower (see p. 188).

Celeriac (see p. 188).

## Carrots

One of the most useful of vegetables for eating raw or cooked, so keep up a supply throughout the year. In addition, the feathery foliage is a great asset in the border.

*Varieties.* For the earliest sowings use 'Rondo', which has round roots. Follow with sowings under cloches using 'Early Nantes' and then outside with 'Berlicum Berjo', which can be sown in succession to be used fresh and will also store well.

*Sowing.* Sow the first crop in late January in modules in the cool greenhouse, sowing six seeds to a cell. Don't thin the seedlings. The second sowing is made in February under cloches, in shallow drills 6 inches (15 cm) apart. The outdoor sowings start in March and go on at monthly intervals until July, again in patches in shallow drills 6 inches (15 cm) apart. The plants from sowings in the open ground are thinned out to 6 inches (15 cm) apart.

*Planting.* The early crop raised in modules is planted in March under cloches, setting the blocks of seedlings 6 inches (15 cm) apart. Make sure the blocks are very well watered before planting.

*Cultivation.* There is nothing to do except weeding and watering. You should take precautions against carrot fly if you've had trouble in the past (see p. 243).

*Harvesting.* Pull the first crops as required, and similarly those that are sown in succession during spring and summer. The final crop is used for storing during the winter. Lift the roots in early November, cut off the tops to leave about $\frac{1}{2}$ inch (13 cm) and store the roots in sand or vermiculite in a frost-free place.

## Cauliflower

The most difficult vegetable of all to grow. You need a fertile soil, the ability to water by hand if necessary and certainly an absence of club root in the soil. But cauliflowers make superb eating and are very attractive vegetables. The secret of success with them is to get the plants growing well and then to *keep* them that way. A single check to growth can spell disaster.

*Varieties.* You'll need several varieties if you want a succession of harvesting. For the earliest crop in summer, use either 'Alpha' or 'Montano'. Follow this with 'Nevada' or 'Dok Elgon' for late summer and autumn cropping, and then 'Veitch's Self-Protecting' for early winter. For late winter you can't beat the very attractive 'Purple Cape', and 'Walcheren Winter' goes through to April.

*Sowing.* Sow the early varieties in the cool greenhouse in late January. Transfer to seed trays at a wider spacing when the seedlings are big enough. The rest can be sown in April or May in short rows.

*Planting.* Plant the early crop as soon as conditions permit in March, first under cloches and later outside. Set the plants in groups with 9–12 inches (23–30 cm) between plants. Later varieties should be planted 2 feet apart when they are about 4 inches (10 cm) tall, again in groups. Never let the transplants get too big, as a check to growth will occur.

*Cultivation.* Water by hand in dry weather. Winter varieties will benefit from a feed of blood, fish and bone meal in February. If sharp frosts are forecast when the curds are mature and ready for cutting, snap a few leaves over them for protection.

*Harvesting.* Cut while the curds are still tight.

## Celeriac

The swollen stem of the celeriac makes a delicious winter vegetable, either grated in salads or cooked.

*Varieties.* 'Snow White' or 'Tellus' are both good varieties.

*Sowing.* As for celery.

*Planting.* Plant outside in groups 10 inches (25 cm) apart.

*Harvesting.* Lift during winter as required. Celeriac is perfectly hardy.

## Celery

Blanched varieties don't suit this type of garden, but self-blanching types, now of excellent quality, are attractive and productive.

*Varieties.* 'Celebrity' is the best, producing long, crisp sticks which will even stand a little frost. Most celery seed is treated with a fungicide, so try to find an untreated source.
*Sowing.* Sow in the greenhouse in a temperature of 65°F (18°C) on the surface of a pot or tray of soilless compost. Just cover with a little vermiculite, as the seeds need light to germinate. Transfer to wider spacings and harden off before planting out.
*Planting.* An early crop can be obtained by planting under cloches or in a frame. The main crop comes in the autumn. Plant out in groups with 9 inches (23 cm) between plants.
*Cultivation.* Keep plants well watered and protect against slugs with a mulch of coarse bark. If frost threatens, cover with spun polypropylene fleece.
*Harvesting.* Pull complete plants as required.

## Chicory

There are two types of chicory, one which is used in autumn and early winter, much like a lettuce, and the forcing variety, which makes excellent salad right through winter.

*Varieties.* For autumn salads use 'Sugar Loaf' and the red type which is sold as 'Radicchio'. Both look wonderful towards the front of the border. For forcing use 'Normato', which produces compact white 'chicons' all winter.
*Sowing.* Sow forcing chicory outside in April, in patches, in shallow drills 6 inches (15 cm) apart and thin to the same distance. Sow the other types outside in June or July in drills 10 inches (25 cm) apart. Don't sow earlier or the plants will run to seed, and in any case, your lettuces will serve you better until the autumn.
*Cultivation.* During the summer, weeding and watering are all that's required. When frost threatens, salad types can be protected with cloches and should then continue to produce good heads throughout the winter.
*Forcing.* Lift the roots in November. Cut off the tops, leaving about ½ inch (13 mm), and store them in sand or vermiculite. Take four or five roots out of store as required during the winter, trim the roots at the bottom to make them about 12 inches (30 cm) long and plunge them into a deep box of moist bark in the greenhouse or even in the kitchen. The warmer they are, the faster they'll grow. The roots should be covered with about 9 inches (23 cm) of bark, so I use a 2 foot (60 cm) deep tub which, during summer, is used on the patio. Then all you have to do is to check periodically for progress and use the chicons when they're about 8 inches (20.5 cm) long.

## Chinese Cabbage

A useful and interesting vegetable for salads or cooking.

*Varieties.* 'Tip Top' and 'Kasumi' are both resistant to bolting.
*Sowing.* Don't sow too early or the plants will run to seed. Sow in May, in small patches where the plants are to mature, in stations 9 inches (23 cm) apart, with two or three seeds per station. Thin to one plant.
*Cultivation.* It's very important to keep the plants moist or they'll run to seed.
*Harvesting.* Cut the hearts eight to ten weeks after sowing.

## Courgettes

A couple of plants will keep cropping throughout the summer to give you delicious courgettes for the asking. What's more, if this wasn't a vegetable, it would be eagerly sought after as an ornamental plant. It has attractive foliage and huge, orange-yellow trumpet-shaped flowers followed by shining fruits in emerald green or brilliant yellow. You may gather that I'm a courgette enthusiast!

*Varieties*. 'Ambassador' gives heavy crops of glossy green, cylindrical fruits, while 'Gold Rush' has early fruits of golden yellow.
*Sowing*. In April, sow individually in 3 inch (7.5 cm) pots of soilless compost, setting the seeds on their sides about 1 inch (2.5 cm) deep. Germinate them in a temperature of about 65°F (18°C). Grow the seedlings on at 50–55°F (10–13°C) and start to harden the young plants off in early May. Plant them out when all danger of frost has passed.
*Planting*. Plant towards the front of the border. If you plant more than one, space them 24 inches (60 cm) apart. You'll need to get at them every other day to harvest the fruits.
*Cultivation*. Keep the plants well watered at all times. Mulch underneath with straw or bark to keep the fruit off the ground and to help deter slugs.
*Harvesting*. Cut the fruits when they're about 6 inches (15 cm) long. Keep cutting at this stage, even if you have to give the fruits away, as this will encourage continuous production.

*Courgette 'Golden Zucchini'.*

## Cucumbers

Cultivation details are on p. 192 with those for marrows and squashes.

## Fennel

Not to be confused with the herb, Florence fennel is grown for its fleshy, bulbous stems, which can be used raw or cooked. It has a delicious, slightly aniseed flavour.

*Varieties*. 'Perfection' is a variety fairly resistant to running to seed. It is often listed in seed catalogues as simply 'fennel' or sometimes 'finocchio'.
*Sowing*. Sow from mid-May to July, in patches, in shallow drills about 9 inches (23 cm) apart and thin the seedlings to the same distance.
*Cultivation*. It's very important to keep the plants well watered or they'll run to seed. When the bulbs start to swell, mulch between the plants with compost and draw it up around the bulbs to keep them tender.
*Harvesting*. Cut the heads three weeks or more after dressing with compost. If the compost is drawn well up the plant, it will stand a certain amount of frost.

## Kale

The modern varieties of this vegetable are definite improvements and make it a useful winter standby.

*Varieties*. 'Dwarf Green Curled' is the best for this type of garden because it's tasty and its curled leaves are very decorative.
*Sowing*. Sow in short rows in April.
*Planting*. Transplant singly or in groups of three towards the middle of the border, setting the plants 2 feet (60 cm) apart.
*Cultivation*. Just keep the plants watered and weed-free.
*Harvesting*. Pull young, tender leaves from the centre of the plants during the winter.

## Kohl Rabi

A much underrated vegetable in my view. It has a fairly bland flavour, I suppose, when cooked and eaten like turnip. But blended and made into a soup, it's delicious. And when chopped raw, it adds an unusual taste to salads. Its peculiar, sputnik-like bulbs make it an interesting plant to grow near the front of the border.

*Varieties.* 'Purple Vienna' has bright purple bulbs and makes an attractive show as well as having a fine flavour. 'Rowel' is juicy and crisp and certainly the best for eating raw.
*Sowing.* Sow in short rows in succession from March to July.
*Planting.* As soon as the seedlings are about 3 inches (7.5 cm) tall, transplant in patches near the front of the border, spacing the plants 9 inches (45 cm) apart.
*Cultivation.* Give the plants plenty of water and keep them weed-free.
*Harvesting.* Pull when the bulbs are a little larger than a golf ball. The smaller they are, the sweeter and crisper they'll be. It is possible to store the later maturing bulbs in vermiculite for several months.

*Trailing marrow (see p. 192) amidst Rudbeckia hirta 'Marmalade'.*

*Lettuce (see p. 192).*

## Land Cress

A vegetable that's not used as much as it should be. It's easy to grow and makes a perfect substitute for watercress. Try it in soups or raw.

*Varieties.* It's sold simply as 'Land Cress' or 'American Cress'.
*Sowing.* Make two sowings in patches near the front of the border in rows 6 inches (15 cm) apart and thin to 6 inches (15 cm). The first should be in April for summer use and the second in September for the winter.
*Cultivation.* Make sure the plants never go short of water.
*Harvesting.* Pick over the plants as required.

## Leeks

A traditional winter vegetable with a fine, mild onion flavour. Some varieties have dark blue leaves which are very decorative.

*Varieties.* 'Giant Winter Wila' is very hardy and has dark blue foliage, but an even better colour can be found with a French variety, 'St Victor', which is really deep blue.
*Sowing.* There are two methods. I sow in modules in the greenhouse in late March, putting six seeds in each cell. When the seedlings appear, don't thin them. They're planted

out as they are and will simply push each other apart during the season to eventually produce perfect leeks. Don't be tempted to sow earlier, as then the plants will run to seed later in the year. The alternative method is to sow outside in short rows in early April for transplanting.

*Planting.* In late April or May, plant out the module-raised plants in groups of three or five blocks (which will give you something like 18–30 plants in all) in the middle of the border with 1 foot (30 cm) between the blocks. There's no need to bury these module-raised plants because they'll blanch each other by being so close together. Those raised outside should be planted in May in groups 6 inches (15 cm) apart, dropping each plant into a 6 inch (15 cm) deep hole made with a dibber.

*Cultivation.* Blanch the stems by mulching with compost as the plants grow. Make sure they never go short of water.

*Harvesting.* Leeks are hardy so they can be pulled any time during the winter as required. If you need to cultivate the space, they can be lifted and heeled in, just covering the roots.

## Lettuces

Certainly the most popular salad vegetable and a succession can be achieved throughout most of the year. Lettuces look very attractive towards the front of the border and there are some coloured varieties available.

*Varieties.* Start by sowing in the greenhouse and later under cloches, using the quick-maturing 'Tom Thumb', a nutty-flavoured cabbage lettuce, or the small crisp cos variety 'Little Gem'. Follow this during the summer with 'Saladin', a fine crisp variety, or, if you prefer the softer, butterhead types, I would recommend 'Sigmaball'. I have little success with lettuce overwintered outside but would certainly grow 'Plus' in a cold frame in winter and 'Kellys' in the greenhouse for harvesting in April. If you prefer a cut-and-come-again type, grow the attractive 'Red Salad Bowl' or

the crinkly leafed 'Lollo Rossa'.

*Sowing.* Start sowing in gentle heat in late January. The next sowing is made under cloches in late February and then outside in short rows from March until August. Thin the plants in rows to 6 inches (15 cm) apart for the early crops and 9 inches (23 cm) for the 'Saladin'. Sow in the cold frame in October and in the greenhouse border in November. During the summer, make sure you sow in short rows with about two weeks between sowings, to achieve a succession of harvesting.

*Planting.* Young lettuces raised in the greenhouse should be planted under cloches in February, setting them 6 inches (15 cm) apart. The thinnings from the plants sown outside should also be replanted, and these will mature slightly later than the ones left in. Set the early varieties 6 inches (15 cm) apart and the later ones 9 inches (23 cm) apart. All should be planted in groups of about five or six near the front of the border.

*Cultivation.* Make sure the plants are regularly weeded and watered.

*Harvesting.* Cut when you can feel that the hearts are hard. The cut-and-come-again varieties can be picked over as required.

## Marrows, Squashes and Cucumbers

I've grouped these types together because they're very similar and are grown in exactly the same way. They can all be grown up the pergola or rose arch, or on a wigwam of stout poles in the border. Grown this way they take up little room and look very dramatic indeed.

*Varieties.* Marrows are very much alike in flavour, so choose the most attractive. I like 'Long Green Striped', which is striped green and yellow, or 'Table Dainty', which produces smaller fruits that are otherwise similar in appearance. 'Sunburst' is a custard squash, round and flat with scalloped edges, and looks marvellous growing up the pergola. So too do the yellow, rugby-ball fruits of

'Vegetable Spaghetti', a delicious squash which will keep until Christmas. The best climbing cucumber is 'Chinese Long Green'.

*Sowing.* Sow in the greenhouse in mid-April, putting two seeds on their sides 1 inch (2.5 cm) deep in a 4 inch (10 cm) pot of soilless compost. They need a temperature of 70°F (21°C).

*Planting.* Harden the plants off in the cold frame and plant out when all danger of frost has passed. Set the plants either against canes attached to the side of the pergola or arbour, or on a stout wooden tripod, with at least 2 feet (60 cm) between the supports.

*Cultivation.* The plants must be tied to the canes regularly as they grow and the side-shoots should be trimmed to leave two leaves. Pinch out the tops when the plants reach the top of the canes or the tripod.

*Harvesting.* Pick regularly. Leave some fruits to ripen in the autumn and store them in a frost-free place until Christmas.

## Onions

Onions are probably the most used vegetable in the kitchen. They're easy to grow and to keep for a long time. Unfortunately, though they last in store until April, sometimes May and even June if you're lucky, that's not quite long enough for a year-round supply. So special steps have to be taken.

*Varieties.* For the main crop, raised from seed, the best variety is still 'Hygro', which produces good sized bulbs which store well. For a really attractive addition to the borders, grow the deep crimson 'Brunswick' or 'North Holland Blood Red', together with the white-skinned 'Albion', both of which produce good sized bulbs which store well. In fact the red varieties have always stored the best of all types in my own garden. If you decide to use sets, I would recommend 'Sturon' or 'Giant Fen Globe'.

To enable you to harvest early to ensure continuity, you'll need to grow an early-maturing type like 'Unwins First Early' which is obtainable as a set. The alternative way of making sure you always have something available for cooking is to grow shallots as well (see p. 194).

*Sowing.* In late January or early February, sow into modules (see p. 146). There should be six to eight seeds per cell, and germinate them at a temperature of about 60°F (15°C). When they germinate, don't thin them.

Outside, in March or April, sow in shallow drills near the front of the border. The drills should be about 3 inches (7.5 cm) apart and the plants thinned to 3 inches (7.5 cm) in the rows.

*Planting.* Plant out module-sown plants in threes with each group of plants 1 foot (30 cm) apart, in a patch near the front of the border. Onion foliage looks particularly good when contrasted with rounded leaves, like those of Heuchera or Tellima, or with low-growing flowers, like white or blue Lobelia.

Plant maincrop sets in March or April, about 3 inches (7.5 cm) apart in patches of five to nine, again near the front. Early-maturing sets are best planted in the autumn as soon as they arrive, which is normally during September.

*Cultivation.* Be careful to keep the plants weed-free and well watered. Autumn-planted sets will benefit from an extra feed of blood, fish and bone meal in February.

*Harvesting.* Lift early varieties in June and use straight away as required. August-maturing varieties should be allowed to ripen naturally. When the foliage falls over and begins to brown, put a fork underneath the clumps and lift them to break the roots. Then allow them to dry until the skin is dry and papery. In wet weather it may be necessary to lay them out on the greenhouse staging. When they are quite dry and well ripened in the sun, either string them into ropes or put them in open trays and store them in a frost-free place. Remember that well ripened and dried bulbs will store much longer.

## Salad Onions

Useful for flavourings, garnishes and summer salads.

*Varieties.* 'White Lisbon' is still the best variety for successional sowings, while the 'Winter Hardy White Lisbon' can be sown in autumn to overwinter.
*Sowing.* Start by sowing in modules in late January, using six to eight seeds per cell. Then make sowings outside about once a month from March to July for pulling during summer. Sow them in rows in patches in the front of the border, with 3 inches (7.5 cm) between rows – and don't thin. Alternatively, broadcast sow in a small patch. A sowing of the hardy variety can be made in the same way in August for pulling in May.
*Planting.* Plant module-grown plants 6 inches (15 cm) apart in April.
*Cultivation.* Weed and water.
*Harvesting.* Pull and use immediately.

## Pickling Onions

Useful for producing delicious small onions for pickling as a more economical alternative to shallots.

*Varieties.* 'Giant Zittau' is a popular, brown-skinned variety with an excellent flavour, while 'Paris Silverskin' looks good in the border and is used for 'cocktail' onions.
*Sowing.* Sow quite thickly in patches at the front of the border, either in rows 1 inch (2.5 cm) apart or broadcast. Cover the seed with a shallow layer of sieved soil. There's no need to thin.
*Harvesting.* Pull cocktail onions when they're marble sized and the others when they're a little larger. Pickle them straight away.

## Shallots

These have the great advantage that they mature as early as June, so filling the gap when onions are often not available. They are appreciated by gourmet cooks too.

*Varieties.* Shallots are always grown from sets rather than seed. The most readily available variety, 'Giant Long Keeping Yellow', produces plenty of good sized bulbs which store well. 'Giant Long Keeping Red' sets are usually slightly harder to come by. They are not the bright red of red onions, and of no greater value as a decorative plant than the brown-skinned, so-called yellow variety. However, some cooks seem to prefer them. The old exhibition variety 'Hative de Niort' is sometimes offered by seedsmen. Though it produces larger bulbs, these do not store as well as the others.
*Planting.* Shallots are perfectly hardy so can go in as soon as they arrive in spring. February or March plantings will yield some bulbs in June. Plant in patches of five to nine near the front of the border, with about 4 inches (10 cm) between sets.
*Cultivation.* Simply keep the bulbs weed-free and watered. In May, draw the soil away from the base of the bulbs to assist ripening.
*Harvesting.* Lift the whole crop when the foliage has gone brown. Store in onion nets begged from the greengrocer or in open trays.

*Shallot*

*Pepper 'Early Prolific' (see p. 196).*

## Parsnips

An indispensable winter root vegetable but, it has to be admitted, not the most beautiful plant in the world. When the foliage is young it looks fine, but later it becomes brown at the edges and very tatty. So I like to grow parsnips in patches nearer to the middle of the border. Early on they'll look quite acceptable and later they can be masked by medium sized annuals like petunias or salvias. They remain in the ground over winter, so the annuals are then replaced with biennials such as wall-flowers.

*Varieties.* Choose a variety resistant to canker, like 'White Gem' or 'Tender and True'.
*Sowing.* In March or April, sow in patches near the middle of the border in rows 6 inches (15 cm) apart and thin to the same distance.
*Cultivation.* Protect the roots against carrot fly (see p. 243).
*Harvesting.* Parsnips are hardy and benefit from a touch of frost which improves the flavour. So the roots can be left in the ground over winter, though this leaves them subject to attack from slugs and wireworms. The best way is to lift them in December, after a good frost, and store them in a box of vermiculite.

## Hamburg Parsley

This is a little-known vegetable, which is a pity since it's as easy to grow as parsnips and has a more subtle flavour with a hint of aniseed. Grow it in the same way as parsnips.

## Peas

If you don't have a lot of room, I suppose this is one to miss out. However, I would be very sorry to do so because some varieties are extremely attractive as well as being quite delicious. Certainly it is well worth finding a space for the mangetout types.

*Varieties.* One of the earliest of the standard varieties for podding is the sweetly flavoured 'Douce Provence', which grows to about 2 feet (60 cm) and could be followed by the 2½ foot (75 cm) tall maincrop variety 'Onward'.

The best of the mangetout varieties for this garden is 'Carouby de Maussane'. It's not the heaviest cropper, but it produces superb purple flowers, which alone make the plant worth-while, plus the most delicious flat pods which remain on the plant for weeks without going stringy. It looks terrific growing to 5 feet (150 cm) tall on the pergola.
*Sowing.* To beat the slugs, it's best to raise the plants in sweet-pea tubes or small pots in the greenhouse. Sow the earliest varieties in early March and the later ones in April. Alterna-tively, sow against netting supported on the pergola or the fence, in stations 1 foot (30 cm) apart, setting two seeds per station. Sow early varieties in March and maincrop in April, with a later sowing in May.
*Planting.* Plant out pot-raised plants in April or May.
*Cultivation.* Fix the support netting at sowing time or soon after. You may need to help the

plants on their way in the very early stages. Cut the plants down after harvesting, leaving the roots in the soil to provide extra nitrogen. Compost the haulm.

*Harvesting.* Pick both the crop for podding and the mange-tout types regularly while they are still young and sweet.

## Peppers

A crop for the cold greenhouse or frame in all but the warmest parts. These attractive tasty fruits are not difficult and they crop well.

*Varieties.* 'Ace' and 'Early Prolific' are two good standards, producing large green fruits which later turn red. 'Redskin' is a superb newish introduction which will produce good crops in 7 inch (18 cm) pots on the windowsill, though they'll do better in the greenhouse. Varieties of chilli peppers are much alike. You should only need one or two plants.

*Sowing.* Sow in February at a temperature of 65–70°F (18–21°C). Prick out the seedlings into seed trays, spacing them about 2 inches (5 cm) apart as soon as the seed-leaves are large enough to handle.

*Potting.* After about three weeks, pot on into 3 inch (7.5 cm) pots of soilless compost. Then continue to transfer the plants to the next sized pot when the roots cover the outside of the root-ball. Peppers have a small root system and won't like being put straight into a large pot where they'll be surrounded by cold, wet compost, so potting up gradually is essential. The final pot should be 7–9 inches (18–23 cm).

*Cultivation.* Stake and tie the plants as they grow. Feed at every watering with a liquid fertilizer. Ventilate freely in hot weather or even put the plants outside. Don't allow more than six to eight fruits per plant.

*Harvesting.* Pick the fruits as required. If left to mature they'll turn bright red. Pick chilli peppers as needed and, at the end of the season, hang them in a cool, dry, airy shed to dry before storing them in airtight jars.

## Radish

Quick maturing, easy and attractive in the mixed border. They should be grown near the front where the bright red roots make a fine sight.

*Varieties.* The old favourite 'French Breakfast' is still the best, producing attractive roots of red and white with a mild flavour.

*Sowing.* Make the first sowing in 5 inch (12.5 cm) pots in the greenhouse in late January and harvest from the pots. At the same time sow in modules, about six seeds per cell. The first sowing outside is made in February under cloches and thenceforth outside at fortnightly intervals until September. Being so quick they're ideal for filling gaps between crops, so they should be sown wherever there's a space. Generally aim to sow at the front of the border in patches, broadcasting the seed and lightly covering with soil or compost.

*Planting.* Plant out the module-sown plants under cloches in February, setting them 2 inches (5 cm) apart.

*Cultivation.* Don't thin the plants but make sure they're weeded and watered.

*Harvesting.* Pull the roots selectively, taking the largest and leaving the rest to grow.

## Potatoes

Maincrop potatoes are not for small gardens, but you should certainly grow some early varieties. They taste very much better dug fresh.

*Varieties.* Check with gardeners locally because the flavour does vary from place to place. I favour 'Concord', which is heavy cropping and delicious. The foliage is very attractive, especially when placed next to taller herbaceous plants like some of the euphorbias.

*Planting.* In March, set one, two or three tubers in patches near the middle of the border. Plant with a trowel, setting the tubers as deeply as you can manage and about 1 foot (30 cm) apart.

*Cultivation*. Give the plants plenty of water and an extra dressing of blood, fish and bone meal in April.

*Harvesting*. Dig in late May or early June. For the first few pickings, scrape a little soil away and remove those tubers you need, leaving the rest to grow on. After mid-June, the whole plant can be dug. They don't store well, losing flavour all the time, so dig only as you need them.

## Salsify and Scorzonera

I include these two delicious roots together because they're very similar and grown in just the same way. Like parsnips, they're not especially attractive, so put them near the middle among annual flowers. They produce long roots which are considered a gourmet delicacy.

*Varieties*. Few are offered and all are much the same. I grow the white-rooted salsify 'Mammoth' and the black-rooted scorzonera 'Habil'.

*Sowing*. Sow in patches in shallow drills 6 inches (15 cm) apart in April or May. Thin to 6 inches (15 cm) apart.

*Cultivation*. Just keep weed-free and watered.

*Harvesting*. Dig the roots in December and store them in vermiculite.

## Spinach

A great crop to grow because it yields well and also looks attractive. It tastes much better grown organically and harvested fresh, and it certainly does you a power of good.

*Varieties*. For growing during the summer, choose 'Symphony', which produces beautiful large leaves and is slow to run to seed. For late sowings or difficult soil, grow spinach beet, which is generally sold simply as 'perpetual spinach'. It's a biennial so it won't run to seed.

*Sowing*. Make the first sowing in modules in late January or February. Sow two seeds per cell, and after germination thin to one seedling. Sowings can be made under cloches in February and thenceforth outside at monthly intervals (unless you eat a lot!) from March until July. Finally, make a sowing of spinach beet to cover with cloches in August or September to harvest next March or April. Sow in patches, just a little back from the front of the border, in shallow drills about 9 inches (23 cm) apart and thin to the same distance.

*Planting*. Plant the module-grown plants under cloches in March, setting them about 9 inches (23 cm) apart. Make sure you have thinned to one plant per cell in this case because there's a tendency to run to seed earlier if there's too much competition between plants.

*Cultivation*. It's important to make sure that spinach doesn't go short of water, otherwise it'll run to seed.

*Harvesting*. Pull a few leaves from the outside of each plant, leaving the rest to grow on, rather than stripping one plant completely. Cook and eat as soon after picking as possible for the best flavour and texture.

## Swede

Not a very attractive plant really, so it is best sown in the middle of the border and masked with annual flowers. It's well worthwhile for its delicious winter roots.

*Varieties*. 'Marian' is the one I would recommend since it's resistant to club root and mildew. There's little discernible difference in flavour between varieties.

*Sowing*. Delay sowing until May or June to avoid the worst of the mildew attack. Then sow in patches in shallow drills 9 inches (23 cm) apart. Thin to the same distance.

*Cultivation*. Keep watered and weed-free.

*Harvesting*. Swedes can stay in the ground over winter when a touch of frost will improve the flavour. If you wish to lift them to cultivate, store the roots in vermiculite.

*Salsify (see p. 197).*

## Sweet Corn.

Modern, early-ripening varieties make the growing of sweet corn possible in all but the coldest areas. They look attractive in the middle of borders, especially underplanted with flowers like tagetes or English marigolds.

*Varieties.* 'Early Xtra Sweet' is a tasty variety, but it must be grown on its own to avoid cross-pollination which spoils the flavour.
*Sowing.* Start the plants off in the greenhouse in April, sowing two seeds per 3 inch (7.5 cm) pot at a temperature of 65–70°F (18–21°C). Thin to leave one seedling per pot.
*Planting.* Plant in early June about 18 inches (45 cm) apart in threes.
*Cultivation.* Water well in dry weather.
*Harvesting.* When the tassels (the male flowers) on the end of the cobs turn black, they're ripe to eat. Pick and cook straight away.

## Swiss Chard

Also called silver or seakale beet, this is an invaluable vegetable for autumn and early spring harvesting when there's often little else.

It produces large, green, crinkled leaves with white stems which make a handsome addition to the border. There is also a red type, ruby or rhubarb chard, which has bright red stems and could happily be grown purely as an ornamental plant.

*Varieties.* A newish variety, 'Fordhook Giant', is an excellent improvement on the old Swiss chard varieties. The red type is sold simply as 'Ruby' or 'Rhubarb Chard'.
*Sowing.* In April and again in July, sow in shallow drills 1 foot (30 cm) apart just a little away from the front of the border. Thin to the same distance.
*Cultivation.* For the most succulent stems, keep the plants well watered.
*Harvesting.* Pull the leaves, detaching the stems from the base of the plant. Take the outside leaves, picking over all the plants to leave more to grow on. It's often recommended that the leaves and stems be cooked separately, but to me they taste just as good cooked whole.

## Tomatoes

Deservedly the most popular greenhouse crop. It's possible to produce heavy yields of excellent fruit throughout the summer. Outside stick to bush varieties which are attractive in leaf and dramatically beautiful in fruit.

*Varieties.* Don't bother with the commercial varieties which are bred for heavy yields and looks. There are much better varieties bred for flavour. In the greenhouse, there is a wide choice. For large fruits I grow the old favourite and by far the tastiest, 'Ailsa Craig', and I would never be without the delicious small-fruited variety 'Gardener's Delight'. But my recommendation would be to grow these in pots. If you grow them in the greenhouse borders, it's best to stick to disease-resistant varieties like 'Piranto'.

Outside, grow bush varieties like 'Red Alert' and 'Tornado'.

*Sowing*. Greenhouse varieties should be sown in February in pots of soilless compost and at a temperature of 65°F (18°C). Prick the seedlings out as soon as the seed-leaves are big enough to handle. Sow outdoor varieties in the same way but in March.

*Potting*. Pot on into 3 inch (7.5 cm) pots when the plants have made two proper leaves, using soilless compost. Outdoor varieties can remain in these pots until planting time. When the roots cover the outside of the root-ball, greenhouse varieties can be potted into their final, 9 inch (23 cm) pots.

*Planting*. When danger of frost has passed, plant outdoor varieties a little back from the front of the border. Set them 2 feet (60 cm) apart, either singly or in groups of three. They need no support.

*Cultivation*. Greenhouse varieties must be fed with liquid fertilizer at each watering. Support them with canes which reach to the top of the greenhouse and are fixed to wires. Rub out side-shoots which form in the joints between the leaves and the stem. Pinch out the tops of the plants when they reach the top of the canes. Remove any bottom leaves that become yellow or brown at the edges. When the plants are in flower, gently shake the canes each morning to spread pollen from flower to flower. Outdoor varieties need no maintenance short of weeding and watering. It's a good idea to mulch underneath them with straw or bark to keep the fruit off the ground.

*Harvesting*. Pick regularly to encourage the production of more fruit. At the end of the season, outdoor plants can be covered with cloches to prolong ripening. Unripe fruits can be ripened after picking simply by taking them indoors.

## Turnips

Easy to grow and very good eating too. The roots of some varieties are also very attractive in the borders. Sow them just a little back from the front.

*Varieties*. For the earliest crops and for successional sowings, use 'Milan Purple Top', whose roots have bright reddish purple tops, which look very attractive in the borders. For keeping, use 'Golden Ball', which has superbly flavoured yellow flesh.

*Sowing*. In late January, sow the earliest crop in the greenhouse, in modules, using two or three seeds per cell. Germinate them at a temperature of 60°F (15°C). The first outdoor sowing is made under cloches in February. Sow in drills 6 inches (15 cm) apart and thin to the same distance for small roots. Then sow without cover in small patches at monthly intervals from March to July at the same distances.

*Planting*. Plant module-sown plants under cloches in February, setting the blocks 9 inches (23 cm) apart.

*Cultivation*. Keep the plants well watered and weed-free.

*Harvesting*. Pull the spring and summer roots when they're still quite small for the best flavour. Those for storage can be left to grow to about the size of a tennis ball. They should be lifted in early November and stored in vermiculite.

*Turnip* 'Milan Purple Top'.

# Chapter 8

## TREE FRUIT

You don't need a large garden to be as near self-sufficient in fruit as the climate will allow. Modern fruit trees are a fraction of the size of the big, gnarled old things one used to have to climb up with a ladder. They'll produce as much fruit in a much smaller space. But the big secret is the way you grow them.

By choosing different shapes of tree, you can make use of your fences and walls. You can edge your paths with trees and grow them free-standing. They need take up only a few inches of soil, leaving plenty of room to grow things around and underneath them.

### ✤ BUYING TREES ✤

In most cases it's best to start out with one or at most two-year-old trees though you may prefer to buy fan-trained trees already formed, which will save a lot of time and trouble. Bear in mind that young trees are full of the vigour of youth and will get established and start cropping much earlier than tired old four- or five-year-olds. They'll be smaller and some of them may not even have side-branches, looking like a single bare stick in winter. But that size of tree is still a much better buy.

Check the varieties carefully before making your choice, so that where you're growing more than one you can stagger the harvesting period to extend it as long as possible. It's not a bad idea to take local advice on varieties because those that do well in warmer areas will often fail where it's cold and vice versa. Remember also that some fruits need two or more varieties to ensure good pollination.

Tree fruit varieties are always budded onto a special rootstock. This will control the eventual size of the tree and the length of time it will take to come into cropping. Where appropriate I have recommended rootstocks. If the nurseryman or garden centre can't tell you which it is, then shop elsewhere.

### ✤ TREE SHAPES ✤

Fruit trees can be pruned to almost any shape you want. The pruning is not difficult once you've mastered a few basic rules and the regular pruning will always increase the crop considerably. In the ornamental kitchen garden, you'll be looking for trees that will give maximum yields in as small a space as possible, and look terrific all year round. It sounds like a tall order, but in fact it's very simple. You're starting, after all, with the advantage that a well-grown tree will give you three good displays of colour every year. There's the blossom in spring, the glossy green leaves in summer and the fruit in autumn.

*Cordons.* I've chosen these first because, once you've mastered the pruning of cordon apples and pears for example, you've mastered the pruning of all the other shapes too. A cordon is basically a single stem, generally grown at an angle of about 45 degrees to the ground, and pruned hard every summer to remove all but short stubs of side-shoots.

They can be trained against a fence or wall, or on a post and wire support, and should be planted $2\frac{1}{2}$ feet (75 cm) apart.

*Cordon apple.*

*Fans.* A very popular way to grow many types of fruit (see p. 26). The trees can be bought half-trained – a highly recommended method to avoid getting bogged down in the technicalities of the initial shaping. They, too, are grown against wires fixed to posts or to the wall or fence. This is one of the most attractive ways to grow fruit and takes up next to no room in the border. Plant about 10–12 feet (3–3.6 m) apart.

*Espaliers.* Much like fans only the 'arms' are trained horizontally in a series of 'tiers'. It's an attractive and space-saving way, especially for apples and pears. Plant 10–12 feet (3–3.6 m) apart.

*Step-overs.* These are single-tier espaliers which grow about 9 inches (23 cm) above the ground and can be used to edge a path or a border in an attractive, space-saving and simple way. Plant about 10 feet (3 m) apart.

*Pillars.* For apples only at the moment. A new type of apple has been developed which produces only short side-branches from a single stem. They thus form straight pillars which can be planted as closely as 2 feet (60 cm) apart. They have limited value but are important for very small gardens.

*Pillar or ballerina apple.*

*Lollipops.* This is an 'invention' of mine, where a tree is trained around a couple of hoops to form a perfect, ball-shaped head. The four branches are then hard pruned to make an attractive formal shape. Lollipops serve as a good illustration of the versatility of fruit trees.

Not all these shapes are suitable for all fruits, and it's best to stick to those recommended for each type. Apples and pears are by far the easiest, so when you're allotting space for each type, remember that they can go more or less anywhere.

Notice that I haven't recommended growing free-standing trees. I've left them out deliberately because they are not ideal where space is limited, as it generally is these days, and recommendations for growing them are available in any fruit book.

## Supports

Fixing wires to the fence is no problem. Simply put staples into the posts and run the wires through them. The wires should start about 2 feet (60 cm) from the ground and continue at 1 foot (30 cm) intervals to the top of the fence. You'll be using the wires for ornamental climbers as well, no doubt, and for those you will probably need to fix vertical wires as well, to make a square mesh.

Fixing wires to a brick or stone wall will require more effort. 'Vine-eyes' are metal tags with a hole in one end. They're simply driven into the mortar and the wires are pushed through the holes. You'll need them at about 6 foot (180 cm) intervals along the wall. They

*A strong post and wire support for fruit.*

are only suitable for old mortar: on new houses you'll need to drill a hole with a masonry drill, plug it and screw in a strong hook; fix wooden battens and staple wires to those.

The trees should not be tied directly to the wires since this will chafe the bark. Instead, fix bamboo canes where you wish to train the trees and tie the branches to those with soft string (nylon twine will cut into the bark).

To build a post and wire support, you'll need strong posts, preferably pressure-treated with wood preservative, about 8 feet (240 cm) long. Drive them 18 inches (45 cm) into the ground and strut the two end posts. Intermediate posts should be at about 9 feet (270 cm) intervals. Fix the wires with staples.

The structure for step-overs is much simpler, as you need only one wire 9 inches (23 cm) from the ground.

Lollipops are free-standing but they need no staking as the hoops hold the tree steady. They are suitable only for apples and pears (see p. 207 for how to make the supports).

*Apples and pears can be trained on a metal arch where they'll make an attractive feature. After planting, treat them just like cordons.*

## 🌸 APPLES 🌸

Certainly the most popular fruit in Britain and the cooler, wetter parts of the world. Apples are best grown as cordons, espaliers, step-overs or lollipops.

### Varieties

Even in a small ornamental kitchen garden you should be able to grow several varieties, so choose a range that will give good pollination and prolong the period of harvesting.

*Apple 'Katy'.*

The varieties in my first list are in order of maturity. All will pollinate each other. Note that all these flower mid-season so may possibly be subject to frost damage in colder areas. It would be worth choosing from the second list if you have problems with late frosts. You'll see, incidentally, that I have not included Britain's favourite variety, 'Cox's Orange Pippin'. It's a poor grower and yields are generally much smaller than other varieties. But worst of all, for a garden that's grown organically, it's very prone indeed to mildew. Leave that one to the commercial grower.

### Early-flowering varieties

*'Discovery'*. The best early variety by far, maturing in August/September. It has crisp, juicy flesh and a green skin with a bright red flush, making it an attractive fruit. It drops its fruit more readily than most, so leave it unthinned. Like all early varieties, it's best eaten straight from the tree.

*'Katy'*. The most reliable cropper I have grown, producing huge yields every year. The fruit is red flushed and delicious. Not to be missed.

*'James Grieve'*. Not a commercial apple because it doesn't travel well, but excellent eaten from the tree. It's also one of the best pollinators of all. The flesh is juicy, crisp and well flavoured and the skin is yellow striped orange. It shows some resistance to frost damage so it's a useful variety for northern gardeners. Matures September/October.

*Apple 'James Grieve'.*

'*Jupiter*'. A new variety bred as a replacement for 'Cox's Orange Pippin'. The fruits are orange-red with a superb 'Cox' flavour. It produces three times the yield of 'Cox' and keeps until January. Not a good pollinator. Ready in October.

'*Fiesta*'. Much like 'Jupiter', with a similar 'Cox' flavour. It produces heavy yields and pollinates other varieties well. It's ready in October and keeps until March.

'*Kent*'. Another product of the search for a better yielding, easier to grow variety than the popular 'Cox'. The wonderful flavour improves with storage. It's ready in November and keeps till February or March.

'*Bramley's Seedling*'. This is still the best cooker, though it makes a vigorous tree. The apples are bright green and have a superb flavour when cooked. Unfortunately it will not pollinate other trees but will receive pollen from any of the above varieties. It's ready in November and keeps until March.

If you live in a colder area, you may find it an advantage to stick with late-flowering varieties. But you should not mix from these two lists or you won't get full pollination.

## Late-flowering varieties

'*Merton Charm*'. A recent variety with crisp, juicy, greenish-yellow fruit with a fine flavour. They are ready to pick in September and should be eaten straight from the tree.

'*Orleans Reinette*'. An ancient French variety with superb flavour and quality. It matures in November and will keep until January.

'*Ashmeads Kernel*'. Another old variety but certainly none the worse for that. It's a well-flavoured russet apple, ready in December and keeping until March.

'*Suntan*'. Another fine new variety which has consistently kept the longest for me. It has a fine 'Cox' flavour which improves with storage. It matures in November and will keep easily until March.

'*Howgate Wonder*'. A cooking variety that produces enormous fruit. It doesn't have quite the flavour of 'Bramley' but is well worthwhile in cold areas. It crops in November and keeps until March.

If you have any problems with pollination, perhaps because you don't have space for more than one tree, plant the flowering crab *Malus* 'Golden Hornet' which will pollinate most varieties.

The best crab apple for culinary purposes is *Malus* 'John Downie'. Both these can be grown exactly like apples.

## Rootstocks

The introduction of rootstocks that would restrict the growth of apple trees and bring them into cropping earlier in their lives revolutionized fruit growing. Though the research was aimed at commercial fruit farmers, it benefited gardeners enormously too.

There are several different stocks to choose from but only two, in my view, that gardeners need remember.

M27 will produce small trees which crop in the second year. It is only for use on very fertile soil where trees will be staked all their lives.

MM106 makes slightly larger trees which also start to crop in year two. It has a stronger root system and is suitable for all apples on soil which is not of the highest fertility.

Check the rootstock when you buy the trees and if the nursery or garden centre can't tell you which they are, go somewhere else where they can.

## Planting

It's best to buy your trees from a specialist grower, during the dormant season. The trees will then arrive bare-rooted. Soak them in a bucket of water for an hour before planting. Plant against the supports in the normal way (see p. 123), but make sure that the join between the variety and the rootstock is well above ground level. It's vital that the variety should not root into the soil or the effect of the rootstock will be lost. Bear in mind that in this garden mulching will be carried out regularly and this could raise the soil level, so keep the planting on the high side.

If you have to buy plants in containers, they should be planted in exactly the way described for ornamentals (see p. 123), but again, keep the grafting point well above ground.

Cordons are planted at an angle of about 30 degrees from the ground, and immediately tied to the canes. After a few years, when they have reached the tops of the canes, they need to be lowered to 45 degrees, so allow for this when planting. All trees should immediately be tied to their supports with soft string.

## Pruning

All the trees grown in the ornamental kitchen garden will be trained on an intensive system. That means that, after the initial pruning in the first year or so, all the major pruning is done during the summer. Normally the best time is during August or September. Always use a sharp pair of secateurs for pruning and always cut back to just above a bud. If you leave a long snag, it will die back and could introduce disease into the tree.

*Cordons.* These are grown as a single stem and pruned to create a series of fruiting 'spurs' along the length of the tree. Plant the young trees in the winter and, immediately after planting, cut back the main stem to remove about a third of the previous year's growth. It's not difficult to recognize where the new growth starts. (If you buy a one-year-old there is only the previous year's growth of course.) If there are any side-shoots, cut them back to leave them 3 inches (7.5 cm) long. That's all the winter-pruning you'll have to do. From now on it's all done in the summer.

## PRUNING CORDON APPLES

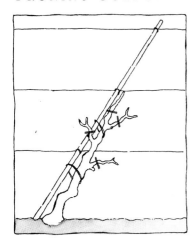

**1** *Cordons should have side-shoots cut back to 3 inches (7.5 cm) after planting. Thereafter, prune only in summer.*

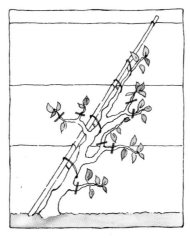

**2** *The first summer, cut back side-shoots arising from main stem to 3 inches (7.5 cm) and shoots coming from them to 1 inch (2.5 cm).*

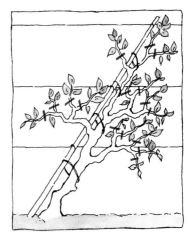

**3** *Every summer prune side-shoots as before. Allow main stem to grow till it reaches the end of the cane, then cut back like the side-shoots.*

In August or early September, cut back all new shoots arising from the main stem to leave them 3 inches (7.5 cm) long, and any that are coming from side-shoots to 1 inch (2.5 cm) long. And that's all there is to it. In this way, you'll build up a number of short, twiggy growths all the way along the stem. These are called 'spurs' and it's here that the fruit is borne.

Leave the growing tip of the main stem alone until it has reached as far as you want it to grow, which will generally be to the end of the cane. Then cut that back too, in the summer, treating it just like the side-shoots. At the same time, the canes can be lowered to 45 degrees to further restrict growth.

I've made a point of explaining the pruning of cordons first because, once you've grasped that, all the other shapes naturally follow. You simply treat each branch as if it were a cordon.

*Espaliers.* You can, of course, buy espaliers already pruned. But they're very expensive and not nearly as much fun as doing your own.

Put up the wire supports first, either on the fence or on a special structure of posts, with the wires 1 foot (30 cm) apart.

Again, you should start with one or two-year-old trees and, in the first winter, cut the main stem back to leave it 2 inches (5 cm) above the first wire.

During the following summer, several shoots will grow out and the three top shoots should be retained. Put a vertical cane in behind the tree and tie another at a 45 degree angle on each side of it. Train the first shoot vertically up the middle cane and the other two, one each side, to the other two canes. This forms the first tier.

In the second winter, the main, central shoot should again be cut back to 2 inches (5 cm) above the second wire and the process is repeated to form the second tier, with the third being made the next year and so on. When you reach as high as you want to go, just allow the two horizontal shoots to grow instead of three.

In the summer, simply treat each side-branch as if it were a cordon, cutting back to 3 inches (7.5 cm) and 1 inch (2.5 cm) to form fruiting spurs.

*Step-overs.* These are simply single-tier espaliers. Again, you can buy them ready-trained, but it's very easy to do your own.

---

## PRUNING ESPALIER APPLES

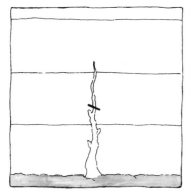

**1** *Espalier 'maidens' are pruned to about 2 inches (5 cm) above the first wire immediately after planting.*

**2** *In the first summer, train the two side-branches to 45° and the centre branch straight up. Prune side-branches to 3 inches (7.5 cm).*

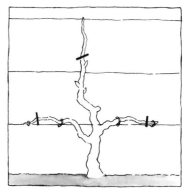

**3** *In the second winter, tie first tier of side-shoots to wires and prune main stem to 2 inches (5 cm) above second wire. Afterwards prune side-branches like cordons.*

This time, fix the wire about 9 inches (23 cm) above the ground. This results in a tree about 1 foot (30 cm) tall, which is easy to step over if you want to get to the border.

Then, after planting in the winter, cut back to 2 inches (5 cm) above the wire but this time, instead of training in the three shoots, just retain two to tie in to the horizontal wires. Again, in summer, treat each branch as if it were a cordon.

*Lollipops.* This is my name for a tree with a rounded, formal head. Initially you'll need a couple of hoops around which the four main branches are trained.

The hoops are made with $\frac{1}{2}$ inch (13 mm) alkathene water pipe, which is obtainable from the builders' merchant. Cut two 6 foot (180 cm) lengths and push a piece of dowelling about 2 inches (5 cm) long into one end. Bend the pipe into a circle and push the other end

over the dowelling. The pipe will obligingly form a perfect circle. Make two circles and tie them together with nylon twine so that they are at right angles. Then tie each one to two 6 foot (180 cm) canes to support them above the tree.

Prune a young tree to leave the stem about 4–5 feet (120–150 cm) above ground level. Then push the canes into the ground so that the two circles rest immediately above the pruned tree. During the summer, shoots will grow out and the top four should be tied into the hoops.

Eventually, when they reach the top, cut the growing tip off and either tie or even graft all four together. After a year, the branches will have stiffened into shape and the hoops can be removed. From then on, just as with all the other shapes, treat each of the branches like a cordon, pruning each summer to produce fruiting spurs.

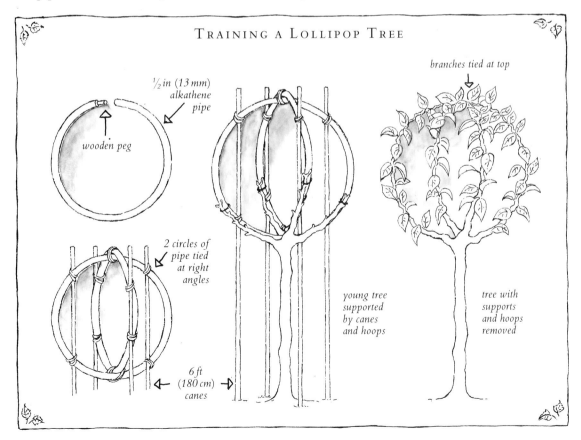

### TRAINING A LOLLIPOP TREE

wooden peg

$\frac{1}{2}$ in (13 mm) alkathene pipe

2 circles of pipe tied at right angles

6 ft (180 cm) canes

branches tied at top

young tree supported by canes and hoops

tree with supports and hoops removed

## Nicking and notching

In order to train trees in exactly the way you want, they have to co-operate. Normally there's no problem, but sometimes they can stubbornly refuse to grow where you want a branch. You'll see a bud there but it simply doesn't grow out. This can actually be controlled by the gardener by harnessing the tree's natural function.

In order to make sure that the tree grows upwards towards the light, nature has equipped it with a mechanism called 'apical dominance'. It sends down a growth-inhibiting substance from the growing point to all the buds below, so effectively reducing their growth and allowing the top bud to take most of the tree's energy to grow upwards. If you cut off the supply of this inhibitor to the bud you want to grow out, the effect will be lost and the bud will be free to develop vigorously.

The inhibitor is carried in tissue just below the bark, so just cut a small notch above the bud to direct the inhibitor around it and away Conversely, if you want to stop the bud growing, nick underneath to concentrate the inhibitor round it. May is the best month to do this job.

*Notching just above a bud.*

## Feeding

It's important to maintain a high state of fertility around the trees, not just for them but also because they'll be providing some competition for the flowers and vegetables you'll want to grow around them. So make sure you mulch well each spring with plenty of manure or compost. There's no need to go out of your way to apply fertilizer, because in this garden you'll be doing that anyway when you sow or plant around the trees.

## Thinning

Thinning the fruit is not really necessary unless you want larger apples. Most people, I'm sure, prefer them a bit on the small side, except perhaps the cookers. If you do decide to thin, leave the job until the so-called 'June drop'. I generally find that the 'June drop' happens in July here, but you will certainly know when it does because the tree will be surrounded by dozens of tiny apples. Eating apples should be thinned to leave the fruits about 4 inches (10 cm) apart and cookers a little wider. Start by removing any misshapen fruit in each cluster and then take out the large central one. But I'm certain that most gardeners would rather leave the job to nature and, if you finish up with lots of small apples, well so be it.

## Harvesting and storing

Early varieties don't store for more than a few weeks and are much better eaten straight from the tree. Storing varieties are best kept in polythene bags. Pick only perfect apples and do so very carefully. Always place them *gently* into a basket lined with soft cloth.

Put no more than about 2 lb (900 gm) of apples into a polythene bag, seal the top and prick a couple of pin-holes in each bag; don't be tempted to do more. You need one pin-hole per 1 lb (450 gm) of apples. Put the bags into a cold but just frost-free shed.

## ❧ PEARS ❧

Pears are more difficult to grow than apples and require higher temperatures for perfect results. They do very well in warmer areas but in a more moderate climate it's best to grow them on a south or west-facing wall or fence. They are slower in growth than apples and flower earlier, and so are more subject to the frost problem. But provided they're grown on a wall or fence, even that is not insoluble. They're best grown as fans or espaliers but in warmer gardens will make good step-overs, cordons, and lollipops too. They're otherwise grown in much the same way as apples. The white flowers are a very welcome sight in the garden as a reminder that spring really is just around the corner.

### Varieties

Just like apples, pears need a pollinator to provide a full crop. It's true that the variety 'Conference' will give quite a good crop on its own pollen, but the fruit is always mis-shapen and the crop is not as good as an adequately pollinated one. Pears will store for only a very short while, so it's even more important to choose carefully to try to provide as long a harvesting period as possible.

Since pears flower earlier than apples, it's even more important to take advantage of local knowledge and to choose late-flowering varieties if necessary.

### Early-flowering varieties

'*Conference*'. Certainly the most popular pear these days because it crops well and will store for a little longer than most. It produces long, green, tapering pears which gradually yellow with age. The flavour is good but not excep-tional. If grown without a pollinator it will produce fair crops. It's ready for picking from mid-October to the end of November.

'*Williams Bon Chretien*'. An old favourite and one of the best flavoured of them all. It forms large, juicy fruits but has only a short period of picking, being ready during September.

'*Beth*'. A newish variety which has always produced very well in my own garden. It's flavour and texture is much like 'Williams' and it crops at about the same time, though it keeps a little longer.

'*Merton Pride*'. Another fairly new variety with a fine flavour, but not a heavy cropper. Unlike the other varieties which will all pollinate each other, this one won't, though it will accept pollen from the rest. So if you do decide to grow it, you'll need three trees of different varieties. It's ready for picking during late September.

### Late-flowering varieties

'*Gorham*'. An old variety with a good flavour, ready from the middle of September. It's best if picked a little early and ripened off the tree,

'*Onward*'. A fairly new variety producing quite large crops with an excellent flavour. Unfortunately it doesn't keep too long.

'*Doyenné du Comice*'. A slightly tender variety that really needs to be grown as a fan on a south-facing wall, but well worth the trouble for its superb flavour and texture. It's ready in October and will keep until late November.

### Rootstocks

Pears are budded or grafted onto quince root-stocks. The most common is Quince A, which is fairly vigorous but, since pears are not as fast growing as apples, this is suitable for most gardens. Certainly it's the one to use on soils that are anything less than very fertile. Quince C is more dwarfing, if you want a very small tree. Like dwarfing stocks for apples, it encourages the trees to come into fruit earlier in their lives. Generally though, it's best to stick to Quince A.

## Planting

Plant pears in exactly the way described for apples (p. 205). If you're growing them as fans, which is certainly the way I would recommend, and you have room for two, plant them about 10 feet (3 m) apart.

## Pruning

As with espaliers, you can buy fan-trained trees from most specialist nurserymen. Alternatively, start with a one or two-year-old tree and train your own from scratch. Pears are quite accommodating for this kind of training because they tend to produce buds fairly close together.

So, instead of going through the tortuous method necessary for peaches or nectarines, I would always take the easy way out. Simply prune the tree back to leave six buds on the main stem in the winter immediately after planting. Then tie long canes to the horizontal wires in the shape of a fan, with three or four canes on each side of the tree. When the shoots develop the following summer, tie them in to the canes to form the fan. In subsequent years, continue to tie the shoots until they reach the ends of the canes.

*Pear 'Gorham'.*

In the summer, the pruning can start a little earlier than for the apples, generally in August or early September. And then you simply treat each branch as if it were a cordon, pruning side-shoots that arise directly from the branch to 3 inches (7.5 cm), and anything coming from those to 1 inch (2.5 cm).

As ornamental plants, fan-trained pears offer great value. They look good even in winter when the fan shape is revealed. The branches are, of course, covered in white blossom in early spring and, with a bit of luck, attractive fruit in autumn. Even the leaves oblige in autumn with good yellow colouring.

*Pear 'Doyenné du Comice'.*

## Frost protection

In the colder parts of the country it's absolutely essential to protect the blossom of pears from frost. If you're lucky enough to have a south-facing wall, the problem won't be quite as acute since the wall will absorb heat in the day and release it at night, but even then some precautions are advisable,

*Protect against frost with clear polythene.*

The easiest way is to staple a sheet of clear polythene to two stout poles at least 8 feet (240 cm) long. Keep them handy, rolled up and leaning against the wall beside the tree during the early spring. Then keep an eye on the weather forecast and, when frost is threatened, simply unroll the polythene and lean the posts against the wall on each side of the tree. That will nearly always be enough to save the crop.

## Harvesting and storing

Getting pears to the peak of condition for eating is not easy and requires a little trial and error and experience. If you like your pears soft and juicy, you need to be able to judge just the right time to pick them and also to eat them. Early ripeners like 'Williams' and 'Merton Pride' should be picked a little before they're quite ripe, when they still appear green and hard. Put them on a shelf in the coldest place you've got. They still need to be protected from frost, of course, but at that time of year it's unlikely that there will be frost severe enough to harm them.

They will look as if they're storing perfectly for a month or two but don't be misled. Often they look fine on the outside but have become soft and mushy inside. So leave them for no more than a couple of weeks before bringing them into room temperature for the final ripening. They'll take two or three days before they're at their juicy best, so bring them inside in succession over the two weeks.

Later-maturing varieties are stored in much the same way but should not be picked until they're completely ripe. Inspect the trees often, lifting a few fruits gently to test them. When they part from the tree with the gentlest of twists, they're ready for picking.

Though pears will not keep well fresh, bear in mind that it is possible to freeze them and they bottle extremely well.

*Pears should be stored unwrapped in an open box. Put them in a cold but frost-free place. They will keep only a month or two.*

## 🪲 QUINCES 🪲

The Japanese Quince (*Chaenomeles japonica*) is widely grown as an ornamental plant, and there are several very decorative varieties. It's also worth while making room for the closely related, culinary type of quince (*Cydonia oblonga*), because the flavour is so very much better. The pink or white blossom looks very pretty in late spring and there's another display in autumn when the big yellow fruits shine from laden branches. Almost as a bonus, the fruits make superb jams and jelly, they can be cooked in pies or flans and they make excellent wine too. They're very easy to grow if you follow the instructions for pears. Since they come into bloom much later than pears they generally escape frosts, so there's normally no need to arrange protection.

### Varieties

Quinces don't need another variety to pollinate them, so you only need one plant. The variety 'Vranja' is the most popular and widely offered, having an excellent flavour and coming into bearing very early in its life. If you live in a cold area and can get hold of the variety 'Apple Shaped', you'll find it quite a bit hardier. It produces round fruits with quite a good flavour.

### Rootstocks

Quinces are grown on their own roots.

### Planting

While it's possible to grow quinces as small, free-standing trees, they'll do much better in a fan shape on a south- or west-facing wall.

### Pruning

Prune exactly as for pears.

### Harvesting and storing

The fruits are ready to pick when they turn yellow and begin to have a distinct and very pleasant aroma. Like all fruit, pick them carefully and store them in boxes in as cold a place as you can so long as it isn't prone to frost. It's best to keep them away from other fruit or the flavour may be spoiled.

Quinces won't store for long but can be frozen or bottled and, of course, processed into jam, jelly or wine.

## 🪲 PEACHES 🪲

Peaches and nectarines are seen by many gardeners as the real aristocrats of the fruit garden. In colder areas they require the protection of a south-facing wall and they're not the easiest fruits to grow. But my goodness, they're certainly worth the trouble.

I've included the two fruits together because they're grown in exactly the same way and, indeed, are very similar in all respects. A nectarine is really no more than a hairless peach with a superlative flavour. Both are best grown as fans in the ornamental kitchen garden. Alternatively, grow one of the newer dwarf varieties in a pot, where it can be protected from the fungus disease that often ravages peaches. They have superb, deep pink flowers in the early spring.

### Peach varieties

'*Duke of York*'. An early variety with large, deep crimson fruits and yellow flesh. The flavour is excellent.

'*Peregrine*'. Large, deep red fruits which are very juicy with an excellent flavour. It crops a little later than 'Duke of York'.

'*Rochester*'. A good variety for gardeners in colder areas as it's one of the hardiest and flowers just a little later than the others, though not late enough to escape frost damage. The flavour is not quite as good as the others.

## Nectarine varieties

'*Early Rivers*' is greenish, flushed red when ripe and with yellow flesh. Excellent flavour.

'*Lord Napier*'. One for the warmer parts only and even then it deserves a south-facing wall. It's the best flavoured of them all.

There are one or two new varieties of genetically dwarf peaches now available, which can be grown in tubs. The ones I have tried are the peaches 'Garden Lady' and 'Bonanza' and the nectarine 'Nectarella'. They produce quite good crops of fairly well flavoured peaches but have one big disadvantage. In my experience they are more prone to the fungus disease peach leaf curl. This causes bad red blistering on the leaves which eventually fall off. The disease makes the trees useless for an organic garden (sprays forbidden) if you're going to grow them outside. However, the spores of the fungus are carried on rain, and if you can keep the trees in a greenhouse during early January to late May, they'll escape. So grow them in pots if you have room in the greenhouse to overwinter them.

## Rootstocks

For normal sized trees, choose the semi-dwarfing St Julien A. If you have a large wall to cover, look for trees grown on the more vigorous Brompton. If you want an especially small tree, some nurserymen now offer peaches on the dwarfing stock Pixy.

## Planting

Always plant against a south-facing wall. If you decide to grow more than one tree, allow about 10 feet (3 m) between them. It's worth while preparing the site well for peaches, especially if your soil is heavy, as they hate

bad drainage. Dig out a big hole, break up the bottom with a fork and work in some coarse gravel. When you refill, mix in plenty of good compost or manure.

Often the south-facing wall is the one devoted to the patio, with just a few slabs left out near the wall to provide planting pockets. With only the width of a paving slab to work in, the preparation of the soil is difficult. I know it's a tall order, but if you can think of preparing a good planting area before you even lay the concrete base for the paving, you'll have better success with the trees.

## Pruning

If you find the instructions for pruning peaches the traditional way totally incomprehensible, you're forgiven. So do I. However, if you remember one fact, peach pruning can be very easy, so for heaven's sake don't be put off.

I would always start with a ready-trained tree. It takes several years to produce the fan shape and it's only after you have done so that you start pruning to produce fruit. So it's much better to let the nurseryman take all that time and trouble. You can generally buy trees that are trained with three or four branches either side and then you simply tie them in to canes as described for pears (see p. 210).

When it comes to pruning for fruit, you must always bear in mind that the fruit is borne on wood the tree made the year before. Once you know that it's simple.

In the first summer, aim to get shoots about 4 inches (10 cm) apart along each of the branches. Any extra ones should be rubbed off while they're still soft. Tie in the shoots you retain. You should also rub out any shoots that are growing directly into the wall or directly away from it.

In the second summer, it's those shoots that will bear fruit. Wait until they're about 4–6 inches (10–15 cm) long and check that there's a shoot growing out from near the base. Then pinch out the tip of the shoot. The one that's growing near the base is the replacement shoot that will bear the fruit next year, so just leave it to grow. After fruiting, prune out the shoot that has borne fruit and tie in the one growing from the base, and the process starts again. And that's really all there is to it.

## Cultivation

In cold springs, you'll need to give the peaches plenty of attention. If the weather is keeping insects away, it's best to hand-pollinate the open flowers. Choose a sunny day if there is one and go over the tree just touching the insides of the flowers with a soft paintbrush to transfer pollen from one to another.

You'll also need to keep an eye on the weather forecast. In the event of a frost warning, cover the trees with polythene in the way described for pears (see p. 211).

## Harvesting

When the peaches colour up, they must be tested for ripeness every day, since you must

avoid them falling and bruising. Just gently cup your hand underneath and give the fruits a slight lift and a twist. If they come away easily they're ripe. They'll keep for a day or two in a cool place.

*Peach 'Rochester'.*

PRUNING PEACHES

**1** *Ready-trained tree with main branches tied to canes and fixed to horizontal wires.*

**2** *On established trees in summer selected side-shoots are allowed to grow 4–6 leaves and then pinched back. Replacement shoot near base is allowed to grow.*

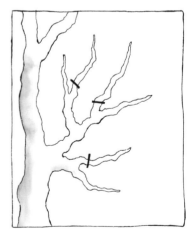

**3** *In winter, cut out shoots that have fruited and tie the replacements on to canes.*

## 🦎 PLUMS AND APRICOTS 🦎

Plums and apricots have been grouped together here because they're grown in much the same way. The biggest difference is that, while plums are tough and hardy, apricots will do best grown as fans against a south-facing wall. I would grow plums as fans, too, but for a different reason.

Perhaps their greatest enemy is the bull-finch – one of those birds we've been trying to tempt into our garden! But in winter and early spring they can strip a tree of its buds in next to no time. Obviously it would be quite a problem to net a big tree but simple if the tree is grown against the wall or a fence. Also,

plums flower in April when there will be a constant risk of frost damage, so it's useful to be able to employ the covering method described for pears and peaches. With that proviso, plums can be grown facing east or west. They look superb in blossom in the spring, in leaf in summer and then in fruit, so they're well worth the fence-space.

**Varieties**

Some varieties are self-fertile and I would recommend sticking to them unless you have some particular preference, when, of course, you'll need to grow two trees of different varieties.

*Plum 'Marjorie's Seedling'.*

'*Denniston's Superb*'. An early variety producing green fruits with a red flush and a very good flavour. It flowers early so you'll have to be on your guard against frost.

'*Czar*'. Generally classed as a cooking variety though I like its fresh flavour when eaten straight from the tree. It flowers late and shows some frost resistance, so it's a good choice for colder gardens. The fruits are large, deep purple and with a slightly acid flavour. It crops in early August.

'*Victoria*'. The most popular of all and excellent for cooking and eating fresh. The fruits are large and deep red with a superb flavour, and it consistently yields heavy crops. It's ready in early September.

'*Marjorie's Seedling*'. Another variety classed as a cooker but with a good flavour for eating fresh too. It has the great advantage of flowering late and could well miss the worst of the frosts. It produces large, deep blue fruits in September or early October.

'*Moorpark*'. One of the most popular apricots, producing large, round, yellow fruits with a red flush. This one is also self-fertile.

## Rootstocks

Apricots are generally grafted on St Julien A, which is ideal for fan-trained trees as they're less vigorous than plums. However, plums make big trees and so I would recommend the newer stock Pixy, which makes trees about half or even two thirds the size – unless, that is, you have a very big space to fill.

## Planting

Plant plums in the way described for apples (see p. 205), bearing in mind the previous remarks about the aspect. Apricots, like peaches, detest poor drainage, so its worthwhile preparing the planting space in the way described for peaches (see p. 213).

## Pruning

Once again, it's wise to start with ready-trained trees to save a lot of time and trouble. They're readily available from fruit specialists.

Plums suffer from a fungus disease called silverleaf, which will severely debilitate and eventually kill the trees. It enters through open wounds so, to reduce the risk of infection to

---

TRAINING AND PRUNING PLUMS AND APRICOTS

**1** *Branches tied to canes fixed to horizontal wires.*

**2** *In summer, pinch out shoots after they've made 6 leaves.*

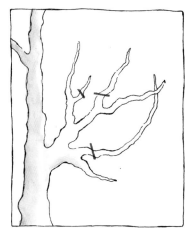

**3** *In autumn, cut back pinched shoots by half. Remove overcrowded or crossing wood.*

a minimum, pruning should be done when the tree is growing strongly and will callus over quickly. The best time is between April and the end of August.

Tie the side-branches to canes in the fan shape as described for pears (see p. 210). In April, remove any shoots that are growing directly towards or away from the wall and then simply tie in shoots to cover the wall. Pinch out any shoots that are overcrowded or not needed. When a shoot outgrows its space, pinch out the growing tip.

## Cultivation

Net the trees against birds both in the winter to deter bullfinches and in the summer to prevent all kinds of birds attacking the fruit. Protect the blossoms from frost, especially in the case of apricots. Mulch generously with compost to retain moisture each spring.

## Harvesting

If you grow plums for bottling or jam-making, it's best to pick the fruits just before they're ripe. Fruits for eating should be allowed to ripen and be eaten straight from the tree. They will keep for only a few days. The time to pick apricots is a matter for argument. Some people like them when they're slightly under-ripe and firm, while others prefer them soft and juicy. They can be dried or bottled and make very good jam.

## CHERRIES

Cherries, both sweet and acid, should always, in the ornamental kitchen garden, be grown as fans on the fence or wall. Even on the new semi-dwarfing rootstocks they make big trees if they're grown as free-standing specimens and that makes them impossible to cover with bird netting. And if you don't do that, you stand little chance, particularly in this garden, of eating any fruit yourself. The birds you've attracted, who always get up earlier in the morning than you, are bound to get there first. Grown on the fence, cherries are easy to protect. They make a very attractive show too, with a mass of blossom in the spring, the colour of the fruits in summer and a bonus of rich leaf colours in autumn.

## Varieties

There is only one reliable self-fertile cherry, so that's the one to go for, since you're unlikely to want two trees in a small garden. 'Stella' is a fairly vigorous grower and perhaps not the best flavoured of all, though quite acceptable. It's fruits are quite large and black, and they're ready for picking in July.

Since it's very likely that you'll be growing an acid cherry to make use of your north-facing fence, another alternative is to grow the sweet variety that is pollinated by it. 'Bigarreau Gaucher' produces large black cherries with an excellent flavour. It has the advantage of late flowering, so frost damage is less likely. It's pollinated by 'Morello' and is ready for picking in July.

'Morello' is the most popular acid cherry and quite delicious when cooked or made into jam. It's self-fertile and will produce good crops of cherries as well as very attractive spring flowers on a north-facing fence or wall. It's ready for picking in July or August.

## Rootstocks

Most cherries now are budded onto the semi-dwarfing rootstock Colt. It should be noted that it does by no means produce dwarf trees like the apples grown on really dwarfing stocks. But it does tend to bring the trees into bearing a little earlier in their lives and they finish up about a third smaller than those on other stocks. Colt is suitable for both sweet and acid cherries.

## Planting

Plant sweet cherries on a west-facing fence and acid types on a north-facing one. If you decide to grow two trees, it's best to leave about 12 feet (3.6 m) between sweet cherries, though 'Morello', which is rather smaller, can go in 8 feet (2.4 m) apart. As with other fruit trees, make sure the union between the rootstock and the variety is well above the ground because regular mulching will raise the soil level. Cherries are rather prone to virus diseases so make sure the nurseryman can guarantee that his stock is virus-free.

## Pruning

Like plums, cherries are prone to silverleaf disease and to bacterial canker, so the less pruning that's done the better. In any case, postpone pruning until the plants are growing vigorously from April to August.

Sweet cherries are pruned and trained just like plums (see p. 216). Acid cherries fruit on wood they made the previous year, so they must be pruned like peaches (see p. 213), though the side-shoots can be left closer together at about 2 inches (5 cm) apart.

## Cultivation

There's little to do except to protect the trees from frost with a polythene screen and from birds by draping netting over the tree in June. In dry weather it will pay to hand-water if you can.

*Netting will protect against birds.*

*Cherry 'Morello'.*

## Harvesting

Allow cherries to stay on the tree as long as possible in order to develop their full sweetness and flavour, though catch them before they split. Take them off the tree with the stalk intact but beware of taking part of the twig with it since this can create an entry point for fungus disease. The best bet is to cut them off with scissors. They will keep only a few days but can be successfully preserved by bottling or making into jam.

Even though the average fan can produce about 15 lbs (480 g), I have yet to meet the gardener who can't happily eat all he grows straight from the tree!

## 🜪 CITRUS FRUITS 🜪

Citrus fruits are, of course, associated with warmer countries but they can be grown very well in a more temperate climate. In fact they prefer to be on the cool side and hate wildly fluctuating temperatures. A night temperature of 40°F (5°C) and a little higher during the day will suit them admirably. They can therefore be grown in pots in the greenhouse in winter and can happily spend the summer outside where they make a most attractive and interesting patio plant.

They are all grown as bushes using much the same cultivation techniques.

### Types and varieties

*Oranges.* 'Washington Navel' is one of the best, with very juicy, sweet and almost seedless flesh. 'Late Valencia' produces large, juicy fruits which hold on the tree for a long period. 'Seville' is the best of the bitter oranges for making marmalades and preserves.

*Mandarin oranges.* 'Satsuma' is a dwarf, weeping, Japanese tree producing small fruits with an excellent 'tangerine' flavour. 'Encore' is a recent introduction from California producing rich, juicy fruits that are orange with darker spots.

*Lemons.* 'Meyer's' is certainly the best for temperate climates. It's compact and prolific and flowers almost continuously, producing medium sized fruit with a very good flavour. 'Quatre Saisons' is a popular variety from the Mediterranean which is very prolific.

*Limes.* 'Tahiti' is a large, sweet, seedless lime which makes a compact but very prolific bush. Keep it at a higher temperature in winter than other citrus plants. If you can't provide sufficient winter heat, grow a limequat. The variety 'Eustis' is very prolific, producing fruits slightly smaller than the lime but with the same aromatic flavour. It's more cold tolerant and easier to grow.

*Grapefruit.* 'Golden Special' is a large, yellow, very juicy variety from New Zealand. It's very prolific when well grown.

### Planting

Citrus plants prefer slightly acid conditions. So grow them in an acid compost in a container no less than 15 inches (38 cm) in diameter. They like good drainage, too. A mix of 2 parts good soil to 1 part of coarse grit and garden compost or a peat alternative would do well. If in addition you can mix an extra part of manure in, it'll do nothing but good. I like to plant into terracotta pots as they allow more air through the compost than plastic and look beautiful on the patio.

'Meyer's Lemon'.

## Cultivation

Try to keep the plants cool at all times. In winter they must stay in the greenhouse at a minimum temperature of 40°F (5°C). After the danger of frost has passed, they'll be much better outside. Bring them in again in October.

Young plants are averse to too much fertilizer, which could scorch their roots. Feed with a liquid animal manure and make sure the plants don't dry out.

If you can do it, spray the plants with water each morning, except when they're in flower.

## Pruning

Carry out pruning in winter and after fruits have been harvested. The winter-pruning consists of thinning out overcrowded branches and removing any that are dead or diseased as well as those that are growing into the centre of the bush.

After picking fruit, prune back the branch you picked from, to leave it about 4 inches (10 cm) long.

## Harvesting and storing

Oranges and grapefruits can be harvested when the fruits are well coloured by twisting them gently off the tree, but lemons and limes are best snipped off with a pair of secateurs. In fact, you can leave the fruits on the trees for quite a long time – up to six months sometimes – and they won't deteriorate.

To store them, put them in boxes and cover them with a few inches of dry sand. Put the boxes in a cool but frost-free place and they'll keep in good condition for about two months.

##  MULBERRIES

Mulberries are only for the larger garden. They make wonderful dome-headed trees but, alas, a majestic 20–30 feet (6–9 m) across. The trees are slow growing, but could cause problems in a small space within 10 years. If you have the room there are few more attractive fruiting tress. They can, however, be grown as fans on a south-facing wall.

## Varieties

The best fruits come from the hardiest species, so stick with the black mulberry, *Morus nigra*, offered by many general nurserymen and fruit specialists. The only variety I have seen is 'Large Black'. They're grown on their own roots and are self-fertile.

## Planting

Standard trees are often grown in the lawn to prevent the fruit from bruising when it falls. Fans should preferably be planted against a south wall, though a west-facing one will do. Container-grown plants will transplant best.

## Pruning

Plant fans against a pattern of canes as recommended for pears (see p. 210). Tie in four or five branches and allow shoots to grow from these at about 1 foot (30 cm) intervals to cover the wall. When side-shoots arise from these, they are summer-pruned just like pears, but this time leave the shoots a little longer at about 4–5 inches (10–12.5 cm).

Standards need little or no pruning, though some side-shoots can be shortened in July to create a series of fruiting spurs.

## Harvesting

The fruits are ready to harvest in August or September and can be carefully picked by hand from fan-trained trees. With large trees it's probably best to follow the old custom of laying a sheet on the grass and allowing the fruit to fall onto it. They won't keep for long but can be bottled or made into jam.

## MEDLARS

Medlars are wonderfully evocative trees and I would grow one for its historical associations alone. They were widely grown in the six-teenth century when they were valued as a fruit and a flavouring and also for medicinal purposes. But it has to be admitted that Cobbett much later described the fruit as being 'only one degree better than a rotten apple'. They're an acquired taste!

Though the fruit doesn't appeal to every-one's taste, medlars are worth growing for their decorative value. They form a small, free-standing tree, with angular, twisted branches that are attractive even in winter. Then in May and June the tree is covered in pale pink flowers, and in the autumn the leaves turn a rich russet red.

### Varieties

Probably the best is the variety 'Nottingham'. It produces small, pear-shaped fruits with a very fine flavour. 'Royal' yields probably the best of all and the fruits are quite well flavoured too.

### Rootstocks

Medlars are either budded onto pear or quince stocks or grown on their own roots. The rootstock seems to make little difference to the size of the tree.

### Planting

Medlars are quite hardy, and so can be planted anywhere where a little height is needed.

### Pruning

Little pruning is needed. Simply remove dead, diseased or overcrowded wood in the winter and cut back to shape up the tree.

### Harvesting

The fruits are ready for harvesting in early November and they should be picked when they come away from the tree quite easily. They'll still be hard at this stage.

Now they must be stored in sand, with just their stalks poking out, for about three weeks. They'll then be soft and ready to eat. This process is known as 'bletting', and it's this that generally puts people off because the fruit turns brown and looks rotten. However, if you can bring yourself to taste one, you'll experience a pleasant, slightly apple-like flavour.

They don't store long after that but can be made into a delicious jelly which is much sought after by connoisseurs for flavouring game dishes.

*Medlar 'Nottingham'.*

# Chapter 9

# SOFT FRUIT – AND SOME OTHERS

The principle of the ornamental kitchen garden is that, to earn its place, every plant and artefact must be beautiful as well as productive. With some soft fruit that's a tall order.

It has to be said that there's little to thrill the soul of an artist in a raspberry cane and nothing to stir the blood in a tangle of blackberry. Yet it would be quite out of the question for anyone aiming at near self-sufficiency

*A fig is worth growing for its foliage alone.*

to miss them out. So they have to be made as attractive as possible and, in some cases, either hidden from view or camouflaged.

Of course, beauty in the garden is very much in the eye of the beholder. I wouldn't be without a blackcurrant bush or two, for example, just for the rich smell they impart when you pass by, especially on a wet day. And I can still get a thrill from the foliage of a gooseberry bush in spring when it has all the fresh green promise of youth.

And – let's give credit where it's due – there are one or two soft fruits that are decidedly beautiful. I would, for example, grow a fig on my wall for its foliage alone even if it never produced a fruit. I actually do grow grape vines just for their foliage.

Still, here and there I have had to cudgel my brains to try to find ways to make some of the soft fruit acceptable. I hope you think I've succeeded in my endeavours.

## BUYING PLANTS

When buying soft fruit, the same rules apply as for tree fruit, as outlined in Chapter 8. First, it'll pay hands down to buy from a fruit specialist. Most fruits are subject to virus diseases and are covered by the Ministry of Agriculture scheme that guarantees clean plants. If your source of supply can't confirm that the plants are virus tested, it's best to go elsewhere.

Again, in most cases it also pays to buy vigorous young trees from a nursery rather than tired old specimens from the garden centre. Some garden centres do now stock young trees in pots and they're good value, but anything more than two years old is best left alone. And it makes sense to buy at the right time of the year. There's absolutely no point, for example, in buying strawberries in April. They won't produce fruit that year, so you might as well get virus tested plants that you know will be healthy and full of the vigour of youth, at the right time, in late summer. It's the same with most soft fruit.

There are many new varieties available because research stations have been busy breeding them for the commercial grower. But, as with vegetables, the commercial grower's varieties are not necessarily best for the garden. The black currant variety 'Jet', for example, was made popular by nurserymen a few years back, mainly because it was grown in large numbers for the trade and gardeners got what was left. But the main attribute of 'Jet' was that the sprigs of fruit stuck out from the bush in a way that made them easy to harvest mechanically. Not a great advantage to the gardener.

## 🐦 MAKING SPACE 🐦

Soft fruit bushes do take up a lot of space in the garden, so I've tried to find ways to grow them so that this problem is reduced. Like tree fruit, some of them can be grown on the fence as cordons or fans. Some others can be grown as standards. This means that the 'bush' is grafted onto a long stem, so that the space beneath it can be utilized. Done like this, gooseberries look rather attractive too.

Raspberries caused me quite a problem because, in my small garden, wherever I wanted to put a row they excluded valuable light from a large part of the garden. I solved that by growing them in a circle. Again, the pillar of green thus created looks really good.

Strawberries proved to be a problem

because they do take up a lot of room and they can't be grown as cordons on the fence or as standards. I simply had to find a space for them because I wouldn't want to be without fresh strawberries. If you're even more restricted than I am, you can grow them in containers, or grow one of the smaller, decorative varieties.

I gave up growing figs and grapes in my greenhouse for a while because they inevitably take up such a lot of room when they're grown as permanent fixtures. But I eventually found a way of growing even those so that they could be stood outside all summer and I could devote my greenhouse space to tomatoes and another fruit I can't resist – melons.

## 🐦 PROBLEMS 🐦

Soft fruit bushes are notoriously subject to a million-and-one pests and diseases. So are they a good idea in an organic garden? Well, I can honestly say that in the ten years that I've been growing my soft fruit organically I've never had a problem that couldn't be solved.

On occasion I've had to pick off caterpillars by hand. Once in a while I've thrown away a slug-damaged strawberry but that has never happened enough to worry me. In one hair-raising incident I lost all the leaves from my gooseberries because of mildew. But even that I've learned to overcome by growing resistant varieties.

The only safeguard I employ now is to net almost everything against birds, to water well in dry weather to help keep away the mildew, and to spray with liquid seaweed every fortnight. I believe strongly that a healthy, strong plant will have much more chance of surviving attacks from diseases and that, provided I don't poison them with chemicals, the birds, the ground beetles, the ladybirds and the hoverflies will keep my plants free from pests. They haven't let me down yet.

## ❧ STRAWBERRIES ❧

Strawberries are about the most accommodating of soft fruits. They can be grown in the borders or in containers on the patio, and even in hanging baskets – and they'll produce a full crop of fruit just nine months after planting. They're easy to grow and, with one exception, will set a full crop on their own pollen. The foliage is very attractive, too, especially alongside low-growing flowering plants. And there's the bonus of attractive white flowers in spring and red fruits to follow.

**Varieties**

New varieties now available to gardeners mean that strawberries can be harvested from June until October with hardly a break. In fact, if they're forced in the greenhouse and under cloches it's possible to have them as early as May.

'*Pantagruella*'. The earliest of all and the one I would recommend for forcing. It's not especially heavy cropping and the fruit is perhaps not quite as well-flavoured as the mid-season varieties. But, as they're the first of the year when strawberries are extremely expensive to buy, who's going to argue?

'*Idil*'. An early summer variety which bears heavy crops with a good flavour. I've grown it for a few years now and the most notable feature is its freedom from disease – an important consideration in a no-spray garden.

'*Elsanta*'. A mid-season variety now being taken up widely by commercial growers. It's a vigorous grower, a heavy cropper and the flavour is good. It's said to be prone to mildew, though I have never had trouble on my heavy soil. If you have a light soil, it would pay to manure it well prior to planting (which you're going to do anyway), and to water in dry weather.

'*Hapil*'. Crops at about the same time as 'Elsanta' and has less trouble with mildew. The flavour is superb, too, though it's said to be prone to verticillium wilt and red spider mite. Again, I have not noticed any problems.

'*Pandora*'. A recently introduced variety which bridges the gap between the summer and the autumn varieties that was hitherto barren. It crops well and has an excellent flavour but is alone in needing another variety as a pollinator. That's no problem, though, because all the mid-summer ones will serve.

'*Aromel*'. Without doubt the best of the autumn-fruiting varieties. My plants always want to fruit in spring as well, but I remove the flowers to save the plants' strength until September and October. The fruits are large and the flavour is nothing short of superb.

'*Serenata*'. An odd man out but tailor-made for the ornamental kitchen garden. It produces masses of small plants which quickly cover the ground to form effective ground cover. The foliage is attractive but the outstanding feature is that the numerous flowers are deep pink and borne for most of the summer. The fruit, which comes in early summer and again in late summer into autumn, is small but the flavour is quite wonderful. It has a slightly musky taste which is not found in other varieties. Highly recommended.

**Planting**

If you go to the garden centre, you'll find it's possible to buy strawberry plants just about all the year round. There's certainly no point in doing so, though. The time to plant is August or September and it's always best to buy from a fruit specialist or at least where the plants can be guaranteed virus-free. Strawberries are quite prone to virus diseases, so it really is important to start clean.

If you plant in August or September, you'll be able to harvest a full crop the following year. Leave it much later and you'll have to remove the flowers in the spring to make sure you build up the plants for the following year.

I have planted strawberries in a long row at the back of a narrow border, but I prefer them planted in groups together with the flowers. They look very attractive in threes, but remember that they're quite vigorous plants, so put them at least 18 inches (45 cm) apart.

When planting, it's important to ensure that the 'crown' of the plant is exactly at soil level. Too shallow and the frost will push the plants out of the soil; too deep and the crown will rot off. Plant firmly and water in well. Check after hard frosts that the plants haven't lifted.

*Plant strawberries with the 'crown' at soil level.*

## Cultivation

Strawberries need little attention except to guard against pests. Our friend the slug and the birds will both want to have a go at your precious fruits. So, as soon as the first small fruits have set, put a good layer of straw underneath the plants, tucking it well beneath the leaves to raise the fruit off the ground. An alternative is to use special strawberry mats made of felt of plastic, both of which are obtainable in the garden centre. Either material will serve to keep the fruit from being splashed with mud and to ensure that it's out of the way of slugs – well, as far as you *can* ensure that.

Don't get over-enthusiastic and mulch under the plants too early. If you do it when they're flowering, you'll insulate the flowers from the residual warmth of the soil and this could cause frost damage.

Birds, always a problem, are easily controlled by netting the plants. Try to stretch the netting tightly rather than just draping it loosely over the plants. This will avoid entangling the legs and feet of inquisitive birds.

When the fruit is beginning to swell, it will pay to give the plants a good watering but, again, don't do it too early. If you apply too much water before flowering has finished, you'll encourage rank, leafy growth and a poor crop.

After harvesting, mats should be removed if you've used them and the plants should be trimmed over with shears, cutting off all the old leaves just above the crown. It seems a bit drastic at the time but they'll soon recover and produce a new crop of leaves. Then remove all the cut leaves and straw if you've used it and put them all on the compost heap. Then clean up any weeds you may find and the plants are ready to face the winter.

*Raise strawberries off the ground with a mulch of straw.*

*Strawberry 'Serenata'.*

## Harvesting

Pick over the crop regularly, taking the fruits with stalk attached. If you pull off the fruits leaving the white 'plug' inside, it's likely to attract fungus disease.

Strawberries will not store except in jam. It is possible to freeze them but they always go soft and sloppy and taste *awful*.

## Forcing

The first crops will come from early varieties that have been forced in the greenhouse. These can come from runners from your stock plants, which are quite easy to root.

Just sink a pot of compost in the soil next to the plant and, in July, find a runner and hold it down onto the surface of the compost with a wire pin. It will root in a few weeks and can then be severed from its parent. I don't recommend doing this for replacing plants outside, because of the risk of virus disease. It's much better to lessen that chance by buying in fresh, virus-tested plants from a known source. But plants that are forced are going to be thrown away afterwards anyway, so there will be no harm done.

Whether you do that or buy plants in for the purpose, they should be potted in August into 7 inch (18 cm) pots of soilless compost and left outside. During the winter, it's essential to keep them dry but cold, so either put them in the well-ventilated cold frame or leave them out turned on their sides.

They shouldn't go into the greenhouse until February because they need a cold spell to initiate fruit. By that time there should have been a few good frosts and they can go into either a cold or heated house and all you have to do is to wait to pick the fruit. They'll never crop very prolifically, but they'll be worth their weight in gold.

After those come the plants forced under cloches or in the cold frame. Again, use an early variety and don't start to protect them until February. After fruiting, it's best to dig

*Strawberry 'Hapil'.*

up the plants and throw them away.

If you're growing autumn-fruiting varieties, plant those where they can be cloched too, as you should be able to prolong the season by protecting the last fruits.

## Container growing

Plants can be grown in tubs and hanging baskets where they look very attractive indeed mixed in with annual flowers. Put them somewhere near the front of the tubs where the fruit will hang down over the edge so that it looks good and can be seen for picking.

Bear in mind that, as with all plants in containers, they'll need to be watered regularly and fed with liquid animal manure about once a month. The difficulty is that the flowering plants may want a little more feeding than the strawberries and there's no way to feed one without the other, so something must take pot luck. I would suggest the strawberries.

Strawberry barrels are popular and look very elegant on the patio, but they do have one snag. It's always quite difficult to water the plants right down at the bottom of the container. Start by using a well-draining compost. I would suggest something like a mixture of equal parts of good soil, garden compost and coarse grit. Then, before filling the container, put a piece of plastic drainpipe in the centre, raised slightly above the bottom of the pot. Then you can simply pour water down the pipe to water the bottom.

Even this is not always successful. I eventually resorted to mixing the planting. In the top levels I grew strawberries but down at the bottom, where the soil would be drier, I planted houseleeks (*Sempervivum*) which thrived in the drier conditions and looked very effective too.

## BLACKCURRANTS

A delicious fruit, full of vitamin C, easy to grow and very prolific, but alas, not very beautiful. I have yet to find a way of making the blackcurrant bush anything other than it really is – a fairly ordinary green bush with insignificant flowers. In fairness, though, the shining black fruit is attractive and the smell of the whole plant is wonderful. I have seen it grown as a sort of fan on a wall, but at best it looks ungainly and is not very happy that way. Stick to growing it as a bush and content yourself with a great aroma and more fruit than you could possibly hope for.

### Varieties

'*Ben Sarek*'. A new variety which will soon become the most widely grown in gardens because of its compact shape. It is a much smaller bush than usual but bears excellent crops of very tasty berries.

'*Ben More*' is a larger variety but could be better for gardens in colder areas as it flowers late. It's heavy cropping and well-flavoured.

*Blackcurrant 'Ben More'.*

'Ben Lomond' is much the same as 'Ben More' in flavour and size but flowers earlier. It generally yields better, however, and therefore could be a good choice for warmer gardens.

## Planting

Once more it'll pay to buy plants from a fruit specialist. Not only will he have a wider range of varieties, he'll be able to guarantee freedom from virus disease. Buy one-year-old plants and always shun the tired two and three-year-olds that are sometimes seen in garden centres.

Blackcurrants are grown as a 'stool', the aim being to encourage lots of young shoots from the base of the plant. Plant them about 2 inches (5 cm) lower than they grew on the nursery. In the ornamental kitchen garden they are best planted individually rather than in groups. They can then be surrounded by flowering plants both for aesthetic reasons and to help camouflage them from pests. If you do decide to plant more than one bush, however, remember that they need at last 4 feet (120 cm)) between them, though 'Ben Sarek' can go in at 3 feet (90 cm) intervals. The normal practice in this garden, of course, is to prepare the soil well with manure or compost and it's even more important for black-currants. They're very heavy feeders, so give them a good sprinkling of blood, fish and bone fertilizer, too. While it's possible to buy plants from the garden centre at any time, it's best to plant in the dormant season.

## Pruning

Immediately after planting, cut all the shoots hard back to within 1 inch (2.5 cm) of the ground. This will mean that they'll bear no fruit in the current year but will spend their energies getting established and making fresh new growth for fruiting the following year.

In the first winter there will be very little to do. Just remove any shoots that are really weak. The second winter, after the crop has been harvested, you can start hard-pruning and this should, from now on, be repeated annually in the winter. Cut right out all branches that have borne fruit, leaving only new young branches for fruiting the next season.

On older bushes you may find that you have to cut back to a strong, low side-shoot growing out of the old wood if there's little new wood growing directly from the base.

## Cultivation

When the fruits are beginning to swell, it'll pay to water well. And, of course, the bushes should be kept clear of weeds at all times. Give the plants a feed with blood, fish and bone meal each February and mulch with compost or manure. You'll need to watch out for birds because bullfinches in particular strip the buds in spring and, later on, all kinds of birds will be after the fruits. The answer is to net them but, again, try to pull the netting tight to avoid birds getting caught in it.

## Harvesting

Pick the fruit with the stalks still on. They can easily be removed later with a table fork. Blackcurrants can be preserved by bottling and in jam and they also freeze quite well.

## Propagation

To ease the budget, you could buy just one bush and use the prunings to make hardwood cuttings. Do the job in the winter, cutting off young shoots of the current season's wood. Trim them top and bottom with sharp secateurs to leave them about 8 inches (20 cm) long. Cut below a bud at the bottom and above one at the top. Leave all the growth buds on and put the cuttings into a sand-lined trench outside, so that just the top three buds show. Firm them in with your heel and leave them until the following autumn when they can be replanted in their fruiting positions.

## ❧ GOOSEBERRIES, RED ❧ CURRANTS, WHITE CURRANTS

Gooseberries can be grown in attractive shapes and are the earliest bushes to fruit, so they are very welcome after a winter of frozen, bottled or, perish the thought, *bought* produce. Red currants and white currants are very attractive when in fruit – so much so that it always seems a pity to harvest the brilliant red or shining silver berries to eat. All are grown in exactly the same way.

### Varieties

When choosing gooseberries, the most important factor to consider, before yield or flavour even, is the inbuilt resistance to mildew. Gooseberries are a martyr to American gooseberry mildew, which coats the leaves with a white felt from which they don't recover. However, there are now varieties which show a real resistance to the disease and it's these that I would recommend every time. They can be prone to virus diseases, so buy from a source that can guarantee freedom from these.

*'Jubilee'*. A recent introduction which is very similar to the popular old variety 'Careless', but with a good resistance to mildew. The variety has also been cleaned of virus disease, so it's one of the best bets for the organic gardener. It produces heavy crops of large yellow berries which can be used for cooking or, if left to ripen, for eating fresh.

*'Invicta'*. Another new variety with good resistance to mildew. It too gives good yields of large, white, well-flavoured berries. It has the one disadvantage for this garden that it's quite a wide-spreading bush and is covered in fairly vicious spines.

*'Red Lake'*. The best of the red currants, with heavy crops of juicy, well-flavoured berries borne on long, easy-to-pick sprigs.

*'White Versailles'*. About the only widely available variety of white currant, a fruit which has gone out of favour recently. The fruits are excellent eaten fresh or cooked and make an attractive display in the borders.

### Planting

Gooseberries and currants can be grown in different ways to make the best of the space available. Whichever way you decide to do it, buy the plants in the autumn and plant them, unlike blackcurrants, at the same level they grew on the nursery. Gooseberries and red and white currants are grown on a 'leg' – a short stem to make weeding underneath easier and to keep the fruit off the ground.

If you decide to grow them as ordinary bushes, plant them about 4 feet (120 cm) apart. This is a suitable way for big gardens, but in smaller spaces where growing room is at a premium you'll save space by growing them as cordons or standards. You can buy cordons already trained as three-armed 'triple-cordons' and this is certainly the best bet. Plant them against a south, east or west-facing wall, setting the plants 3 feet (90 cm) apart.

Standards form a bushy head on a 3–4 foot (90–120 cm) stem. They can be planted as close as 5 feet (150 cm) apart, but in the ornamental kitchen garden they will probably look better well separated. When they're planted, make sure they have a strong stake right to the head of the plant and that the stem is firmly tied to it with proper tree or standard rose ties. When the plants are full of fruit there will be a great deal of weight to support. I have only seen standards of gooseberries for sale, though there's no reason why currants should not be grown in this way too.

*Red currant 'Red Lake', a heavy cropper with a good flavour.*

## Pruning

Bushes need little attention. Aim to keep the centre of the bush open by pruning out dead, diseased, crossing or overcrowded wood in winter. It pays to shorten the main branches by about a third of their length, cutting back to a downward or outward-facing bud for erect varieties and to an upward-facing one for drooping types. Do this in the winter too.

Standards are pruned in the same way, but standing up!

Cordons are great fun, look good and take up no more than 6 inches (15 cm) of space, so they're well worth a little extra trouble. Unlike apples, the 'arms' are grown vertically rather than at an angle to the ground.

Triple cordons look something like a trident and each arm should be trained so that they're spaced 1 foot (30 cm) apart. If you can only get double cordons, they're done in exactly the same way except that the plants will be 2 feet (60 cm) apart with still 1 foot (30 cm) between each arm. Fix wires to the wall to take 6 foot (180 cm) canes spaced at 1 foot (30 cm) intervals. Tie the branches to the canes and cut back by about a third each winter.

In August, cut back all side-shoots that have grown from the main branches to leave just three buds. In this way you'll build up a system of fruiting spurs in the same way as described for apples (see p. 205).

## Cultivation

There's virtually nothing to do short of weeding and watering and, like black currants, mulching and feeding in February and, of course, netting against birds.

## Harvesting

Start to pick some gooseberries a little before they're fully ripe, leaving room for those remaining to grow. Use the immature fruits for cooking. Those for dessert purposes should be left to ripen fully. They won't keep for long except bottled or as jam. Currants are harvested and removed from their stalks in the same way as black currants (see p. 228).

## Propagation

Take cuttings of gooseberries and currants in the way described for black currants though just a little earlier, in September. Before planting, examine the roots and remove any suckers that may be developing.

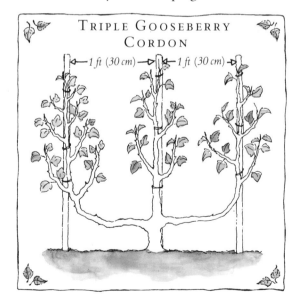

TRIPLE GOOSEBERRY CORDON

—1 ft (30 cm)—  —1 ft (30 cm)—

## 🌿 RASPBERRIES 🌿

You couldn't even consider doing without raspberries. There are few more delicious fruits and, if you plant a few varieties, they'll continue right through to the first frosts. Unfortunately, they have two distinct disadvantages.

They are not the most beautiful of plants at the best of times and should not really qualify for the ornamental kitchen garden since they certainly fail the beauty test. They are also extremely difficult to fit into a very small garden. In my plan I found that, wherever I wanted to put a row, they would not only stop me getting at the other plants behind them, but they'd block out most of the sunshine from those in front of them too. So a bit of lateral thinking was called for.

Why put them in a straight line at all? Well, the answer, of course, is that it's the easiest way to support them. But with a little thought, it wasn't difficult to devise a circular support for them, so that they could be grown as a pillar instead of a row. They don't crop quite so well in this form, because the middle of the circle gets no sun, but they cut out the

*Raspberries grown around a pillar.*

minimum amount of light from other plants and, when they have leaves on, they form a green pillar which looks quite attractive. I have to admit that this aesthetic joy is short lived, because as soon as the new canes begin to grow they look a mess again. But it's at least a verdant green mess, which I can live with. Grown in this way they certainly qualify.

### Summer-fruiting varieties

'*Glen Clova*'. This is a variety which has served me very well over the years. It's full of vigour, reaching 9 feet (270 cm) when established, though it can, of course, be cut back if you want to reduce its height. The fruits are large and have an excellent flavour and the yields are heavy. It crops early in the season.

*Raspberry '*Glen Clova*'.*

'*Glen Prosen*'. A mid-season variety which has spine-free canes and good sized fruit with a fine flavour. It's resistant to greenfly and fairly disease resistant too – always important in an entirely organic garden.

'*Malling Leo*'. A late-fruiting variety with large, firm berries with a sweet, aromatic flavour. It's resistant to aphids.

## Supports

Raspberries must be supported on a post and wire structure. The posts should stand 6 feet (180 cm) above ground level. The wires should be fixed so that the bottom one is 2 feet (60 cm) from the ground with another at the top of the post and one in the middle. If you have room to grow raspberries in a row, the end-posts should be firmly strutted and the intermediate ones should be driven in 10 feet (3 m) apart. To grow them as a column,

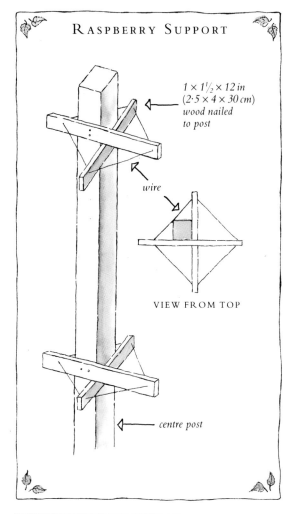

RASPBERRY SUPPORT

1 × 1½ × 12 in
(2·5 × 4 × 30 cm)
*wood nailed to post*

*wire*

VIEW FROM TOP

*centre post*

nail three crosses 3 feet (90 cm) long to a single post at the heights you want the wires. Drill holes in the ends of the arms of the crosses and pass a piece of wire through them to allow you to attach the raspberry canes (see drawing).

## Planting

Buy the canes from a fruit specialist in the autumn or winter and plant them against the supports, setting them 1½ feet (45 cm) apart. After planting, cut them down to leave about 6 inches (15 cm).

## Cultivation

In the first season, new shoots will arise from the base of the plant. Select enough strong ones to tie in to the wires so that they finish 4 inches (10 cm) apart. Cut out any weak or overcrowded ones. It's likely that in the first year the canes won't reach the top wire, but they certainly will as soon as the plants are established.

Feed with blood, fish and bone meal in February and mulch well with compost or manure. If you find any suckers coming up away from the plant, where they can't be used, it's best to pull them out bodily if you can.

## Pruning

There's no pruning to do in the first year. The canes you have tied in will fruit the following year and, at the same time, strong young suckers will again grow up from the base. Wait until you have picked all the fruit and then cut out the fruited canes and tie in the best of the strong young shoots to take their place. If they reach higher than the top of the supports, cut them off about 3 inches (7.5 cm) above the top wire. The old canes can be shredded and used as a weed-suppressing mulch.

## Autumn-fruiting varieties

All the old autumn-fruiting varieties have now been superseded by the recent 'Autumn Bliss'. It actually crops about three times as heavily as 'Heritage' and 'Zeva', the old types.

The canes are weaker in growth than the summer-fruiting ones and the method of growing them quite different. Plant them in a circle, setting the plants about 1 foot (30 cm) apart. There's no need to support them, though they may need to be tied to a central cane with a piece of string round the whole clump if the site is exposed. If you have the room, they can, of course, also be grown in a row.

These raspberries fruit on the current season's wood, so the pruning is very simple. Just cut them hard back to the ground in February, when you give them a feed and a mulch like the summer varieties.

*Pruning autumn-fruiting raspberries.*

## Harvesting

Pull off the fruits leaving the plugs behind. There's little risk of disease this time because the canes will be cut right out shortly afterwards. They don't store except in the freezer, or bottled, and of course they can be made into jam.

 **BRIAR FRUITS**

Briar fruits include blackberries, loganberries and a few other hybrid berries, all of which are grown in the same way. I have to say that in my opinion they're only really suitable for the larger garden. They take up a lot of fence space or they have to be grown on a post and wire structure which takes up a lot of room. Some are quite attractive when in flower and fruit but I have never found a way to grow them in a compact form. Perhaps one day someone will come up with a 'blackberry tree', but it's certainly not available at present. It's also true to say that the flavour of cultivated blackberries is not quite as good as those collected from the hedgerows, though loganberries and tayberries are delicious. Of course, if you grow them in your garden you do at least know that they haven't been sprayed with some noxious agricultural chemical, which is more than you can say for those collected from the hedgerow.

## Varieties

*'Ashton Cross'.* The best of the blackberries for flavour, with very nearly the wild, slightly acid taste. The fruits are somewhat smaller than some other cultivated varieties and the canes are perhaps thinner and slightly less vigorous. It is, however, very high yielding and ready from early August until the end of September.

*Medana Tayberry.* This is a cross between a blackberry and a raspberry. It produces very large fruits with a good flavour when cooked but perhaps a little acid to eat fresh. This is also ready from July to mid-August.

*LY654* is still the best loganberry. The number refers to the trial number it was given at East Malling Research Station where it was developed. For some reason, no one has thought to give it a name! It's thornless so it's

*Loganberry fruits are ready from July to mid-August.*

## Planting

Plant in the autumn against a post-and-wire structure or a sunny fence with supporting wires at 1 foot (30 cm) intervals. Select an easily accessible place because the plants will need to be tied in regularly. (Be sure to buy virus-free plants from a fruit specialist.)

## Training

After planting, cut the canes down to leave about 6 inches (15 cm). When the shoots start to grow, train them onto the wires. If you plant two, put them about 10 feet (3 m) apart. There are two alternative ways of training.

The fruit is borne on one-year-old wood, after which the fruit-bearing shoots are cut out and the new shoots tied into their place to fruit the next season. The easiest way is to train the shoots into the shape of half a fan, with all the first year's shoots being tied on the right of centre. The next year's shoots are tied on the other side, to the left of centre, so it's easy to see which to cut out.

Alternatively, train the shoots into a normal fan and bunch the new shoots into the middle so that they grow straight up. Then, when the old wood has been cut out, they are spread out and tied in their place.

easy to handle, and that, believe me, is a real blessing! Having been cleaned of virus, it's heavy cropping and delicious. I would grow this instead of a blackberry if space was limited. It's ready from July to mid-August.

## TRAINING BRIAR FRUIT

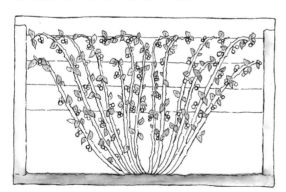

**1** *Fan: one-year-old fruiting wood splayed out in a fan, while new wood is trained in the centre.*

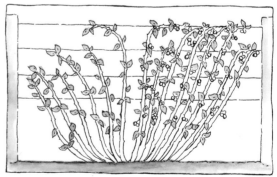

**2** *Alternative method: fruiting wood trained to right, new wood to left.*

Whichever way you do it, it's essential to tie in the new shoots progressively as they grow. If you leave them to form a tangled heap on the ground and then try to unravel them and tie them in, you'll never succeed.

## Cultivation

Feed during February with blood, fish and bone meal and mulch underneath the plants with compost or manure. Water well, especially when the fruits begin to swell, and make sure the plants are kept weed-free. Protect from birds with netting when the fruits begin to colour. This is quite important since at that time of year moisture is likely to be scarce so birds find it through the juice in fruits.

## Harvesting

Harvest the fruits progressively as they ripen. They can be taken off the plug, as the canes will be cut out afterwards. None of the berries will keep unless made into jam or preserves (they freeze quite well).

## RHUBARB

Rhubarb is a delicious 'fruit', always the first of the year to mature, so very welcome just for that. It's also a strikingly beautiful plant. The large leaves and red stems add a strong focal point to the border. They look especially good alongside spiky foliage such as that of flag irises or even chives and onions.

## Varieties

*'Early Victoria'*. An old variety but has still not been surpassed for the first crops of the year. It's sweet and tender, especially when forced.

*'Cawood Delight'*. A strong-growing maincrop variety with deep red stems of excellent quality. It has been cleaned of virus so is vigorous and reliable.

## Planting

Plant the crowns in winter, either bare-rooted or from containers. They are best placed near the middle of the border.

## Cultivation

This is the easiest of plants to grow and requires only weeding and watering.

## Forcing

Forced stems have very much less acid in them and this gives them a very delicate flavour. They'll also come earlier, of course. Force them simply by covering the crowns in late January or February with plastic bins or, preferably, with terracotta forcers, which look marvellous in the garden.

## Harvesting

Pull the stems right from the bottom when they have reached a usable size but never strip the whole plant. After forcing, allow the crown to rest for a year before forcing again: you'll need at least two crowns.

*Using a terracotta forcer on rhubarb.*

## ❧ GRAPES ❧

If ever there was a fruit tailor-made for the ornamental kitchen garden, this is it. Grape vines are extremely decorative in leaf all the season. They start out fresh green and turn to rich russet-purple in autumn. The flowers are not much to look at, but I don't have to tell you how attractive the fruits are. They can be grown outside, though in cooler areas only as wine-making grapes, and they look marvellous trailing through the pergola or rose arbour mixed in with roses and honeysuckle.

They can also be grown in the greenhouse and it's here that dessert grapes can easily be produced even in colder areas. They require very little heat. In a big greenhouse they could be grown in the border and trained into the roof where they'll shade the rest of the plants in summer. In smaller spaces they can be grown as standards on a tall stem, to make a 'grape-tree'.

### Varieties

For outside –
'Madeleine Angevine'. A vigorous variety producing heavy crops of white grapes, which make excellent spicy wine. A good variety for colder areas. Highly recommended.

Grape 'Black Hamburg'.

'Mueller-Thurgau'. Not a suitable variety for wet areas but, if it's given a warm wall, it will produce excellent quality white grapes.

'Siegerebbe'. A honey-sweet grape that can be used for wine or dessert. But it's subject to fungus attack and wasps. It ripens very early.

'Brandt'. A variety producing masses of small red grapes which are good for eating and wine. It has spectacular autumn foliage.

For inside –

'Black Hamburg'. A well-known black grape for the greenhouse. It unfailingly produces good bunches of fine quality grapes, excellent for dessert. It does very well in pots.

'Buckland Sweetwater'. An early white variety producing amber berries of excellent quality.

'Muscat of Alexandria'. A late variety that really needs a little heat to grow it perfectly. The amber berries are of superb quality.

### Planting

Plant outdoor grapes against the pergola or arbour in November or December and cut them down to about 9 inches (23 cm). Prune before the end of January to avoid bleeding. Greenhouse grapes can be planted in the border in the same way and pruned back to leave three buds. Plant at the end of the greenhouse with the idea of training the rods either into the roof or along the back of the staging.

If you intend to grow in pots, it's best really to buy a ready-grown plant. Pot it into a mixture of 3 parts of good garden soil, 2 of garden compost and 1 of coarse grit, using clay pots at least 9 inches (23 cm) in diameter.

### Training

Plants grown up the pergola can be left to their own devices but will not produce so much fruit as those you prune and train. Allow the main stem to grow up over the pergola but reduce the side-shoots to two leaves past the first bunch of grapes you see. This is a job to do when the bunch has just set. If no bunch appears, pinch the shoot at five leaves. If side-shoots are less than about 9 inches (23 cm) apart, it's best to remove some. At the end of the season, once the leaves have fallen, prune the side-shoots back to leave just two good buds. The second bud is an insurance policy and the shoot it makes the following year should be pinched back as soon as the first shoot produces its bunch of grapes.

In the greenhouse allow one main stem (or rod) to grow up into the roof or alternatively train two along the sides of the house about 3 feet (90 cm) above the ground. Again, allow the side-shoots to develop about 9 inches (23 cm) apart and pinch back to two leaves past the first bunch of grapes or at five leaves if no bunch appears. In the winter, prune back to leave two buds.

If you grow a standard in a pot, use your judgement to produce a well-shaped head. When you buy the plant the head will already be formed, so allow one shoot to come from each joint and, when it produces its grapes, allow it to make two more leaves and then pinch it back. Again, after leaf fall, prune the fruited shoots to leave one good bud.

## Cultivation

There's not a great deal to do outside, short of weeding and watering. Grapes are not gross feeders, so fertilizer is seldom necessary in the ornamental kitchen garden where a high level of fertility is maintained for the other plants.

In the greenhouse, make sure that the plants do not become a tangled mess as this will reduce air flow. If this happens, the leaves and fruits will be prone to mildew. So ventilate freely in summer and pinch and tie regularly.

In summer, plants in pots can go outside. Feed greenhouse plants with liquid animal manure once a fortnight.

For dessert grapes, some thinning of the berries will be necessary. Remove a few small berries with scissors, to allow the remainder to grow bigger. Start when they are the size of pearl barley and remove all berries that are facing inwards. Look at them again when they're the size of peas and remove any that are touching.

## Harvesting

Several weeks after the grapes have coloured, they can be harvested. They will not keep, so use them straight away.

TRAINING GRAPES

**1** *At the end of the season prune side-shoots to leave 2 good buds.*

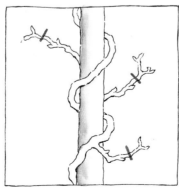

**2** *Pinch out side-shoots 2 leaves past bunch of grapes.*

THINNING GRAPES

*Thin grapes with a small pair of scissors.*

## ❧ FIGS ❧

Another plant that fits into our scheme perfectly. The foliage of a fig is so exotically beautiful that it would deserve its place in the garden even without fruit. Yet it's easy to produce good fruits outside on a south or west-facing wall in warmer parts. Even in cold areas, you'll produce superb fruits with little trouble in the greenhouse.

### Varieties

*'Brown Turkey'*. One of the most reliable varieties, very prolific and early to ripen. The fruits are large and pear-shaped and quite delicious.

*Fig grown as a standard.*

*'Brunswick'*. Produces very large fruit with yellow flesh and a fine flavour. It's one of the hardiest and therefore a good choice for growing outside. The enormous leaves it produces are very attractive indeed.

### Planting

Outside, figs must be planted against a warm wall. Both inside and out, their roots must be restricted to encourage fruit. The ideal spot is in a space on the patio where a paving slab has been left out. Prepare the soil by digging plenty of coarse grit or rubble into the lower levels and refill with soil improved with manure or compost. Plants are generally pot grown and can be put in at any time.

Inside, it's best to grow them in large clay pots. I grow mine very successfully in an 18 inch (45 cm) pot filled with a compost consisting of equal parts of soil, compost and coarse grit. The pot is placed against the wall where the plant can be trained into a fan shape. It's also possible to buy standards which have been run up on a stem about 4–5 feet (120–150 cm) tall. These are exceptionally good for a small garden where greenhouse space is limited because the plants can be stood outside in summer and only brought in when the weather turns cold. Standing on the patio, they look superb.

### Pruning

Train the shoots of fans into wires about 9 inches (23 cm) apart on the wall. They can be tied in with soft string. Pruning consists of removing old wood to encourage vigorous growth from the bottom and this is done after leaf fall. It's sometimes also necessary to pinch back over-vigorous young shoots in summer. The fruit is carried on young shoots so the aim should be to create a succession of them by cutting out the old wood. Standards need to be judiciously pruned to maintain the shape and this is a case of cutting back older wood to a couple of buds after the main shape of the head has been formed.

## Cultivation

Water generously in spring and summer but very little in winter. When the fruit starts to swell in early summer, feed weekly with a liquid fertilizer. The fruits of figs outside actually take two seasons to develop in colder areas. So if you see tiny fruits in winter, leave them on because these will swell to form eatable fruit the following summer. If the fruits are too big they will be spoiled by frost but it could be worthwhile providing protection with a sheet of polythene fixed to two posts when frost is threatened. Fruits will generally ripen in the same season if the plants are in the greenhouse during colder weather.

## Harvesting

Pick the fruits when they're soft and aromatic. They can be stored by drying.

## MELONS

Melons must be grown in the greenhouse or in a cold frame heated by a hotbed (see p. 64). They will produce plenty of good fruits and can grown in the same conditions as tomatoes, so they will fit in with the general greenhouse regime very well. The plants resemble cucumbers but they require less water, better drainage and a lower humidity than cucumbers. In the ornamental kitchen garden, it's best to stick to the smaller fruited types which are easier to grow with other crops.

## Varieties

'Sweetheart'. A small fruited variety producing good crops of delicious yellow fruits.

'Ogen' also produces fruits but these are green with a faint netting on the skin. They have a very fine, distinctive flavour.

## Raising

Sow the seeds in March or April in a temperature of 70°F (21°C), setting two seeds to each 3 inch (7.5 cm) pot of soilless compost. When they come through, thin to leave the strongest seedling. Pot on progressively into the next sized pot until they are ready to go into their final 9 inch (23 cm) pots. They will do well in soilless composts but you will have to be careful not to overwater.

## Cultivation

Tie the plants regularly, either to a cane or to a string fixed to a wire in the roof and 'planted' under the root-ball. In a cold frame, the shoots are allowed to run over the surface of the soil but should be trimmed in the same way as those growing in the greenhouse.

As the plants develop, trim the side-shoots to leave two leaves. Feed with a liquid fertilizer at every watering after the plants have been in the pots for six weeks. Pollinate the female flowers by removing a male flower, pulling back the petals and pushing it into the open female flower. The female has a tiny embryo fruit behind it. Allow only four to six fruits per plant. Once they have formed, the main stem of the plant can be stopped too.

## Harvesting

You'll know when the fruits are ripe and ready to cut by the superb aroma that fills the greenhouse. Press the flower end of the fruit to feel whether it has gone soft. When it has, it's ready to cut. If the fruit is lying on the ground, it's a good idea to protect it from soil organisms by resting it on a piece of slate or wood. The fruits should be eaten straight away.

# Chapter 10

## CONTROL OF PESTS, WEEDS AND DISEASES

Chemical pesticides are specifically designed to kill. Some of them act on the nervous system of insects, some affect the digestive system and there are others which act in different ways. Whatever they do, they're *all* poisons, and therefore present some kind of danger to us too. Of course the chemical companies will claim that they are all rigorously tested and are used in such weak dilutions that there's no risk to human beings at all. What I say is, just look at the protective clothing you're supposed to wear. Rubber gloves, goggles, face masks, overalls, sometimes even breathing equipment. The modern tractor driver looks like a spaceman when he's dressed for work.

But even if chemical pesticides were entirely safe for us, there's no doubt that many of them kill just about every other living thing they touch. I'm quite certain that most of us gardeners are not so arrogant as to believe we have the right to do that. We are not lords of all we survey, but just a link in a long and wonderful chain of life.

The ornamental kitchen gardener *has* to be an organic gardener who is pleased to share his garden with the wildlife around him. Of course we want to fill our plots with birds, bees, butterflies and other insects and you can't do that if you smother everything with poison.

So throw away the chemicals and start again, this time looking at the problem of pest control with a benign eye. Everything, but *everything* has a right to his space and his span on earth and, if you respect all the living things you share your garden with, you'll never need a chemical again. That I promise.

## 🏵 HUSBANDRY 🏵

I strongly believe, and I'm sure that even the chemical addicts would have to agree with me, that a healthy plant will survive attacks from pests and diseases far better than a weakly one. It stands to reason. So rule number one is to grow strong, healthy plants.

First of all, you must maintain a high state of fertility by the methods we've already discussed. Lots of organic matter and the use of organic fertilizers, excluding all others, will produce plants that are tough and healthy. Force-feeding with chemicals leads to soft, sappy growth that's attractive to insect pests and will readily succumb to fungus attack.

But you must also know when to admit defeat. Ideally, raise your plants yourself and use only the strongest ones. If a plant is weak when you plant it out, it's likely never to recover.

Check the acidity of the garden with a lime test kit fairly regularly. Keep the soil somewhere around pH 6.5 if you can, and then only grow those plants that like the conditions. If you find you're struggling with a plant that won't grow whatever you try, throw it out. It could be the introducer of disease to the rest of the garden.

Organic gardeners are often not, by nature, clean and meticulous people. When you're enjoying your gardening as much as I think you will, you're often too busy growing things to worry about cleaning up. But you should make time. When you cut a cabbage, pull out the root, shred it or bash it with a hammer and put it on the compost heap. Sitting in the soil with an open wound, it invites disease. When you've finished the pruning, pick up the bits and put those through the shredder too. When you've done with a dozen pots for the season, dunk them in a tub of very hot water and clean them up. In other words, try to eliminate all the hiding places that disease may lurk.

But while you're doing that, don't also eliminate homes for other wildlife. While I agree that the old leaves stuck under the hedge may be a safe haven for slugs, they'll also be home to ground beetles, perhaps hedgehogs, frogs and toads. All of them are the gardener's friends, so put up with the slugs for their sake.

Make a habit of carefully inspecting your plants quite regularly, especially those that are likely to be attacked at a certain time. Cabbages, for example, are bound to be prey to greenfly most of the year. So turn a few leaves from time to time, looking for egg clusters. When you see them, just rub them off with your thumb and then, having found one, search the rest of the plants.

In the same way look out for caterpillars on most plants. Gooseberries are likely to be attacked by the brown caterpillars of gooseberry sawfly but, if you get them early enough, you can control them with nothing more than thumb and forefinger.

Check also for fungus diseases. As soon as you see a brown leaf on an apple tree, pick it off and confine it to the dustbin. If you see the tell-tale silvery marks of mildew on the shoots, it's worth while cutting them out and getting rid of them completely.

As soon as you see signs of potato blight you should take immediate action. If you're just growing earlies as I suggest you do, you won't be troubled, but maincrop varieties do sometimes succumb late in the season. It's worthwhile cutting off leaves that show signs of brown patches which are the typical symptoms. It shouldn't be long before the whole crop can be lifted and, in my view, it's better

to accept very slightly smaller tubers than risk infecting the whole crop.

You can get your wildlife friends to do a bit of this early clearing up work for you. If you keep the hoe going to stir up the soil, especially at the beginning of the year, you'll not only keep the young weed seedlings down, but you'll also turn up wireworms, cockchafers and especially slugs and snails and their eggs. The birds will thank you very much and scoff the lot.

Finally a bit of husbandry that may or may not be worthwhile. I have been spraying my garden about once a fortnight with liquid seaweed. It will add something in the way of nutrients and growth promotors, but there's also another reason. Seaweed contains an alginate which makes is stick fast to leaves when it's sprayed on. I wonder if insects and even fungus could be deterred from the covered leaves because they don't have the same taste, touch or smell as the ones they're used to. Now I put that forward as an idea only. I haven't yet had the chance to test it scientifically. But I do know that since I've been doing it my problems have been reduced.

## Rotation

I'm not a great believer in rotating crops in a small garden. This is a good system, I'm sure, for organic farmers who can move their cabbages, say, from one side of the village to the other, but in the tiny space of a garden it just doesn't work. As I've said, it's simply sensible to avoid following one crop just harvested with exactly the same thing or similar. But you can do a lot with camouflage.

In many instances, pests locate their host plants either by smell or by sight. Surrounding them with other plants of a completely different type – flowers among vegetables, for example – confuses them and they'll often fly off in search of something a bit more promising. So resist the temptation to plant or sow in anything other than small blocks. Really, the fewer plants per block the better.

## ENCOURAGING YOUR ALLIES

In the main, the ornamental kitchen gardener's strategy should be to grow as wide a diversity of plants as possible and never to use noxious chemicals. That's a sure-fire way of building up a balance of wildlife so that no one species becomes a threat. But there are one or two special friends who should be encouraged.

Hoverflies are among the best controllers of greenfly. They lay their eggs in clutches of greenfly, so that when the larvae hatch out they have an instant meal on tap. And they get through a lot of greenfly. As I pointed out in Chapter 5, the adult female needs a feed of pollen before she lays and, since she only has a short feeding tube, flowers with an open structure are what she'll be looking for. Poached Egg Plant, dwarf Convolvulus and French and English Marigolds are best.

Hoverflies, by the way, have a cunning method of defence against their own predators. They dress up as wasps, with striped abdomens, though they are a little smaller generally. So if you see hundreds of small wasps buzzing around your plants, don't worry and for heaven's sake don't kill them.

Ladybirds and lacewings also eat plenty of aphids and other insect pests but I know of no specific plant to attract them. Just maintain a wide diversity.

Of course, once you get all these insects into the garden, you'll automatically attract the birds too. They'll clear up greenfly, most caterpillars, and slugs and snails. But there are some allies who should be protected against the birds. The defence policy here is far more complex than NATO will ever be!

Ground beetles are wonderful friends to have. They don't look it, I'm afraid, with large, shining black bodies and often cruel looking jaws. If you were a slug or a caterpillar, you would certainly have cause for concern, but gardeners have nothing whatever to fear. Ground beetles are extremely good at devouring slugs, snails and caterpillars

*Seven-spot ladybirds making a meal of aphids on a rose bud.*

and will also have a go at cockchafer grubs and wireworms, so should be encouraged.

Since they're carnivores, there's not a lot you can do to encourage them into the garden, though there are bound to be plenty about naturally. But one thing you can and must do is to provide them with shelter. They hunt during the night, but by day they're prey to our other allies, the birds. So give them plenty of ground cover, a few slates or flat stones they can crawl under.

Hedgehogs are more difficult. These are transient creatures who may come to stay for a few days, even for a few months, but, like the gipsies, can't be tied down. You may be able to encourage them to stay some time by feeding them with bread and milk (*not* good for them), or dog food (much better), and indeed, they can become quite tame. But if you do feed them well, they have no need to hunt so, though you may enjoy watching them, they'll become drones I'm afraid.

The best way to encourage them and keep them working is, again, to provide shelter. If you can arrange a small pile of logs or bits of wood for them to crawl into and make a home, they may be tempted to raise a family. And you should always check your compost heap and especially your unlit bonfire to make sure it hasn't become a hedgehog house before you set light to it.

Frogs are excellent slug-eaters and will keep your garden pretty clear once you've established a colony. They will also eat plenty of insects, but they appear to be pretty indiscriminate and won't just stick to the pests!

They want water, of course, so you must have a pond. Make sure that it has plenty of weed in it so that the spawn can be fairly near the surface. If it's a steep-sided pool, like a beer-barrel, see that it has a means for the tiny frogs to get out. The ideal thing is a marginal plant in a pot which has its surface just slightly above the water level.

To establish the frogs, beg a little spawn from a friend or contact your local naturalist society which is bound to be able to help. What you must never do is to collect it from the wild. After the spawn has hatched, the tadpoles will grow and become frogs that will return every year to your pond to breed.

Toads have much the same habits though they prefer deeper water in which to breed. A pool 2 foot (60 cm) deep is ideal. The spawn differs in that frog spawn is found in large, amorphous lumps while toad spawn comes in long strings.

## PHYSICAL PEST CONTROLS

Many pests can be kept away from crops by physical methods. I've already suggested that birds should be kept from crops by netting. This can be a somewhat distressing way of doing it since there's nothing worse than watching a trapped bird get more and more enmeshed as it struggles to free itself. Try to stretch the netting tightly or weigh it down firmly to the ground so that there are no openings for birds to get in.

Black cotton is sometimes suggested and this certainly does work, but it has the same dangers for birds who simply can't see it. That is why it's so effective – they lose confidence when they touch the cotton without being able to see what it is.

Scarecrows and flashing mirrors, etc., are effective for a short while. But birds very quickly become used to them, so you'll have to keep moving them about.

Spun polypropylene sheeting is an ideal way of protecting many crops from all birds and flying insects, but it has the one disadvantage that it doesn't look attractive. In the ornamental kitchen garden it's not quite so bad since you'll only be using small pieces. Even so, the garden could look like the face of a man with an unsteady hand after shaving!

To get over the problem, I have used a very thin, perforated polythene which is green in colour. It doesn't look nearly as bad, and in fact it blends in with the surrounding foliage quite nicely. If you can support it so that it doesn't touch the plants, it'll be more effective.

The snag with it is that it doesn't give protection from frost early in the season and can tend to raise the temperature a bit too much in the height of the summer. In cooler areas, it's perfect.

### Carrot-fly

The larvae of the carrot-fly make brown tunnels in the roots of carrots, in bad cases completely ruining them. They can be controlled to some extent by putting a polythene barrier around the plants. It seems that the female carrot-fly skims along close to the ground looking for suitable crops, but if she comes to a physical barrier she flies up and over the top and misses them completely. Well, I agree it sounds a bit too good to be true, but I've tried it and it does reduce the damage by about 80 per cent. All you have to do is to grow 20 per cent more than you need. In fact the method works better in the ornamental kitchen garden because the carrots will be grown in a patch rather than a row and can be encircled with the barrier.

To make the barrier, simply put six canes into the ground around the plants and fix an 18 inch (45 cm) high clear polythene sheet to them. There's no need to cover the top. If your patch of carrots is no more than about 1 foot (30 cm) in diameter, you'll probably escape altogether. So successful has this method been for me, that I have now invested in some rigid plastic which I've glued together to form a circle. Then I can dispense with the canes and slip the plastic collar over the crop.

You should also remember that there's no need to protect carrots all the time. The eggs are laid in two batches, the first in late May and the second in August to September. If the carrots are lifted before late May there's no need to worry, and those sown in mid-June and lifted before the middle of August will generally escape.

*Protecting against carrot-fly.*

### Cabbage-root fly
Cabbage-root fly maggots eat the roots of cabbages, cauliflowers, and all other members of the same family. The first symptom is wilting and finally the collapse of the plants. When you pull them up, the roots are often virtually non-existent.

The female insect lays her eggs right next to the cabbage stem, just below the surface of the soil. Then, when the eggs hatch, the larvae can start to feed immediately. If you can prevent her laying her eggs near to the plant, she'll lay them in someone else's garden. For this purpose, you can buy special felt discs from the garden centre or you can make your own from foam rubber carpet underlay. Just cut it into 6 inch (15 cm) squares, then make a slit to the middle and a small cross slit so that the foam can be fitted snugly round the stem. Note that the operative word is 'snugly'. If it's a loose fit, the fly will still be able to lay. The other advantage with the foam rubber is that it provides a hiding place for ground beetles who also eat cabbage-root fly larvae.

### Winter moths
Winter moths and other insects on fruit trees can be trapped with a grease band or a strip of grease applied with a special gun. This method is effective against wingless insects since they can't pass the sticky barrier and get caught as they crawl up the tree trunk.

### Vine weevil
Vine weevil in the greenhouse can also be caught this way. These are really troublesome pests which lay their eggs in the compost of many pot plants. The grubs hatch out and rapidly devour the roots, completely destroying the plants. They're extremely difficult to control, even with poisons, but the organic gardener has the perfect answer. The female weevil is wingless, so to get onto the staging to get at your pots she has to climb up one of the legs. If you simply put a band of grease around each leg, you'll catch the lot. If you feel that this would put you in danger of soiling your clothes with grease when you brush against the staging, as an alternative put each leg into a small bowl of water.

## Peach leaf curl

Peaches and nectarines can be effectively protected against peach leaf curl, the debilitating fungus disease that causes red blisters on the leaves which eventually turn black and drop off. The spores are carried on rain, so all you have to do is to protect the trees from rain during the crucial time which is from early January to June. It sounds a tall order, but if your trees are fan trained against a wall or fence, it's not too difficult to arrange some kind of awning over the top. In some cases the trees will be fairly well protected by the eaves of the house.

If that's impossible, another way is to grow dwarf varieties in pots and to keep them inside until June. The dwarf varieties in my experience are much more prone to peach leaf curl than the normal ones, so they're virtually useless for growing outside. But they're ideal for growing in pots and that way can escape the disease completely.

*Peach leaf curl.*

## ❦ RESISTANT VARIETIES ❧

There are quite a few varieties of fruit and vegetables which have had a certain amount of pest and disease resistance bred into them. I'm certain that the near future will see many more produced by the technique of genetic engineering. The seed catalogues and the mail order fruit lists will give details and this is another reason why it's much better to buy through a catalogue than from the garden centre. Ideally, when buying fruit, pay the specialist nursery a visit and pick a brain or two.

The same applies to certain trees, shrubs and especially to roses. Always reject a young rose if you see the dark brown patches that are a sure sign of blackspot, or the grey powder on leaves and shoots which means mildew. They are symptoms first of all of the poor husbandry of the nursery selling them but, more importantly, also a good indication that the plants are prone to these diseases. I even go as far, if I find a carrier of either disease in my garden, as to dig it up and throw it out in favour of something more resistant. So consult the rose catalogue carefully.

## ❦ BIOLOGICAL PEST CONTROL ❧

Another technique that is bound to develop rapidly now is the biological control of pests and diseases. Already it's possible to introduce a predator to prey on insect pests and to set one fungus to fight another. This is mainly used at the moment in the greenhouse for the obvious reason that the insect predators can't fly away as they would outside. But there are one or two that can be used in the open too.

### Caterpillars

*Bacillus thuringiensis* is a bacterium which you can buy in powder form in a sachet just like a powdered insecticide. When it's mixed with water and sprayed onto the plants it becomes active in the control of caterpillars. It only acts on caterpillars, and does so by attacking their digestive system. They stop feeding as soon as they're sprayed and eventually die. It's particularly useful against the cabbage white butterfly caterpillars.

### Silverleaf disease

*Trichoderma* is a fungus used to control silverleaf disease, which attacks plums and cherries in particular but also apples, apricots and almonds. It shows first as a silvering of the leaves which eventually turn brown and this is followed by die-back. When an infected branch is cut off, a brown or purplish stain can be seen in the wood.

The *Trichoderma* fungus used to kill it can be bought in the form of pellets which are injected into the trunk of the tree. Drill a series of holes 4 inches (10 cm) apart round the trunk in the form of a spiral. Insert three pellets per hole and seal the hole again with putty or tree wound paint to stop birds pinching the pellets.

It's also possible to buy the fungus in powder form which can be mixed into a paste

*Drilling holes for pellets to kill silverleaf disease.*

and used to paint the wounds of pruning cuts: a worthwhile precaution on vulnerable trees.

### Whitefly

*Encarsia formosa* is a small wasp about the size of a whitefly, the greenhouse pest it controls. Whiteflies suck the sap of many plants, causing a general decline.

The wasp actually lays its eggs inside the whitefly scales and each female will parasitize about 50 whitefly. You buy the predators on bits of tobacco leaves which are hung in the greenhouse about halfway up the attacked plants but out of direct sunshine and where they won't be sprayed with water. They work best in warm temperatures because over 70°F (21°C) the predator will breed faster than the pest, but below that the reverse is true.

### Red spider mite

*Phytoseuilus persimilis* is a small mite which is used to control the greenhouse pest red spider mite. Red spider is a tiny red coloured mite which is only just visible with a hand lens. If the plants are badly infested, they can be seen as a red haze or, in very bad cases, the whole plant becomes covered with a web. The mites suck the sap of plants, severely debilitating them.

The predator mites are generally supplied on pieces of bean leaf. When they arrive, put them in the greenhouse, spreading them over a wide area because they will not move on until they've finished all the mites in one particular area. They eat about 30 each every day. Once introduced, they breed quite rapidly and will normally control red spider for the season.

It has to be said that the biggest problem with this method of control on a garden scale is that once the pests have all disappeared there's no food for the predators, which will then die out. However, it's a very effective way to control pests without chemicals and, in my view, well worth a little extra time and expense.

## SPECIAL METHODS OF PEST CONTROL

There are several special ways that have been developed by organic gardeners to control specific pests. Many of them work very well while some achieve only a degree of control. All are worth trying since they are aimed specifically at one particular pest and will do no harm to other wildlife.

### Slugs

I've tried dozens of ways of controlling slugs and I've been sent hundreds of pet remedies, most of which I've tried. Not one of them is ever going to give complete control but some are definitely worth the extra effort they entail to at least reduce the population. I've already mentioned hoeing, particularly early in the season, to turn up eggs which will be eaten by birds.

Collection is a never-ending job but can still be quite effective in protecting particularly vulnerable crops, especially young seedlings. The most convenient way, I found, was to put a few boards down near the crops. They can be turned over first thing each morning and dozens of slugs are generally to be found sheltering underneath. Pick them up and either put them in a jar of paraffin or transport them somewhere a long way away where they will not harm other folk's plants.

Mulching around plants with soot is quite a good defence but, with the increasing popularity of central heating, it's becoming a scarce commodity. Lime is also effective though not to be recommended because of its effect on the soil acidity. I have found coarse pine bark to have some deterrent effect.

Special young plants can be protected quite well with plastic bottles or, for larger plants, with the piece of rigid plastic glued into a circle that I suggested for carrot-fly control. Make sure you push the plastic well into the ground because slugs can burrow quite effectively.

### Codling Moth

Codling moth is the maggot you find in apples when you bite into them. Not a pleasant sensation. The female lays her eggs in late May or June, so action should be taken before then. Commercial fruit growers use a codling moth trap to indicate when there are enough of the moths about to warrant spraying. This trap is available to gardeners and can be used to trap enough moths to give about 80 per cent control.

It consists of a small roof of corrugated plastic with an insert of sticky paper. On the paper is placed a capsule of the attractant the female puts out when she wants to lure the male for mating. It's called a pheremone. The males detect the pheremone, fly into the trap and are stuck fast. Of course it's the female who does the egg laying, but the effect of catching the males is to prevent mating. And naturally, no mating equals no eggs.

*A pheremone trap for codling moth.*

### Wireworms

Wireworms attack the roots of many plants and can often be found in potato tubers where their burrows cause a lot of damage. The way to trap them is to spear pieces of potato or any root vegetable onto the ends of a number of sticks. Bury the sticks near the crop and the wireworms will burrow into the vegetables on the ends. Then you can dig up the sticks from time to time and get rid of the infested vegetables. This is not a complete control but certainly reduces the problem.

Wireworms are at their worst on land that has just come into cultivation, especially if it was old grassland. They love the roots of grass and this can be used to trap them. At either side of a row of susceptible vegetables, like potatoes, sow a row of corn. You'll be able to get seed either from a friendly farmer or from the pet shop. The wireworms will prefer to attack the roots of the corn rather than the potatoes and you can simply dig up the corn plants and burn them. Again, this is not a hundred per cent effective but the wireworms will decrease naturally once you start cultivating and this helps them on their way.

## Earwigs

Earwigs can do a lot of damage, especially to flower buds which they chew, resulting in deformed flowers. Dahlias and chrysanthemums are particularly susceptible but nothing is immune. Earwigs feed at night and hide during the day, and that habit is used to control them. Put a series of straw-filled flower pots upside-down on top of stakes near the plants. The earwigs will crawl into them at dawn, and during the day you can empty them into a bucket of water.

*A trap for earwigs.*

## Flea beetles

Flea beetles attack seedlings, especially members of the cabbage family. Turnips and Chinese cabbage seem particularly vulnerable. They're called flea beetles because of their habit of jumping into the air when disturbed. Again, this habit is used to control them. As soon as you see the first signs of attack – a number of tiny round holes in the leaves of seedlings – defend yourself with a greasy board. Put a layer of any type of grease thinly over a piece of wood and pass this about 1 inch (2.5 cm) over the top of the plants. The beetles jump upwards and stick on the board.

## Whitefly

Whitefly in the greenhouse can be controlled biologically as described on p. 246, but you can also control small infestations with sticky yellow cards. Whitefly and indeed some other insects are attracted to bright yellow objects. The cards work like an old-fashioned flypaper, holding the insects fast onto the sticky surface. However, once the whitefly find the plants and start feeding, they won't want to be disturbed and they'll forget all about the yellow cards. Each morning, remind them by giving the plants a good shake to unsettle them. This method really does work quite well and is being widely used now by commercial growers.

Another effective way of controlling whitefly and other pests is with the vacuum cleaner. Yes, I know it sounds crazy, but a vacuum tube passed over the plants will suck them off in large numbers. This is another technique now being used by commercial growers, even outdoors, so it has obviously been found to have merit.

## Club root

Club root in members of the cabbage family is impossible to control effectively. Also known as 'finger and toe', the fungus that causes it distorts the roots, creating ugly swellings which eventually turn putrid and rot. The plant either stays very small or collapses. There's no known cure but some measures are effective and acceptable crops can be grown.

First of all, make sure that the land is well limed, since club root thrives on acid soil. Also ensure that the drainage is good, though the method of cultivation described for this type of gardening will automatically do that anyway.

Then start the plants off in pots, growing them on to transplanting size, when they should be filling a 4 inch (10 cm) pot. Naturally you should use good clean compost that has been bought in for this job. The plants will still get attacked by the club root fungus but, because they have a good clean root system to start with, they'll survive to produce acceptable crops. The exception may be cauliflowers which are very fussy indeed and might produce small curds prematurely.

### Root rots

Various root rots of tomatoes may affect greenhouse crops, leading to rotting at the base of the stem or roots, discolouration of the foliage and often a complete collapse. You can grow resistant varieties like 'Piranto', just in case, but if your plants do succumb, it's best to isolate them from the soil by growing in growing bags or pots. You can now buy organic growing bags and composts for pot culture, a few of which contain no peat.

### Apple canker

Apple canker attacks older trees in particular and starts as sunken, discoloured patches on the bark which spread quite rapidly, causing ugly wounds. In summer, white pustules appear. In winter, red fruiting bodies show up too. Eventually the disease will encircle shoots and then they'll die. As soon as you see the disease, cut it out right back to healthy wood and burn what you cut out.

### Fireblight

Fireblight is a bacterial disease of fruit trees and some ornamentals. The leaves turn brown and look as though they've been burned – hence the name. There's no cure. In Britain it's a disease which must be reported, and the tree must be removed.

## CONTROLLING WEEDS

There is no such thing as an organic herbicide, except what nature gave us at birth; use your hands to pull them out or, if the area is large, a hoe. In this garden, you're unlikely to be greatly troubled by weeds after a few years because the planting will be so dense that there will be little space for them. In the early stages, though, you'll have to keep at them.

The time to hoe or pull weeds is when they're small. Don't wait for them to become a real problem and never allow them to seed or you'll multiply your problem a hundredfold. Hoe when the weather is dry and sunny if you can. If you use a Dutch hoe, try to work from the paths or, if the area is large, walk backwards to avoid treading on the seedlings and pushing the roots back into the soil.

You can help reduce work by mulching permanently planted areas with ground bark which is a very effective weed inhibitor if used in layers about 3 inches (7.5 cm) thick. You can also use shredded prunings which, once you've bought the shredder, are free.

If you're faced with a new garden that's infested with weeds, it's wise to start clean. You can do this by growing a crop like potatoes for at least the first year. These are excellent weed controllers since you work the soil first when you plant and then again when you earth up, perhaps twice, and again when you harvest. Also, as soon as the strong-growing plants meet in the rows, they form a perfect canopy which excludes light and further inhibits the weeds.

Alternatively, cover the ground with black plastic sheeting and cut slits to grow plants through it. If you exclude the light from any plant, it will eventually die.

# USEFUL ADDRESSES

## ORGANIZATIONS

*Friends of the Earth,*
26–28 Underwood Street, London N1 7JQ.
Environmental pressure group.

*Henry Doubleday Research Association,*
Ryton Gardens, The National Centre for Organic
Gardening, Ryton-on-Dunsmore, Coventry CV8
3LG.
Information and demonstration gardens on all
aspects of organic gardening. Also supplies
members with most organic products including
seeds, fertilizers and biological controls.

*National Society of Allotment and Leisure Gardeners,*
Hunters Road, Corby, Northamptonshire NN17
1JE.
Advice on allotments.

*Nature Conservancy Council,*
Northminster House, Northminster Road,
Peterborough, Cambridgeshire PE1 1UA.
Information on wild flowers and attracting insects,
etc.

*Northern Horticultural Society,*
Harlow Carr Botanical Gardens, Crag Lane,
Harrogate, N. Yorkshire HG3 1QB.

*Royal Caledonian Horticultural Society,*
3 West Newington Place, Edinburgh EH9 1QT.

*Royal Horticultural Society,*
Vincent Square, London SW1P 2PE.

*Royal Horticultural Society of Ireland,*
Thomas Prior House, Merrion Road,
Dublin 4.

*Royal Society for Nature Conservation,*
The Green, Nettleham, Lincoln LN2 2NR.
Help with native trees and other plants, etc.

*Royal Society for the Protection of Birds,*
The Lodge, Sandy, Bedfordshire SG19 2DL.
Information and literature on attracting birds, etc.

*Soil Association,*
86 Colston Street, Bristol BS1 5BB.
Information on organic gardening and farming.
The recognized authority on organic standards.

## SEEDSMEN

*J. W. Boyce,*
Bush Pasture, Lower Carter Street, Fordham, Ely,
Cambridgeshire CB7 5JU.

*John Chambers Wildflower Seeds,*
15 Westleigh Road, Barton Seagrave, Kettering,
Northamptonshire NN15 5AJ.

*Chiltern Seeds,*
Bortree Stile, Ulverston, Cumbria LA12 7PB.

*Samuel Dobie and Son Ltd,*
Broomhill Way, Torquay, Devon TQ2 7QW.

*Mr Fothergill's Seeds Ltd,*
Gazeley Road, Kentford, Newmarket, Suffolk
CB8 7QB.

*W. W. Johnson and Son,*
London Road, Boston, Lincolnshire PE21 8AD.

*S. E. Marshall and Co Ltd,*
23/24 Regal Road, Wisbech, Cambridgeshire
PE13 2RF.

*W. Robinson and Sons,*
Sunnybank, Forton, Nr. Preston, Lancashire ER3
0BN.

*Suffolk Herbs,* Sawyers Farm, Little Cornard,
Sudbury, Suffolk CO10 0NY.

*Suttons Seeds Ltd,*
Hele Road, Torquay, Devon TQ2 7QJ.

*Thompson and Morgan Ltd,*
London Road, Ipswich, Suffolk 1P2 0BA.

*Unwins Seeds Ltd,*
Histon, Cambridge CB4 4LE.

## GENERAL ORGANIC SUPPLIES

*Chase Organic,*
Shepperton, Middlesex TW17 8AS.

*Cumulus Organics,* Two Mile Lane, Highnam,
Gloucestershire GL2 8DW.

*Dig and Delve Organics,*
Blo Norton, Diss, Norfolk IP22 2BR.

*Organic Garden Centre,*
Watling Street, Hockliffe, Nr. Leighton Buzzard,
Bedfordshire LU7 9NP.

## ORGANIC PEST CONTROL

*Agralan,*
The Old Brickyard, Ashton Keynes, Swindon,
Wiltshire SN6 6QR.

*Bunting Biological Control Ltd,* The Nurseries, Great
Horkesley, Colchester, Essex CO6 4AJ.

*English Woodlands Ltd,*
Burrow Nursery, Cross in Hand, Heathfield,
E. Sussex TN21 0UG.

*Koppert (UK) Ltd,*
1 Wadhurst Business Park, Faircrouch Lane,
Wadhurst, E. Sussex TN5 6PT.

*Natural Pest Control,*
Yapton Road, Barnham, Bognor Regis,
W. Sussex PO22 0BQ.

## FRUIT TREES

*Deacons Nursery,*
Godshill, Isle of Wight PO38 3HW.

*Highfield Nurseries,*
Whitminster, Gloucestershire GL2 7PL.

## SOFT FRUIT

*Ken Muir,* Honeypot Farm, Weeley Heath,
Clacton-on-Sea, Essex CO16 9BJ. Propagator and
distributor of certified fruit stocks. Mail order.

## WOODEN GREENHOUSES

*Banbury Homes and Gardens,*
PO Box 17, Banbury, Oxfordshire OX17 3NS.

*S. Wernick & Sons Ltd.,* Lindon Road, Brownhills,
Walsall, W. Midlands WS8 7BW.

## COLD FRAMES

*Access Frames,*
Crick, Northamptonshire NN6 7BR.

## PAVING

*ECC Quarries Ltd,*
Okus, Swindon, Wiltshire SN1 4JJ.

## CLAY POTS AND RHUBARB FORCERS

*Whichford Potteries,* Whichford, Shipston-on-
Stour, Warwickshire CV36 5PG.

## FRUIT ARCHES

*Agriframes Ltd,* Charlwoods Road, East Grinstead,
W. Sussex RH19 2HG.

## PERGOLA KITS

*Larch-Lap Ltd,*
PO Box 17, Lichfield Street, Stourport-on-Severn,
Worcestershire DY13 9ES.

## FURNITURE

*Andrew Crace Designs,*
51 Bourne Lane, Much Hadham, Hertfordshire
SG10 6ER.

## ORNAMENTAL PLANTS

There are, of course, hundreds of nurseries and
garden centres which sell plants. For particular
requirements, I refer you to *The Plant Finder,*
published by Headmain Ltd, and the Hardy
Plant Society, Lakeside, Gaines Road, Whit-
bourne, Worcestershire WR6 5RD.

# INDEX

Page numbers in *italics* refer to the illustrations